RANGERS: THE MANAGERS

ACKNOWLEDGEMENTS

This book would not have been possible without the assistance and advice of a great many people. I cannot list all those who have helped, but particular thanks are due to Walter Smith, Graeme Souness, Dick Advocaat, John Greig, Alison Muir (née Dallas), Eric Caldow, Davie Wilson, Colin Jackson, Sandy Jardine, Willie Johnston, Willie Henderson, David Robertson, Richard Gough, Ally McCoist, Davie Provan, Alex Willoughby, Ian McColl, the late Bob McPhail, Campbell Ogilvie, Alan Montgomery, 'Tiny' Gallacher, Bill McMurdo, Laura Tarbet, Alex MacDonald, Tom Forsyth, Derek Johnstone, Ian Durrant, Hilda Waddell, William Goodfellow, Robert McElroy, Carol Patton, Gillian Dorricott, Bert van Lingen, Martin Bain, Nick Peel and all at Rangers Football Club who have been tremendously supportive. The photographs have been supplied by the Rangers Picture Library, *The Herald* and First Press Publishing.

Finally, I should also express my thanks for the support of my long-suffering wife Karen and daughters Laura and Louise, who will now see some tangible result to my long hours locked away in the study.

RANGERS
THE MANAGERS

DAVID MASON

MAINSTREAM
PUBLISHING

EDINBURGH AND LONDON

First published in Great Britain in 2000 by
MAINSTREAM PUBLISHING COMPANY (EDINBURGH) LTD
7 Albany Street
Edinburgh EH1 3UG
Under licence from the Rangers Football Club plc

ISBN 1 84018 404 3

A catalogue record for this book is available
from the British Library

Typeset in Hoefler Text
Printed and bound in Great Britain by Butler & Tanner Ltd,
Frome and London

CONTENTS

This book is dedicated to my father, Hector Mason, who first showed me the light that is 'Rangers Football Club'

THE IBROX MANAGERS

Manager of the Rangers Football Club. It is the Holy Grail of football management, a position aspired to by many, but achieved by precious few. Just ten men, in fact. Ten men from widely varying backgrounds, but all with a common goal – to satisfy the great expectations of the fervent followers who regard Rangers as more than a mere football club. To them it is a veritable institution.

It is a role that has always carried immense responsibility and promises the greatest of rewards for those who succeed. But what was a cup filled with fame and fortune for most, with all the adulation and glory that follow success, became a poisoned chalice of disappointment and great discontent for others.

For the countless fans who have faithfully followed the club over its long history, success has always been a double-edged sword. The streaming red, white and blue ribbons on a cascading flow of silverware provide tangible testimony to the achievements of the team. But success is not measured by the honours list alone. In a Scottish society where religious divisions have been polarised into two colours – blue and green – the success of one has almost always been judged against the achievements of the other.

Rangers and Celtic – the Old Firm – share a city, but little else. They carry the hopes of thousands of fans whose very perspective on life is influenced by their determination to achieve superiority. To win is to justify the belief that one section is greater than the other. 'We arra people,' they proudly proclaim. To fail is tantamount to the sufferance of repression, giving a sense of dismay and hopelessness that leaves a void that cannot be filled until the next time – a depression so deep that the Monday after an Old Firm contest traditionally saw the highest levels of absenteeism in the heavy industries of the Clyde. Men might have been ready to face work, but they were not prepared to face their opposites.

This is the great burden that every manager, on both sides of the Old Firm, has assumed. It has always been a role of immense responsibility. No half measures are permitted – or expected.

The position of manager of Rangers has always been about more than the tribal jingoism of its fanatic followers, however. From its earliest days the club has been an integral part of the fabric of the Glasgow society. Formed in 1872, it has shared in the changing fortunes of the city. Its growth has mirrored Glasgow's own development, whose success was Clyde-built in the endeavour of the post-Industrial Revolution era of the late nineteenth century, to the modern affluent metropolis of today.

The tragedies of two World Wars and the two Ibrox disasters added darker hues to the kaleidoscope of life in Govan, but these events were inextricably linked to the development and growth of the club. The managers found that there was much more to their job than selecting players and turning out the best eleven the Light Blues could muster each week. They had to absorb themselves into the fabric of the club, making decisions and formulating ideas and policies that would influence its course. During their tenure, they were, in effect, Rangers, working within a blueprint evolved by the early founders in the formative years.

When the position of manager was created with the incorporation of the club to Limited Liability in 1899, some 27 years after its formation, the ethos of Rangers was already well established. A sense of 'nothing being too good for us' became a perpetual theme as they strove to have the best players, the best stadium and be the best club. But even if the philosophy of Rangers was already well mapped out, the first two managers, William Wilton and William Struth, who between them guided the club for over 55 years, left their own indelible mark on it. The Rangers of today is a reflection of the ideals they pursued. The determination to be the best is embraced within character ideals of smartness and sportsmanship in a stadium that provides the finest of quality.

But while these early pioneers were impressive and the great traditions of Ibrox have prevailed through the years, the accomplishments of successive managers have been reflected by their ability to adjust to the changing face of the game and society. There were some who adapted to the role and embraced the needs for change as circumstances dictated. There were others who did not. There were some whose fortunes were unaffected by their ability or willingness to adapt, their failure only being in the wrong place at the wrong time as Celtic swept all before them.

For those who failed there was little sentiment. Men who had served the club well for many years were cast aside as the demands of the fans and the hawks in the boardroom were unfulfilled. Embarrassed and embittered by the experience, they shunned a return to Ibrox, enduring a period of self-imposed exile from the club they once ruled. Even for some of those who succeeded, the end of their tenure was not the celebratory farewell that their contribution merited. Reflecting the old football cliché that 'you are only as good as your last game', memories of past triumphs are quickly forgotten by the fickle fans of football.

If the price of failure is heavy, however, the rewards for success are immeasurable. Where once the honour of the position eclipsed the importance of financial remuneration, the job now brings terms to match some of the biggest clubs in Europe. But while the position ensures financial security, the real prize remains in the kudos earned among the loyal support as the manager of one of the greatest clubs in the game.

Few men have been given the opportunity to manage Rangers. Those who took up the challenge were men from diverse back-grounds. William Wilton, the great administrator, emerged to guide Rangers as the game itself evolved. Then came William Struth, the athlete who graduated from the training-ground to inherit office in 1920, ruling the club with an iron fist inside a blue velvet glove. He was succeeded by Scot Symon in 1954, the first of the former players who was reared in the traditions of Ibrox and who enjoyed great success before succumbing to a blind adherence to the old ideas he held so true. After that came the fateful Davie White, an aspiring young coach whose tenure in the late 1960s was short-lived. He failed partly as a result of his inexperience, but principally because his time in office coincided with the greatest period in Celtic's history. Another former player, Willie Waddell, returned in 1970 to restore the diminished Ibrox traditions and was rewarded with Rangers' greatest triumph – winning the European Cup-Winners' Cup. As Waddell turned to transform Rangers in the aftermath of the Ibrox Disaster, he passed the reins in 1972 to his assistant, the rugged ex-serviceman Jock Wallace. Wallace led one of the fittest Rangers sides ever to a clean sweep of Scotland's three domestic trophies on two occasions. In 1978, at the height of his success, he departed in controversial circumstances. He was succeeded by John

Greig, another former player who had carried the club through the lean years with remarkable resilience, but even he could not make any impact as boss as he struggled through transitional years with inexperienced youngsters emerging and old stars waning. Not even the return of Wallace five years later could lift Rangers from the doldrums. That only happened with the arrival of the flamboyant Graeme Souness in 1986, the club's first player-manager. Playing the role of international superstar to the letter, he brandished the chequebook and heralded a bright new period of success.

He built a team that the studious Walter Smith inherited in 1991 as he pushed Rangers to unprecedented domestic honours. Smith came to Ibrox with a good track record as an assistant coach to some of the best managers in the country. He delivered little in terms of European competition, however, as British football became infatuated with the concept of the 'European manager'. He was replaced in 1998 by Dick Advocaat, the first foreign coach to manage Rangers. Despite having little familiarity with the traditions, the Dutchman found that his ideals reflected those ingrained in the club he had come to serve.

Every manager who has entered the historic office at the top of the marble staircase inside Ibrox stadium has carried forward the hopes and expectations of the fans and the enormous burden of responsibility the position brings. None dared predict what the future held. None dared contemplate failure. 'Long live the manager of Rangers,' the assembled fans would proclaim as each one took up office. Their voices were equally vociferous if they failed, although less reverent.

Through it all, the manager could enjoy almost regal status. He was the ruler of all he surveyed as he gazed out on the stadium. Nevertheless, for all the importance of the position, it has also been a humbling experience for many. To know the managers is to understand Rangers Football Club. They have been almost one and the same. But while Rangers go on, each of the managers provides just a chapter in the club's long history. What Rangers would have been without them is impossible to say, but what can be stated without fear of contradiction is that each had his own part to play in the development of the great footballing institution.

Ten colourful characters. Ten important characters. This is their story, the story of the Rangers managers.

WILLIAM WILTON

'PRINCE AMONG FOOTBALL MANAGERS' read the banner headline in Glasgow's *Evening Citizen* on Monday, 3 April 1920. Underneath, the grim reality of the weekend's events stunned thousands as the newspaper reported: 'Rangers FC Manager William Wilton Drowned at Gourock'.

As the news spread around the country, many made the sad pilgrimage down the Clyde to see the scene of the tragedy. The crowds gathered with 'melancholy interest' as the battered yawl *Caltha* rocked gently in the harbour, scarcely revealing the intensity of the storm which saw the loss of one of Scottish football's finest administrators.

Wilton had looked forward to the weekend break on the boat after an arduous season. As he left Ibrox on the Saturday evening he had remarked to chairman Sir John Ure Primrose that he was 'fatigued with the heavy season's work'. Victory over Morton in that final match of the season had secured the championship and left Wilton in good spirits as he travelled to Gourock with co-director J.P. Buchanan. They were guests of James Marr, a former Rangers committee member.

The *Caltha* was a tidy vessel of around 19 tonnes and had ample accommodation for the three men plus the skipper and his mate. As they bunked down for the evening an easterly gale blew up and by the early hours the boat was being tossed around in the swell. At some time between 2 and 3 a.m. it was torn from its moorings and Wilton alerted the others. The *Caltha* was driven towards the Caledonian Pier and the men watched helplessly, unable to signal their distress to the shore or other vessels in the vicinity. The little boat was battered against the solid concrete pier with every wave and the anxious party realised that their very lives would depend on them getting ashore. The skipper climbed the mast and then, as the boat rolled towards the quayside, he leapt to the sanctuary of the land. He was followed by each of the remaining passengers in turn, until only Wilton remained. The Rangers boss climbed the mast and frantically reached for a rope thrown by one of his friends on the quayside. As the boat rolled towards the pier, he stretched over, getting a knee on to the quay, but before he could safely alight the mast pulled clear of the landing.

As the *Caltha* heaved on the swell and again rolled towards the pier with its mast leaning tantalisingly close to safety, Wilton reached out once again. Just as it seemed that he had secured a hold the mast pulled away. He lost his grip and plunged into the raging sea.

Marr dived into the swell in an attempt to rescue his friend and managed to grasp him, but the unrelenting waves beat the pair apart. William Wilton disappeared beneath the water with a faint cry. His body was never recovered.

In the aftermath of his untimely death, Wilton received countless tributes from friends and associates from the world of football, but he had a much wider appeal. Many remembered his contribution to other sports and his interests in the Choral Union. He was respected as a fine tenor who sang with the Glasgow Select Choir. But football was Wilton's life and Rangers would quite simply not be the club we see today without his guiding hand on the tiller through the critical early years.

THE FORMATIVE YEARS

To understand Wilton's influence on the growth and development of Rangers we have to turn back the pages of the club records to the 1880s when the young Willie Wilton first pursued his interest in the comparatively new game of association football. Born and raised in Glasgow, he was attracted to the lively young Rangers side that had captured the public's attention by challenging the long-established institutions of Queen's Park and Vale of Leven. He paid his dues and became one of an increasing number of members of the Rangers Football Club.

He certainly had enthusiasm for the game, but it would appear that his vigour was not matched by any real ability on the field of play. He was selected for the second string 'Swifts' eleven but he did not show enough talent to earn a place in the first team. But if his skills on the field were questionable, his organisational abilities on the sidelines were readily appreciated and he was appointed match secretary to the Swifts shortly after joining the club.

During this period, the position of 'manager' did not exist within football clubs. The selecting committee, a group of resolute club members whose enthusiasm and commitment to the task transcended any particular knowledge of the game, chose the team each week. The general committee later ratified their selection, often after lengthy deliberation.

Even though he was match secretary for the Swifts, Wilton was not on the selecting committee. His individual powers may have been restricted, with committees deciding on almost every facet of the club, but it was a situation that he was entirely comfortable with, because he was, in essence, a democrat. As such, the records show that he enthusiastically contributed to every aspect of the organisation of the club.

Wilton's interest and apparent influence in the running of the club were first highlighted in the records of a special meeting of the members in 1887. Concerned at the poor performances that had seen the first eleven slip out of the cup competitions at an early stage, he proposed an increase in the number of people making up the selecting committee. The records highlight that Wilton's argument was 'well presented' and influential. His proposal was carried.

The young William was rapidly gaining respect within the embryonic club as an enthusiast brimming with ideas. A few months later, at the AGM in May 1889, he was put forward for the prestigious position of match secretary of Rangers. It was a key role within the club and one that carried a coveted place on the selecting committee. He found himself in competition for the post with the residing officer, Mr J. Gossland, a respected member of long standing. Wilton, at the age of just 23, was elected by a large majority.

By 1889 he had gained public recognition as 'the energetic secretary of Rangers' and his duties were wide and varied. As match secretary, he was expected to run the line in matches as an 'umpire'. Like the modern-day linesmen, or 'referee's assistants', as they are now known, the umpire's task was thankless and invariably the focus of some pointed criticism. One newspaper of the period commented on the duties of the umpire with a touch of sarcasm, writing that the umpire was 'expected to carry a small banner and give every throw-in to his side'. At least the maligned umpires were perceived to be of some support to their clubs, unlike committeemen who, it was said, were 'men who play the game in the pavilion and tell the players afterwards what they should have done'.

Wilton was never given such guidance from his peers in the committee room for they could not fail to be impressed by the enthusiasm and gusto with which the young man embraced his role. The records of the committee meetings of the time make frequent references to the quality of his work and presentation. His 'report was particularly satisfactory', one minute read, in acknowledgement of Wilton's efforts in steering the team towards wider respectability in the game.

Wilton's involvement in the club's affairs was unbridled. He extended his interests into the broader management of Rangers as it grew in tandem with the expanding appeal of football. The club records show that, even in the early stages of his tenure as match secretary, Wilton's remit extended far beyond the simple task of scheduling games. He was the instigator of the Ibrox sports, in 1889, which became a fixture in the athletics calendar until the 1950s. Such sports days were to become a popular feature in the calendars of most football clubs as stadiums were put to some beneficial use in the close-season summer months. Apart from athletics and cycling, they generally included a five-a-side tournament with entries from most of the major clubs. The Rangers sports day was by far the most important at the time.

As his remit continued to expand out of his enthusiasm for the role and the confidence that the club members had in his abilities, Wilton turned his attention to plans for ground-improvement work at Ibrox. Rangers had moved to the rural lands to the west of the city in 1887 after leaving the Kinning Park ground that had seen them through their early years following initial spells at Glasgow Green and then Burnbank. As the team's support grew with the increasing popularity of the game, it became clear that Ibrox was becoming quite inadequate for the crowds that were being attracted to the stadium. In the first full season at Ibrox, in 1887, crowds typically numbered less than 5,000, although the opening match against Preston North End drew almost 16,000. By 1890, crowds of over 10,000 were common and, as well the growing band of enthusiastic followers, the stadium had to accommodate a battery of pressmen, eager to carry the news. Wilton set about the construction of a new press-box, a contribution to the comfort of the journalists, which was reflected in a number of complimentary comments about the Rangers secretary in the broadsheets.

His greatest efforts were reserved for the ground itself. In his efforts to increase the capacity of Ibrox, Wilton proposed the construction of a new covered stand, with seating for 3,000, to be erected on the south side of the field. The committee accepted his proposal, but they would need the express approval of the club members. Wilton, a respected speaker, was asked to present the proposal at a special meeting of the members. The scheme was passed with little dissent and the project was initiated, albeit on a reduced scale when the costs exceeded the original budgets.

Through Wilton's initiatives and efforts, Rangers had become the most prominent football club in the country. As they prepared to move into the 1890s, the committee proudly announced that the club was 'never in a healthier position' and on the field of play they had a 'better all-round team'. The structure of Scottish competition was, however, about to change.

THE EMERGENCE OF PROFESSIONALISM AND THE NEW LEAGUE STRUCTURE

Within a year of taking office Wilton was elected to represent the club in the discussions concerning the proposed establishment of a football league structure, mirroring the development of the game in England. Cup ties, benefit matches and friendlies had conspired to produce chaos in the Scottish game and the legalisation of professionalism presented both opportunity and uncertainty to the future of the football north of the border.

In March 1890 Wilton and Rangers president John Mellish joined representatives of eleven of Scotland's leading clubs to consider the establishment of a league structure. It seemed a logical, if not necessary, step forward. The clubs had become increasingly concerned that Scottish players were being lured south to join the professional sides there. A league structure had been in operation in England for two years and appeared to be working successfully.

Despite dissenting voices from some clubs, it was ultimately decided that a Scottish football league was the only way to protect the game in the country, and Wilton took an active role in the formation of the new institution, embracing the idea of the league with some vigour and assuming the role of secretary to the new organisation while still maintaining his enthusiasm for his duties at Ibrox.

His involvement in the wider administration of the game provided him with the opportunity to improve the overall organisation of football in Scotland. He was irked when one match at Ibrox was postponed in bad weather simply because the referee did not turn up. He campaigned for the reform of the guidelines for pitch inspections and established procedures similar to those which prevail today.

He also recognised that the professionalism which had been absorbed by the game in England and precipitated the formation of the league structures north and south of the border would inevitably be all-consuming in Scotland. The choice was clear: clubs could either embrace the changing winds of time or resist the moves to uphold the old traditional amateur values. With the exception of Queen's Park, who stubbornly maintained loyalty to the amateur game, the league clubs stated their intentions of going down the road towards professionalism, but the concept needed support from the Scottish Football Association. Wilton sought and received the Rangers committee's approval to put the case to the SFA, highlighting the club's support. He succeeded. By 1893 the SFA took the decision to legalise professionalism in the game.

While Wilton continued to assist the Scottish Football League and even worked feverishly in administration of the SFA, he revelled in his role at Ibrox, which brought him regular acclaim from the press. 'Respected match secretary' and 'the excellent match secretary' were but two references to him in the *Scottish Sport* publication which tracked the progress of the game and clubs in the country.

WILTON'S MAN-MANAGEMENT AND DISCIPLINE

While Wilton's administrative skills and achievements were well documented by the press, his management of the players can only really be appreciated by referring to the club records.

He cared for the players' every interest, from arranging social evenings to the negotiation of their terms. He could also be compassionate in times of trouble. In one instance, he submitted a proposal to the committee that they should defray the costs of the funeral of one young player who had passed away after illness. On another occasion, he raised concerns at the committee meeting over the health of trainer James Taylor and suggested the appointment of an assistant. He also served as best man at the wedding of one of the players, John McPherson, showing beyond doubt his rapport with his men.

But Wilton could also be very hard if he felt a player had let the club down. In 1893, for example, the same John McPherson whose marriage vows had been witnessed by the Rangers secretary, was called to account for his behaviour towards a referee after being sent off. McPherson had remonstrated with the official for some time before eventually leaving the field. Wilton was instructed to write to the player pointing out the unacceptability of his conduct.

A few months later another player, named McCreadie, became similarly involved with an official during a game at Nottingham. Wilton, unable to enforce any action without the backing of the committee, brought the matter to their attention at one of their regular meetings. They backed him and the player was censured. The team respected Wilton and they knew that he expected high standards of behaviour from them and that anyone who breached his unwritten code of discipline would inevitably be brought to task.

One player, Sam Allen, realised in the harshest way that misbehaviour would not be tolerated. The minutes of a board meeting in 1912 tersely record that 'Sam Allen [was] suspended *sine die* for drinking last week'. It is an edict that would cause consternation to many modern players.

There is little doubt that Wilton was the instigator of the disciplinary code that successive managers were to adopt as being the 'Rangers way'. Certain standards of behaviour were expected of them when they represented the club. Wilton did everything in his power to ensure that his players met these standards.

He and the rest of the committee were generally highly respected figures from Glasgow community life who were unstinting in their determination to maintain responsible control over the club. An interesting display of assumed player power emerged late in 1893 when the Swifts, who remained amateurs in the early years of the professional era, approached the committee and demanded promotion to professional terms. It was a move that was hardly practical since the revenues from the small attendances attracted by the second-string matches were barely enough to maintain the kit they wore, let alone pay any wages. Indeed, the Swifts contributed virtually nothing in gate money to the income of the club.

The militant Swifts wrote to the committee on the eve of a cup tie demanding that their terms be met, otherwise they would refuse to appear in the match. The committee stood firm and the team were forced into an embarrassing withdrawal.

The players may have incurred the wrath of Wilton at times, but he would always stand by them if they were maligned. On one occasion he acted to protect some of his players who were suffering a barracking from the crowd. He saw to it that the committee placed plainclothes constables in the offending area until the season was over.

What emerges from the records is the character of a man who was there for his players, but who was a 'club man' first and foremost. He had ideals and standards that had to be attained. These would become enshrined as part of the very traditions of the club.

A FIRST SCOTTISH CUP WIN AND IBROX FLOURISHES

Throughout the formative years, Rangers had made great strides on the field but had little tangible success in reward. Victory in the first League championship, which the club shared with Dumbarton in 1890, was a major achievement, but the premier tournament of the period was the Scottish Cup. Rangers had never succeeded in the tournament until a victory over Celtic in the 1894 final. It was a long time coming, but it signalled the start of a new successful era.

Under Wilton's control, the club marched through the decade, their fortunes flourishing under the new professional set-up. By 1895 crowds at Ibrox exceeded 20,000 for key cup ties against the more prominent sides such as Celtic, Hibernian and Queen's Park. Wilton's efforts that year were rewarded with an honorarium of £25.

Income for the year reached the record total of £5,548 and the players' wages and expenses amounted to just £1,898. Continuous ground improvements stretched the club financially, however, and Wilton led the drive to raise funds to tide them through the barren close-season break.

Around this time, both Rangers and Celtic found their grounds in demand as a neutral venue for cup ties and by a host of minor clubs. In an unambiguous sign of collaboration, the two decided that they would not let out their stadiums unless they received 'full stand drawings'. While Hampden was also available to outside clubs, the 'Celtic Agreement', as it became known in the minutes, established a cartel through which Glasgow's two major clubs could only prosper further, reaping the rewards for their foresight in developing large attractive football grounds.

A few years later, in 1898, they reached a further agreement on gate money although this was precipitated by a dispute rather than by collaboration. Rangers and Celtic were well aware that they were a tremendous draw for football fans in the city, although in this period the games were not afflicted by the hatred and bigotry which was to taint them in the future. A massive crowd estimated at around 50,000 attended the New Year fixture between the sides at Celtic Park. The clubs disagreed over their respective share of the match takings – a dispute which threatened their otherwise healthy relationship.

Wilton proposed that the matter might best be resolved if the clubs agreed to divide the income from each match. Celtic agreed, reinforcing the prevailing view from the outside that the two clubs were, to all intents and purposes, a commercial organisation – or firm. They would soon be known as the Old Firm.

With crowds growing steadily, the Rangers committee became increasingly pressured to extend the ground at Ibrox and further improve the facilities. While Ibrox had an excellent track that was used by runners and cyclists between May and August, at a membership cost of 5/- and 7/6d respectively, the ground was first and foremost a football park. The surface was protected during some of the summer months by closure, but improvements continued almost incessantly in new construction works extending the stadium facilities.

Fifteen turnstiles were procured at a cost of £8/12s/6d each in 1897 as the old pay-boxes disappeared. The committee had their eyes firmly on the use of the ground as a possible venue for an international fixture. Such a coup in bringing the national side to Ibrox would be financially rewarding and would also enhance the standing of Rangers within the game. The committee voted that £800 should be set aside for efforts to secure the fixture. These were successful. That year Scotland met Ireland in a match that attracted 15,000 to Ibrox.

Wilton and his colleagues were justifiably proud of their achievement in raising Ibrox to such prominence in just eleven years. As they moved to secure the lease on their ground, however, they were faced with not only disappointment but also with a sense of opportunity. The landlords required part of the ground occupied by the stadium, but an area of ground extending westwards and amounting to 14.5 acres was offered to Rangers on favourable terms. It would mean the construction of a new stadium.

Architects commissioned to advise on the scheme submitted plans for a new ground with a capacity of 80,000. The project was estimated to cost around £12,000, but it would need the endorsement of the members. With the club's balance-sheet showing only £5,600 on account, the initiative would require a massive injection of funds. It seemed that the only way that the 'gigantic ground scheme' could be realised would be for the club to incorporate. In March 1899 the committee took the proposals to the members. After an initial favourable response the matter was referred to the committee to draw up the articles. The share capital would be £12,000, the indicated cost of the works.

In May 1899, when the dust had settled on the proposals, and architects, engineers and solicitors had worked feverishly in the background to realise the club's ambitions, a rather melancholy membership turned up at the Trades Hall in Glasgow for the final AGM before incorporation. The minutes record that in his final report as match secretary, Willie Wilton 'referred to the doings of the club in the old days, showing what great progress the Light Blues had made in the past two or three seasons'.

The final business of the meeting concerned the appointment of manager and secretary to the new Rangers Football Club Limited. The minutes of the meeting reported that, 'only one name was put forward, that of Mr Wilton, and amidst round after round of applause, [he] was unanimously elected'.

THE FIRST MANAGER OF RANGERS

Wilton took up his new appointment with vigour, resigning from his positions with the League and the SFA to concentrate on Rangers' business. Although he had a new title and carried some added responsibility to the overall administration and well-being of the club, Wilton had effectively assumed the role several years earlier through his increasing development of the position of match secretary.

The main task at hand in his early months in office concerned the construction of what would be known as 'New Ibrox'. The celebrated stadium architect Archibald Leitch was charged with drawing up the blueprint for the new ground. There was some debate as to whether the existing large covered stand could be relocated to the new field, and there was also an expression of interest from Kilmarnock FC in acquiring the grand structure for their own ground improvement plans. Rangers recognised that if they could get a 'fair price' from Kilmarnock for the stand, they may find it cheaper to erect a new stand at Ibrox. After some consultation with Leitch, the club decided to retain the structure, but move it to the new field. The architect received the instruction to proceed with the work and was also advised that 'the turf should be of the finest'.

Work progressed under the strict supervision of William Wilton and was ready for football within seven months. The new ground was opened on 30 December 1899, just two days before the start of a new century which would see Rangers go on to even greater heights.

Into the New Year, the construction work continued as the club strove to extend and improve the facilities at Ibrox. Two new stands were erected on each flank of the ground with the pavilion situated in the south-east corner. The ends of the ground were constructed with sweeping high-banked wooden terracings laid on an iron lattice framework. It was an imposing and attractive ground and Rangers celebrated their new company status and the glamour of their new ground with four successive championships between 1899 and 1902.

The new ground was a huge attraction in itself. In 1902 the average attendance at Ibrox was a healthy 13,000, but Rangers attracted much larger crowds for games against Celtic (30,000) and Hibernian (35,000). The ground was capable of sustaining even larger numbers and Rangers were keen to build on the reputation that Ibrox had gained over the years as a good venue for prestigious matches in the football calendar. They actively canvassed for some big fixtures and were rewarded when the ground was chosen as the venue for the annual Scotland v. England game. They had hosted the fixture, in the past, at 'Old Ibrox' and only two years earlier the game came to 'New Ibrox', but this was the first time that what was known as 'Greater Ibrox' would see such a grand match.

Their success in attracting the international game was followed with an announcement that the Scottish Cup final would also be held at the ground a few weeks later. It seemed that things could not be better for Rangers and Wilton. In fact, as the weeks unfolded, things could not have been worse.

THE FIRST IBROX DISASTER

As the press eagerly anticipated the Scotland–England match, one newspaper expressed hope that the 'magnificent enclosure [would be] taxed to its utmost capacity'. It also reported that there would be room for 'thousands upon thousands' on the terracings and stressed that the concerns which had been raised by some with regard to the safety of the structures were unfounded as the ground had been 'checked by various engineers and tested in matches'. Work to get the stadium ready was conducted from 'daylight to dawn', and it was reported that the preparations were carried out under 'the watchful eye of William Wilton'.

The gates were opened for the fixture at 12.30 p.m. on 4 April 1902, the crowds heeding instructions to arrive early. Marching bands provided pre-match entertainment. What should have been something of a celebration for Wilton and his board turned out, however, to be something quite tragic.

Ibrox was described at the time as being in many ways a replica of the Coliseum in Rome. The field itself was enclosed within an iron paling and outside was a cinder track. Beyond this rose the terraced stands which were broad enough to hold three deep. At each end of the ground the terraces rose to a height of over 40 feet. On the south side, where the present Main Stand is, there was a grandstand, which could hold 6,000. On the opposite side of the ground, a large covered stand had a capacity of 13,000. It was estimated that 80,000 people could watch a match, although it was generally reckoned that the crowd would be unlikely to exceed 70,000.

The ground was, in fact, reportedly full to capacity an hour before kick-off, but still people continued to pour in. As the game commenced, the welded masses of fans swayed and one eyewitness said that the terracing gave the impression of a 'long, rolling wave'. To counteract such swaying, sturdy iron railings divided the terracing and should have limited the capacity in each area, but they were ineffectual that fateful spring day. The continuing swaying wrenched some of the rails from their positions and the wave swept towards the back of the east terracing. With the enormous pressure of the masses directed towards the rear of the structure, the corrugated backing, which was never intended to support such weight, wrenched and then twisted the supports.

An eyewitness account vividly related the subsequent events: 'The game had only been in progress for about ten minutes when I heard a sound behind me as of wood splitting. Looking round, I noticed there was a gulf, but as nobody shouted I could not realise what had happened. I was practically stunned with fear. I had only to step back a couple of yards, and there I saw a chasm at the foot of which were strewn people. All the people for fifty yards on every side then scrambled to get into the arena and on to the cinder track.'

The game was stopped and the players were led from the field. By the time rescuers reached the dreadful scene at the base of the mangled structure, a number of people were seen to be dead and many more lay seriously injured. The final toll showed that 26 had lost their lives and 587 were injured.

The match was played out to a conclusion, raising some criticism, but the intention was to ensure that no panic or rioting ensued.

One story, which emerged in the newspapers in the aftermath, brought some relief to one family. A Falkirk man returned home after seemingly having identified his young son among the dead, and as he set about the tortuous task of arranging the undertaker, the boy walked into the house. Relief for that one family, however, would appear to have resulted in despair for another.

The press coverage in the aftermath of the tragedy rose to a hysterical pitch, with much of the criticism directed at Rangers. William Wilton's feelings at the time are unknown, but it was clear that he was a central figure to the whole episode and must have been distraught by the events. Interviews with the architect Archibald Leitch in the press revealed that he had carried out a safety inspection with Wilton prior to the match and that the ground was considered to be safe.

In a statement a few days after the events of the disaster, Wilton expressed his heartfelt sympathy for all those affected by the tragedy, but said that, although the ground had never had such a big crowd in the past, the particular area affected had experienced that density of fans in the past. He also mentioned that the club had received a certificate from the Govan Burgh Surveyor confirming his satisfaction with the structure.

The subsequent enquiry recognised that there was no particular design fault or any real blame that could be attached to the club. It was concluded that the accident was the result of the swaying movement of the crowd. Nevertheless, it virtually sounded the death knell on the timber-and-iron-lattice style of terracing construction. Clubs, including Rangers, would in the future move towards earth banks.

The SFA set up a fund for the injured and the dependants of the deceased. This was boosted by a separate fund established by Rangers, with William Wilton the principal trustee. He launched himself wholeheartedly into the fund-raising activities, arranging benefit matches, concerts and a variety of other initiatives. Through the auspices of Rangers, he raised over £4,000. Some idea of the true value of this sum can be seen when it is compared to the £12,000 it cost to construct the stadium.

The disaster was certainly a black moment in Wilton's life, but, ironically, tributes that followed his own death in 1920 referred to his remarkable efforts in swelling the disaster fund.

Following the events of 4 April 1902, Rangers recognised that much work would be required to improve safety in the stadium and ensure that they would never face such tragedy again. In order to finance the improvement works, the club put all 22 professional players up for sale. It was a sad end to a great side that had dominated the League championship for three seasons, but the resilience of the team in that difficult 1902–03 season was rewarded with a Scottish Cup win. Wilton now set about the reconstruction of Rangers both on and off the field.

THE REBIRTH OF IBROX AND THE HAMPDEN RIOT

While the team battled to recover from the effects of the disaster, Wilton and his committee continued to pursue ground improvements and in 1904 secured the purchase of Ibrox for the princely sum of £15,000. By the following year the reconstruction works were well under way, with a programme of demolition in the clearance of the old wooden stands for the erection of the massive earth banks that would replace them. By the end of the year Rangers had spent £42,000 on the stadium, a huge increase on the £12,000 which precipitated the incorporation of the club just six years earlier.

While Ibrox remained first and foremost a football ground, the stadium continued to be used for a range of other sports and the renowned Ibrox Sports meeting. Famous athletes from around the world were attracted to the ground and William Wilton took an active part in the close-season organisation of the event. In 1904 Alfred Shrub, a top athlete of the period, pronounced the Ibrox track to be the finest he had ever run on. As if to offer justification to his comments, Shrub proceeded to set world records in the two-mile and four-mile races at the ground.

As the club continued its rehabilitation off the field, success on the field of play was comparatively elusive until 1909 when the team battled through to the Scottish Cup final, and an encounter with Old Firm rivals Celtic. The sides played out 90 minutes with four goals between them but no outright winner. The game went to a replay and a crowd of around 60,000 returned to Hampden, many believing that the match would be played to a conclusion. One Glasgow newspaper had suggested this would be the case, although the SFA rules unequivocally stated that a further replay would be required in the event of a draw.

Almost inevitably, the match ended with the teams all-square, but the uncertainty of the fans on the question of extra-time was compounded by the fact that some players lingered on the field instead of walking straight to the pavilion. At a time when there was already a common belief that the Old Firm were indeed a commercial entity rather than two football clubs, the prevailing view among the fans was that the sides were exploiting the situation for another pay-day. The uncertainties conveyed by the press on the arrangements in the event of a draw were unhelpful.

The partisan crowd quickly became a singularly unruly mob intent on seeking some retribution for the failure of their teams to play to a conclusion. Fences were torn down, pay-boxes were set alight and as the police moved in to attempt to restore order, they were pelted with stones.

The board convened a few days after the match and discussed the 'regrettable riot' which took place at Hampden. Wilton was assigned, with two fellow directors, to approach Celtic with a view to making a public statement. Celtic met the delegation and the following statement was issued: 'Although it was mooted during the week that extra-time might be played in the event of a draw, it was found that the Cup competition rules prevented this. On account of the regrettable occurrences of Saturday, both clubs agree to petition the association that the final tie be abandoned.'

While debates raged on as to whether there should ever have been a second game due to some controversial refereeing decisions in the first match, it all became pointless arguing. The two clubs were acutely embarrassed by the events and wanted to extricate themselves from the issue as quickly as possible.

TRAINING AND PHYSIOTHERAPY IN THE WILTON ERA

While Wilton was involved in the acquisition of players and clearly had a pivotal role in selecting the team, preparing the players for matches was left firmly in the domain of the club trainer, James Wilson. The onset of professionalism altered the traditional routines whereby players would turn up at the stadium in the evenings after doing a hard day's labour. When wages reached a level at which players could dispense with their jobs and concentrate solely on football, the training régime altered with sessions organised for the morning, afternoon and evening. The professional players turned up during the day and those who continued to work attended the stadium in the evening. Some of the professionals also turned in an evening shift.

Many old traditionalists felt that this did little for the game, claiming that the professional player who went to the ground every day would lose his enthusiasm and become 'stereotyped, listless and automatic'. There is little doubt, however, that the regular attendance of the players at the ground provided the trainer with an opportunity to monitor fitness and ensure that injuries were properly dealt with. The Ibrox training records from this period prove fascinating reading and research has shown that the methods were fairly typical of the practices that prevailed more widely throughout the game.

Monday was generally used for recuperation after the rugged play of the Saturday. The players invariably went for a four-mile walk, wearing the obligatory 'heavy sweater'. By the afternoon, with the muscles loosened, they did some sprinting and exercises. These exercises were normally carried out in the gym and were typical of the routines used in training for many sports during that period. Skipping was popular and exercises with the Indian clubs, dumb-bells and ball-punching helped tone and build upper-body strength.

On Tuesdays, the focus was very much directed towards shooting practice in the morning and evening with the afternoon used, again, for exercising. Occasionally the players would have a game of five-a-side and some had their legs massaged, but the programme would be already building towards the weekend match.

On Wednesdays, the trainer took the squad walking and running for four miles before returning to the ground for sprinting in the afternoon. Many of the players enjoyed a hot bath after training, and some returned for the evening session to join the working pros and amateurs.

Thursdays were used to hone shooting skills and the morning session was rounded off with sprinting and exercises into the afternoon. When the players returned to the ground on Friday, the morning was generally set aside for sprinting, with the afternoon set aside as a period of rest. The training records reveal that on one occasion the players complained of 'sore legs' after the heavy sessions of the week and were sent home to relax before the game.

Prior to important matches, the players were usually taken away for 'special training' to the likes of Troon on the west coast or the inland haven of Dunblane Hydro. The coastal resort was favoured because of the 'change of air' which the players felt was beneficial.

Generally, the emphasis lay more on maintaining the fitness of the players rather than on enhancing their footballing skills. This was a criticism that was levelled at most teams around this time. Rangers' training programme allowed only one session in the week to be devoted to the actual improvement of ball skills in five-a-sides and, even then, the coaching was tenuous. One old football worthy of the period questioned why players were not encouraged to 'practise dribbling'. He went further by raising concerns that 'men get nothing like as much actual work with the ball as they need'. This is a criticism that persists to the modern day and it is curious that the common sense that prevailed almost a century ago should not be reflected by significant change in the relative proportions of ball-work and fitness training at many clubs today.

Although the players appeared to be responsible in their attention to their training duties, the trainer felt on at least one occasion that the squad might be distracted by interests elsewhere. He told them all to turn up at the ground one afternoon 'to prevent them going to Ayr races'. It is reminiscent of a similar incident in recent times when Ally McCoist incurred the wrath of Graeme Souness by travelling to Cheltenham races at a time when the manager reckoned the striker should have been in Glasgow.

Certainly in the early days of football, the men traditionally attracted to the game came from rougher stock and training instilled a discipline that they might otherwise not have received. One worthy ventured 'that men have so much time hanging heavily on their hands that, if it were not artificially taken up, would probably be devoted to purposes which would not be conducive to good football later in the week'. At a time when Glasgow had a public bar on every corner, it is not too difficult to imagine the distractions which young men were exposed to.

Apart from that, the records provide no indication that the players in Wilton's era had anything other than a responsible attitude to their training duties. The trainer was in fact the man with whom the players had most contact during the season and invariably a bond developed between them. He pushed them on in training but also attended to their injuries.

After a rigorous training session the players would relax in a hot 'soda bath' or have their aching muscles massaged. Common injuries such as bruising and muscle strains were generally treated by the application of 'hot fomentations' and massaged with oil. It was often said that players 'felt a fine glow of health after a vigorous rubbing down following a good bath'.

More severe injuries were treated by 'steamer' and the players would sit with the injured limb placed inside this primitive but effective contraption for a considerable period. In instances when the injury was beyond the capable treatments of the trainer, the player was referred to the doctor who would administer appropriate attention. As a general rule, the doctor would attend the ground at least once a week, stitching cuts and putting broken limbs in splints.

While the players fought their way back to fitness, the trainer kept a watchful eye on their progress and recorded their condition in his daily report. This was vital information for the selecting committee and Wilton, who were eager to get their very best players on the field. Players approaching full fitness were often noted to be 'running well and kicking all right'.

Clearly, therefore, the players had greater day-to-day contact with the trainer than they did with Wilton, whose attention was focused more firmly on the routine administration of his secretarial duties. James Wilson continued to work with the players on a daily basis, but in 1910 the club offered his position to William Struth of Clyde, with the intention that Wilson would revert to the role of groundsman. It is unclear what precipitated the move, although clearly Rangers identified Struth's capabilities much earlier than is commonly realised. Any difficulties that Wilson would have in accepting the move were lost when Struth declined the offer, while expressing thanks to the committee for their consideration. It was suggested that Struth was reluctant to take the position because he knew that his arrival would result in demotion for James Wilson.

Wilton put the disappointment of his failure to attract Struth behind him and continued with his initiatives to improve Rangers and Ibrox. Forty-two turnstiles were ordered in 1911 as the average attendance at Ibrox rose to over 20,000. Extra rows of terracing were also added to the new earth banks over the next couple of years, and a concrete wall replaced the railings around the track.

Wilton was given funds of up to £500 by the board to seek players for the coming season of 1914–15. The loyal old trainer James Wilson died early in the year and a replacement had to be found. William Struth wrote to the club requesting consideration for the same position he had turned down four years earlier. This time, when the post was offered to him, he accepted. Rangers were ready for a new era, but the world was about to be thrown into a conflict that would have a dramatic effect on everyday life. On 4 August 1914 Britain entered the First World War.

RANGERS DURING THE FIRST WORLD WAR

Britain's entry into the conflict took place shortly after the season commenced and it did not take long for the events to have an impact on the game. With no conscription, the country relied on its young and loyal men volunteering to take up arms.

Just a few days after the outbreak of war, Sir John Ure Primrose, an honorary president of Rangers for many years, sent a letter to the club. He adopted the formal role of recruitment officer and requested that Rangers send two representatives to attend a meeting with other clubs with a view to assisting the war effort. His letter highlighted that the meeting would 'consider what the football clubs can do towards raising recruits for the army at this time of national danger'.

At the same time, the players readied themselves for conflict by setting up a 'rifle club' and Rangers decided to pay the cost of the ammunition. Meanwhile, Wilton attended the meeting along with a fellow director. The clubs agreed to contribute money towards recruitment expenses, but Rangers' involvement in the war effort extended far beyond any token finance.

They sent a dozen footballs, on request, to the soldiers at Aldershot, but what began as a small gesture would eventually turn into a 'vital supply' to the front-line troops. By the end of the war Rangers had sent hundreds of balls to the troops, many purchased through collections at the ground. They may not have been of direct value in winning the war, but the popularity of the Rangers footballs suggests that they were an important contribution to boosting the morale of the troops.

It is curious that, for all horrors of the Great War, football should figure in one of the most poignant moments of truce. A few years back, Paul McCartney had chart success with his Christmas anthem *Pipes of Peace*. The song told the story of a remarkable incident which allegedly took place amidst the pall of death on the fierce battlefields of Belgium. It concerned a brief cessation of the hostilities on Christmas Day when the soldiers of both sides emerged from their cold, dark and dingy trenches to face each other for a kick-about on the battlefield. Details of the event are sketchy, but it is entirely possible that the ball which featured in the story was one of the many that travelled to the front from Ibrox.

Football continued amidst the troubles, providing some entertainment and sense of normality in a country anxious that its young men would return. With huge numbers rushing to join up, attendances at matches suffered and the game descended into financial hardship. Desperate to play their part, however, Rangers instructed that any of their players who felt they wanted to take the king's shilling would continue to be paid by the club, receiving half wages.

With the average attendance dropping from 20,000 to less than 15,000 in that first season, causing income to plummet, the club had to tighten its belt. The assistant trainer and assistant secretary had to be dismissed as the club strove to cut costs. Times were hard but Wilton continued to manage the affairs with true resilience – although he found some of the directors less eager to continue. In private correspondence to a friend just four months into the conflict he wrote: 'There is big agitation in here just now to have the game stopped until the war is over.' Wilton wanted to continue, and Rangers did, serving an important role in maintaining the morale of Glaswegians.

As 1914 drew to a close and an end to the conflict seemed far away, the players were called to attend a board meeting where a letter from the Scottish Football League was read out. It recommended a reduction in players' wages as a result of the 'financial position' of the clubs. Rangers undertook to refund the players at the end of the war, if possible. The players accepted the deal, and then Wilton addressed them on the subject of army recruitment. Many were clearly interested in going to the front because the records show that a number asked Wilton to get details of the terms of service.

As players moved around the country on war duty they became available to play for local clubs. Many Rangers players went off to fight, but most remained in Glasgow to help with the war effort by working in the yards and factories near the stadium. William Wilton and William Struth were not called up as they were considered to be in gainful employment at Ibrox, but they offered to assist at the wartime hospital at Bellahouston. In October 1915 they received a letter from the Red Cross accepting Struth as a masseur and Wilton as an assistant in the general running of the facilities at Bellahouston. Their assistance would only be part-time because they still had key roles to fulfil in the day-to-day running of Rangers.

At the same time, with massive casualties being reported on the front, the board decided to reserve some accommodation at Ibrox for wounded soldiers. During this period Rangers developed a close affinity with the Bellahouston Hospital and the nearby Murrayflats Hospital, probably mainly because of their location but also no doubt as a result of the involvement of Wilton and Struth. No sooner had the two men taken up their positions than the club donated a piano and organ to Bellahouston. A few months later they made a similar gift to Murrayflats.

While Wilton worked hard to keep the soldiers' spirits up with many well-organised concerts, Struth was granted special leave to train in London and enhance his Red Cross work.

Although mainland Britain had not suffered much damage from bombing, Rangers decided it would be prudent to take out 'Aircraft Insurance' for the 'stands, pavilion, walls and pay-boxes'. The premium was £12/10s and the value of the insurance was £12,500.

In recognition of their efforts, the board voted a war bonus to both Wilton and Struth. Wilton received £50, which represented two months' salary. It was a well-deserved award as the manager had thrown himself into his dual role with characteristic vigour. Struth received a smaller bonus in keeping with his standing at the club, but it was no less deserved.

Early in 1917 Struth received a letter instructing him to commit himself to full-time duties for the Red Cross or join the army. He decided that he could best serve with the Red Cross for which he had become a valuable operative.

As the war continued into the spring of 1917, the board rewarded Wilton for his efforts once again, with a £50 increase in his salary, which rose to £350.

The war, meanwhile, continued to have a devastating effect on the community, and, with more and more young men heading east, the average gates fell by another 3,000. Among the Ibrox favourites who went to the front were Andy Cunningham, Dr James Paterson, Jimmy Gordon and William Reid. With his squad depleted, Wilton was left in many instances with only youngsters to fill the gaps in the team. At the AGM the chairman commented that the club's third-place finish in the League was good, 'considering the number of first-class players who had gone to fight for their country and the long hours and arduous work of those left, who were all on war work'.

Wilton went into the new season with two new players – players who would go on to become Rangers legends: Sandy Archibald and Tommy Muirhead. They were joined a month later by Arthur Dixon (Little or L'il Arthur) who would eventually serve the club well as trainer.

In September 1917 Ibrox was honoured to be selected as the venue for an investiture when King George V presented medals to the country's heroes. Thousands attended the ceremony, their flags waving as the King's car carried him around the track, before he stepped out on to the Ibrox turf. It was a great day in the history of Rangers Football Club and one in which Wilton did himself and the club proud with his organisation.

The city of Glasgow recorded its gratitude in a letter stating that the King 'expressed himself as highly pleased with the arrangements'. Two months later Wilton received acknowledgement for his great public standing by being appointed a Justice of the Peace.

As football struggled through the war years, Rangers finally got some reward for their efforts on and off the field by winning the League championship. In a final day of drama, with the Light Blues locked at the top with old rivals Celtic, something had to give. Rangers put aside the nervousness that had characterised their play in the preceding weeks to defeat Clyde at Ibrox. Meanwhile, at Celtic Park, Motherwell held the home side to a draw to send the championship trophy to Ibrox for the first time in five years.

Wilton had done remarkably well to continue his administration and management duties at Ibrox while at the same time providing sterling service to Bellahouston Hospital, but the stresses were taking their toll. In private correspondence he wrote that his 'time had been taken up with Red Cross work and football for the past three years'. The work at the stadium was onerous as he arranged countless benefit matches for a variety of war-relief funds in addition to competitive games. But at the hospital he faced the trauma of dealing with the many casualties who had been sent back from the front.

Through it all, he was seen as a rock upon which others could rely for support in times of trouble. One poignant letter that he received from the sister of Sandy Archibald sought his assistance regarding the stationing of her brother. She enquired, in an anxious tone, if there was any way that Wilton could use his influence to have Sandy assigned to a regiment that would be in less peril. Wilton's reply was sympathetic, if not successful in achieving the young girl's wishes.

Archibald would come through the war without injury, but Walter Tull, the first black player to sign for the club, was killed in action in March 1918. He was the only one of the playing staff to die in the conflict although, like most families let alone clubs, tragedy was to touch many more of those involved at Ibrox. Director William Crichton, for example, lost a son in the early days of the war.

Wilton continued to play a major part in the relief effort, arranging Christmas treats for the wounded soldiers at Bellahouston and sending parcels to 'players on foreign service'. 'Greetings and cigarettes' were sent to players on home service. Still the footballs were despatched to the troops and in the six months prior to March 1918 the board recorded that 125 balls had been sent overseas. Four months later, another 50 were on their way. The troops would soon be able to devote much more of their time to the beautiful game, however. Just four months after the last batch of balls was sent to the front, on the eleventh hour of the eleventh day of the eleventh month, the Great War ended.

EMERGENCE FROM DARKNESS

As the country emerged from the dark days of wartime the popularity of football was revived, with crowds swelled by those young men who had survived the battlefields of Europe. The average attendance at Ibrox returned to pre-war levels, and a bit more. On the field Rangers had a good championship challenge but lost out by a single point to Celtic. The season ended fruitless, but the Light Blues were building a new side.

Before the 1918–19 season had finished, the directors decided to honour William Wilton for his services with a benefit match. It is unclear whether Wilton was entirely supportive of the idea, or perhaps a little embarrassed, but he wrote to Everton, the invited opponents, confirming that the arrangements were to be quite private. In his correspondence he explained, 'The proceeds go as complimentary to the writer after 30 years' service. I do not wish, however, to advertise it as a "Benefit", so it will just be billed as an ordinary match.'

The records show that around 20,000 watched the game, which the Light Blues won comfortably, ensuring a well-deserved payday for Wilton.

Rangers continued their progress to the top of Scottish football in the 1919–20 season with a settled side that included many of the great names who were to be the backbone of the side through the next decade and beyond – Manderson, Archibald, Cairns, Muirhead and Cunningham, and then, in March 1920, a young Davie Meiklejohn. They were to become legends, one and all.

As Rangers marched through the season in style and fought through to the semi-final of the Scottish Cup, the pressure of work built up on Wilton. In early April, the club received a request to play a testimonial match, but the intensity of the fixture card virtually ruled out the possibility of finding a free date. Wilton replied that Rangers would have three games per week up to the end of the season, quite apart from other testimonial commitments. In fact, they played ten matches in April alone with a further four scheduled for the first week in May. And this didn't include several Alliance matches and Second Eleven Cup games.

Wilton continued to build the squad, signing William Orb from Birmingham FC for a fee of £1,500 as the championship drew to a conclusion. There were frustrations, too, and Wilton talked of his 'rotten luck with enquiries at the moment', as he rushed off to attend a meeting in Edinburgh as April drew to a close. His efforts continued with some evenings set aside to talk to other clubs about available players. Wilton was assisted in his acquisition of players by a network of scouts, or what may now loosely be called 'agents'.

On 28 April a draw at Dumbarton was enough for Rangers to secure their tenth League title, with a record points total. Two days later Wilton sent a letter to one of his agents enclosing a money order in settlement of outlays incurred in the acquisition of players. He wrote that it would 'close their little arrangement', but he expressed an interest in any other players that should become available. It was the last letter he would ever write. He closed the small book of correspondence which related his hectic and involved schedule of duties and looked forward to the final game of the League season against Morton. He would never open the book again. It was the May holiday weekend, and the Rangers manager was looking forward to relaxing aboard James Marr's boat. He would leave with director Joseph Buchanan immediately after the game to head down to Gourock. He was never to return.

A few weeks later, at the AGM of the club that Wilton had been so influential in rearing to such great standing, the chairman spoke of 'the deep sense of loss which the club had sustained'. At that, those present stood in silence in respect for a man destined to become revered in Ibrox folklore.

It is doubtful whether Rangers would have become the club that it is today without the endeavours of William Wilton. He established the organisation of the club, seeing it through the traumas of disaster and war, and guiding it towards not just success but also prominence in the game throughout Scotland. The first manager of Rangers, he laid the foundations upon which others would build.

WILLIAM STRUTH

A few years ago I was honoured to assist John Bett, the celebrated actor, playwright and director, in the research for his successful stage play about Rangers, *Follow, Follow.* After he had put the final touches to the script, I read it over to remove any historical inaccuracies. The only area I had misgivings about was a long monologue by Rangers' second manager, William Struth. It was eloquently written, quite emotional in places and suggested a deep affection for the club. I felt that it would sound too scripted – more a caricature than a realistic portrayal of the man.

When I discussed this with Bett, he told me that he had lifted the passage, unaltered, from an acceptance speech that Struth had made when he received the portrait that now hangs prominently in the Ibrox trophy-room, shortly before he died. The portrait was presented to him by the Lord Provost and some friends in recognition of his service to 'Glasgow sport'. Struth had uttered these very words in gratitude for the honour that was bestowed upon him. They provide a remarkable insight into his intense affection for the club, and his expectations of those who served it. He said:

> I have been lucky – lucky in those who were around me from the boardroom to the dressing-room. In time of stress, their unstinted support, unbroken devotion to our club and calmness in adversity eased the task of making Rangers FC the premier club in this country.
>
> To be a Ranger is to sense the sacred trust of upholding all that such a name means in this shrine of football. They must be true in their conception of what the Ibrox tradition seeks from them. No true Ranger has ever failed in the tradition set him.
>
> Our very success, gained you will agree by skill, will draw more people than ever to see it. And that will benefit many more clubs than Rangers. Let the others come after us. We welcome the chase. It is healthy for all of us. We will never

hide from it. Never fear, inevitably we shall have our years
of failure, and when they arrive, we must reveal tolerance
and sanity. No matter the days of anxiety that come our way,
we shall emerge stronger because of the trials to be overcome. That has been the philosophy of the Rangers since
the days of the gallant pioneers.

Struth lived much of his life overlooking Ibrox from his tenement
flat in Copland Road and when he died on 21 September 1956 after
a long illness, he was interred in nearby Craigton Cemetery, close
to his beloved stadium. It is where he would have wished to lie,
because Rangers became a huge part of his life, although he would
have scarcely imagined his destiny when he took up the vacant
position of trainer at the ground forty-two years earlier.

THE ROAD TO IBROX

William Struth was born in Milnathort, Kinross-shire, in 1875 and
lived much of his early life close to Heart of Midlothian's Tynecastle Park. It was inevitable that he would harbour an affection
for the Maroons, although his aptitude in sports tended more
towards athletics than it did to football. In fact, apart from in a
few games as a schoolboy, he scarcely kicked a ball.

Struth was a stonemason, but although this was his trade it was
not his living. By his teens, he was running in local meetings and
picking up prizes, although he still found time to help out in a
variety of odd-jobs. 'I was glad to get a tanner for a couple of hours
digging,' he once said.

Eventually he would gain widespread respect as a champion
athlete, excelling at every distance from the sprint to the mile. At
the half-mile race, he had no equal in his day. He travelled, as a
professional athlete, to competitions throughout the country in
what was tough work for aspiring athletes. 'If we didn't win, we
didn't eat,' he said, and his determination to win was without
question. In one handicap race at Porthcawl, in Wales, unhappy at
the distance he was required to concede, he set off before the gun,
sprinting to the line and straight for the prize table where he
received a £5 voucher before the starter could alert the organisers.
He was told that he could exchange the voucher for cash, so off he
ran to the bank, then grabbed the first train out of town. Years

later he donated £50 to the Porthcawl sports meeting and relived the moment with the officials, who laughed at his exploits. It was said that Struth never failed to repay a debt. His conscience may have been spurred, but the story of the Porthcawl meeting provides an insight to the hardships of professional running in that period and Struth's determination. As he later confessed, he had to win to get the money for his fare out of town.

Struth used to train on the local football ground and he had his own ideas about fitness, which were quite different from those adopted by footballers at the time. He felt that he 'could show them a thing or two' about fitness training.

His first introduction to professional football came in a brief stint as trainer to Hearts. He was a shareholder in the Tynecastle side and no doubt enjoyed his association with the club from across the road, but in 1907 he got the opportunity to train Clyde's players. No one was more surprised than Struth himself. He saw the position advertised and applied. 'I did it for a joke,' he later admitted. 'I was flabbergasted when I received a letter telling me that I had got the job.'

The Shawfield side, a part-time outfit, were in poor shape when Struth arrived. He took up his duties with great enthusiasm, attending to the players and even the condition of the ground. He scrubbed and polished the dressing-rooms twice a week in a demonstration of fastidiousness that would later characterise his reign at Ibrox.

Within a short time, the Clyde team were reckoned to be the fittest in the country and Struth's abilities as a trainer were becoming increasingly known. His impact on Clyde was obvious. They appeared in the Scottish Cup final, the blue riband of Scottish football, twice. His reputation was growing.

In April 1910 Rangers approached him with a view to replacing the long-serving James Wilson as trainer at Ibrox. As mentioned, Struth declined, although the club records show that he was fulsome in gratitude for being considered. He possibly felt uncomfortable that Wilson would be demoted to groundsman, although he was clearly interested in the position. When Wilson died in 1914 after 17 years of solid service, Rangers revived their interest in the Clyde trainer. This time Struth was delighted to accept the position and he was appointed on 11 May 1914.

William Struth immediately formed a close working relationship with the assiduous William Wilton. While Wilton worked feverishly in the administration of the club, Struth toiled mercilessly on the training field. He was a stickler for discipline and pushed the players hard, but, as he later stated, he 'never asked one of them to do anything that [he] couldn't do himself'.

He also set an example in the clean-cut image of 'the Ranger' that prevails today. Players had to be immaculate both on and off the pitch. Smoking and swearing in the dressing-room were unacceptable. On one occasion even the Rangers chairman was asked to remove a cigarette from his mouth when he entered Struth's domain.

Struth's secret for training was in paying meticulous attention to individual players' needs. He studied every one of them and adjusted their training accordingly. It was said that he groomed and trained every player as if he were a racehorse – or a professional runner.

But there was more to Struth than simply a carefully worked-out training régime. He was inspirational and had a magnetism which encouraged players to take the field when they were off-colour in form, or even in health. Struth felt that it was important to keep his men together. Former club captain Tommy Muirhead once said that Struth 'could persuade you to play with a broken ankle'. But he was not being critical: he believed that the manager had got it right. 'He's terrific,' he finished.

A few months after joining Rangers, Struth found himself in a position quite unrelated to that he was appointed to. With the outbreak of the Great War, every football club, like every other organisation, had to adapt and assist in the national emergency. Struth was quickly immersed in the traumas of the war effort, applying his limited but invaluable knowledge of physiotherapy to aid the casualties detained in the nearby Bellahouston Hospital. He learned a lot from the orthopaedic surgeons and doctors there, gaining a knowledge that he was to put to good use in later years. He once performed an emergency dressing-room operation on a player's soft corn using a sterilised penknife. His interest went wider. Whenever a player went to theatre for cartilage operations or similar surgery, he insisted on being there during the procedure.

In the busy Bellahouston Hospital, Struth served capably along-side William Wilton who had taken up a key administrative role there. He threw himself wholeheartedly into his wartime duties, further developing his skills as a masseur and training in advanced physiotherapy. Like Wilton, he served at the hospital by day and returned to the stadium in the evenings to continue the work at Ibrox. The days were long and arduous. It was a stressful time for both men as they strove to keep the team together and maintain some sort of continuity with football life. They recognised that, like other 'entertainments', as football was deemed, the game had a role to play in keeping up morale at a time when the attention of the worried populace would drift to mainland Europe.

Finally, when the war ended, Struth celebrated the return to normality with some silverware that had been strangely elusive throughout much of the conflict. In 1920, in the first full season after the war, Wilton and Struth rejoiced when Rangers secured the championship with a record points total. Struth, as trainer, had every reason to be pleased with the team's performance. The side scored 106 League goals and conceded just 25. Interest in football rose again and the average attendance climbed to around 20,000 from the 15,000 experienced in the final year of war.

Like the manager, Struth looked forward to the May weekend break as Rangers concluded their League campaign with victory over Morton. Unlike Wilton, who perished that fateful evening on the *Cultha*, Struth would return to Ibrox and prepare for a role that he would assume for 34 years: manager of Rangers.

WILLIAM STRUTH: THE NEW MANAGER

The management role that William Wilton had evolved at Ibrox quite simply could not be fulfilled by any other individual. Wilton almost single-handedly ran Rangers using the administrative skills and familiarity he had gained through an association with the club extending over three decades. In fact, his intimate knowledge of the game extended beyond Ibrox to the very corridors of power at the SFA and the Scottish League. He had been an administrator with an interest in the playing-field. Struth was fundamentally a sportsman whose interest in the administration was very much secondary to the performance of the team.

In the aftermath of Wilton's tragic death, the club's directors deliberated over the position. They knew that they could not find a man capable – or, possibly, willing – to take on the onerous duties that Wilton had assumed. They decided that they would create two positions – one of secretary and the other of manager.

Struth was the natural choice as manager, a position ratified in June 1920. The *Evening Times* hailed the move as 'a popular and sensible appointment', and pointed out that Struth was 'a keen student of all phases of athletic life with a wide and varied knowledge of men and matters'. With the manager's position resolved, the directors attended to the administration in the short term, before appointing W. Rogers Simpson as the new secretary.

Struth's graduation to the position of manager was a natural transition from his role on the training-ground where he had served well for a number of years at Tynecastle, Shawfield and, finally, Ibrox. He was ready to relinquish these duties in favour of a more active management role, although the death of Wilton hardly created the circumstances under which he would have expected, or wanted, to attain the position.

Struth took on the job with some trepidation. In the early years he trod warily, keeping his mouth shut and his ears open. He later confessed that he had some doubts in the beginning as to whether he was worthy of the role. Considering what he ultimately achieved, his self-doubt was clearly misplaced. Despite this initial anxiety, though, Struth immersed himself in the position with some vigour. He may not have been the model replacement for Wilton, but he embraced his predecessor's principles to the letter. Nothing but the best would be good enough for Rangers and Struth. He resolved to do what he did best: turn out a fine football team that would be a credit to the blue jersey.

The players found that they were lauded and cosseted by the new manager. A member of the team at the time told of how Struth could never do enough for his 'boys'. If they were playing away, he saw that they had their lunch before the directors and that they had the pick of the bedrooms in the hotel before anyone else at the club had a say on their accommodation. He did everything for them and the respect was reciprocated. It was said that they obeyed without question his commands as trainer or manager. To them he was simply 'the boss'. To him they were 'my boys'.

Struth's transition to the role of manager was painless as far as the club was concerned. To many, he was simply extending his responsibilities over a team that he was already well acquainted with. There would be no tactical changes, because Struth wasn't a man of tactics. He simply picked the best players in the best positions and left it up to them, sending them on to the field with some rousing words.

One player he picked, his first notable signing as manager, was Alan Morton. The diminutive winger was already a big name in Scottish football having served both Queen's Park and Scotland well. At the end of the 1919–20 season speculation was rife that he would relinquish his amateur status and move south like many stars of the period but Bill Struth stepped in and convinced Morton that his future lay in Scotland, where he could continue his studies towards qualifying as a mining engineer. Morton agreed, and he joined Rangers in one of the most important transfers in the club's history. It was the start of a wonderful association as Morton gave Rangers 13 good seasons, carving out a place for himself in Scottish football folklore.

Struth added others to his squad, most notably Willie Robb in goal and Billy McCandless. He took his reshaped side into his first New Year Old Firm fixture at Ibrox, and promptly lost (0–2). Remarkably, it was the only Ne'erday match he would lose to Celtic at the stadium in 34 years of management.

The setback of that defeat did not prevent Struth from leading Rangers to the championship in his first season in control. It was the beginning of a monopoly that the Light Blues had on the title for much of Struth's tenure. They won eight out of the ten championships of the decade and both the Glasgow Cup and Charity Cup made frequent visits to the Ibrox trophy cabinet. The Scottish Cup, however, remained strangely elusive.

William Wilton held the Cup back in 1903, but try as they might, Rangers could not recapture the trophy despite their undoubted dominance of the game at that time. In the pre-war years of Wilton, they succumbed to sides such as Falkirk, Dundee, Clyde and Hibernian, clubs that would not profess superiority over Rangers, but still they succeeded in ending the Ibrox side's hopes of the cup. Even the change of managership did little to alter the team's fortunes in the competition. Struth saw his men lose to the likes of Partick Thistle, Morton, Falkirk, Clyde and St Mirren. It was little wonder that talk of a Scottish Cup hoodoo dogged Rangers at every turn in the competition.

In 1928 the team fought their way to the final for the second time in as many years. Their opponents at Hampden Park would be old rivals Celtic, who had ended their hopes of lifting the trophy in the previous season. A crowd of 118,115, a record for the period, gathered inside the stadium. Celtic played with a stiff wind behind them in the first half and almost took the lead with a shot from outside-right Connolly which goalkeeper Tom Hamilton did well to save. The teams went in at the interval with the scoresheet blank and the tension building.

With just ten minutes played in the second half, Rangers were awarded a penalty when Celtic's McStay punched out a shot from Rangers centre Jimmy Fleming. Davie Meiklejohn, the captain, grasped the ball and the responsibility for possibly the most important spot-kick in the club's history. Regular penalty-takers McPhail and Cunningham stood aside. Who knows what must have gone through Struth's mind as he watched Meiklejohn pause before beginning his run up to take the kick. 'Cometh the hour, cometh the man,' he would frequently tell his players. In that moment, the strength of his captain was put to the test.

It is worth relating Meiklejohn's comments afterwards, as indication of the pressures he had to endure. He described his feelings as follows: 'I saw, in a flash, the whole picture of our striving to win the Cup. I saw all the dire flicks of fortune which had beaten us when we should have won. That ball should have been in the net. It was on the penalty-spot instead. If I scored, we would win; if I failed, we could be beaten. It was a moment of agony.'

Meiklejohn hit the ball well and true, and it blasted into the net behind Celtic's young keeper, John Thompson. The captain's assessment of the importance of the kick was correct. Rangers went on from there to score three more times, smashing all remnants of the hoodoo. It had taken the club 25 years to win the Cup and now not only had they finally achieved their goal, but they had concluded their first League and Cup double.

At the end of the match, Struth saluted his heroes with tears in his eyes. Never again would there be talk of a hoodoo – in fact,

Rangers developed the kind of familiarisation for the trophy that they had previously reserved for the championship. In the next eight years they won the Cup a further five times.

At the end of the season Struth took his players on an American tour, during which they played ten games without defeat. Wherever they travelled they were greeted by thousands of exiled Scots, all delighted to see their heroes from the old land. The trip served to bond Struth and his players even more than before and they returned to see a new Ibrox growing in stature. Work was well under way on a new grandstand that would provide 19 rows of tip-up seating for 10,500.

Struth used his trade as a mason to assess the construction. 'It is all good Welsh brick and it cost £95,000 to build. Moreover, it will be here long after the others have gone,' he would say in defiance of those who suggested that the new grandstand was too ostentatious and grandiose for a football club. With the building today given 'listed' status and still standing proudly on Edmiston Drive, Struth's words were truly prophetic.

The new grandstand was officially opened by the Lord Provost, Sir David Mason OBE, on 1 January 1929. The facilities surpassed anything else available in Scotland at the time. The players, too, were well catered for. They found an ample dressing-room with a plunge bath measuring twelve and a half by six and a half feet and three feet deep, with the water heated by a special boiler in the basement. The new structure also provided facilities for the directors and guests and an office for the manager. It was a room that Struth was to treat like home for much of the remainder of his life.

THE 1930s

Bill Struth settled into his new accommodation and quickly found himself a companion – a canary. The bird flew in his window one day and into its own little piece of history. The manager captured the lost bird and placed it in a cage that he hung by the window, suspended from a hook in the top frame. The hook remains there today. Struth would occasionally give the bird a little tipple of whisky that had it chirping merrily. The spirit appeared to have no ill effects on the health of the canary, which lived for a long time.

Struth would sit by the fireside in his little home for long hours as he worked through the administrative duties of the team affairs.

Indeed, it seemed to many that he never went home at all. In the office he had a wardrobe in which he kept several suits. Such was his attention to his appearance that he would often be seen in two different suits over the course of a day. He was quite justifiably called the Beau Brummel of football.

As the administrative duties mounted at Ibrox, Struth knew that he would need some assistance. Occasionally he would take the short walk round to a little shop attached to Peacock's Bakery in Copland Road. He got to know the office manager and asked if there was anyone who could assist at Ibrox part-time. The bakery office boss suggested an Alison Dallas. She would become the heart of Rangers' administrative responsibilities for the remainder of Struth's management.

While Mrs Dallas eased the burdens of the paperwork, Struth continued to nurture the skills of 'his boys'. He retained the back-bone of the side that had been so successful through the 1920s and he continued to introduce new blood as his older players faded. In July 1931 he signed a young fair-haired centre-forward from the Irish side Coleraine. His name was Sam English. English had a remarkable start to his Rangers career, scoring two goals on his début and then grabbing five in a 7–3 win over Morton in only his fourth game. By the time Celtic came to Ibrox on 5 September 1931 for the first Old Firm game of the season, English had scored twelve goals in eight games.

In a largely uneventful first half Rangers and Celtic stood level at 0–0. Five minutes into the second half, English broke forward and rushed in on goal, bracing himself to shoot. Celtic's courage-ous young goalkeeper John Thompson rushed out to block the shot. In a sickening collision, Thompson's head struck English's knee, leaving the Rangers player limping away in pain, while the goalkeeper lay motionless on the turf.

Twenty-three-year-old Thompson was rushed to hospital but was pronounced dead later that evening. He had a depressed skull fracture. In the aftermath, emotive words from Celtic manager Willie Maley threw doubt on English's intent, but newsreel footage later confirmed what just about everyone had accepted – that it was an accident. It had been the second serious injury suffered by the goalkeeper in similar circumstances – a year earlier he had sustained a fractured jaw in another courageous dive at the feet of an onrushing forward. On that occasion, Thompson survived. His luck ran out at Ibrox.

The incident left a huge scar on the life of Sam English and although he continued his remarkable scoring rate, he never really recovered from the incident. Family members recently talked of the deep anguish he continued to suffer until his death.

The event also cut deep into Struth. While he refrained from any public antipathy with Maley, who was a good friend, he provided some comfort and support for English. He did not forget Thompson, though. Some time after Struth's own death, the club received a number of his personal effects. Included within a collection of old photographs was a sketch of John Thompson.

Struth put the trauma of the goalkeeper's tragic death behind him and continued to pursue the honours that the supporters so craved. Gillick and Venters were added to the side as old warhorses Morton, Fleming and Archibald departed. In 1933–34 Struth achieved possibly his greatest success with a clean sweep of all the major trophies. In 1931 he had won the three principal cups, the League championship, the Scottish Cup and Glasgow Cup. This time he added the Charity Cup as well. It was the culmination of a remarkably successful three-year spell in which the team won ten out of the twelve trophies they competed for.

The victories continued through the 1930s as Struth found more new stars through his network of scouts. Shaw, Duncanson, Woodburn, Waddell and Symon came in as the old guard drifted away. Attendances continued to rise and in 1939 a record 118,730 were attracted to the Ne'erday Old Firm fixture at Ibrox. The dark clouds of war were gathering, however, and football would soon descend into a void of uncertainty. Undeterred by the anxieties of war, Struth utilised all of the experience gained during the last conflict when he and Wilton had nursed the club through the difficult years to provide a rallying point for the community. He would once again be a tower of strength to Rangers.

IBROX: FOCUS OF THE COMMUNITY IN THE WAR YEARS

When Britain entered the fray on 3 September 1939, football was cast into the turmoil of a people coming to terms with impending conflict. Within days the game was suspended, before the SFA capitulated and agreed to set up a regionalised league. Clubs based in the west and south formed one league, while those in the east and north joined a northern league. The concept of a western division, which featured the Glasgow clubs and those south of the main conurbation, was not popular with the Edinburgh sides who lost the revenue generated by matches with the Old Firm. Within a year they would be incorporated in a southern league.

The conscription to service of players throughout the country necessitated the cancellation of contracts. The players were to all intents and purposes free agents, and moved around the country to wherever they were stationed. For those remaining in Scotland, wages were capped at £2 per week. Many went off to war and served valiantly, but many others remained at home to provide at least some degree of normality in the crisis of war.

Struth had first-hand experience of the role that football could play in maintaining public morale during wartime. Although above the age where he could make a practical contribution to the effort in applying his medical skills as he had done in the 1914–18 conflict, he recognised the importance of the club to the community. Normalisation could only be pursued if the team had the main body of its peacetime personnel.

Using his long-standing contacts in the shipyards and factories of Govan, Struth placed a number of his boys in what were known as 'reserved occupations'. Some critics believed that his motives were simply to put his players beyond the draft. While many remained, a number of first-team stars joined the armed forces. They included Tom McKillop, Davie Kinnear, James Galloway, Chris McNee, Joe Johnston and Willie Thornton. The last in particular distinguished himself well in battle, earning the Military Medal. As the war continued, more Rangers players joined the conflict.

The free movement of players during the war years saw several stars guest for Rangers, including the great Stanley Matthews who went on to win a Charity Cup medal in 1941. Former Ranger Torry Gillick also returned from Everton to guest for the side, and Jimmy Caskie made an early appearance before eventually signing for Rangers in 1945.

Throughout the war the club played many charity matches, raising funds for a variety of good causes including the Clydeside Air-Raid Distress Fund and the Lord Provost's Central Relief

Fund. Rangers might have been a good draw for fund-raising and a boon for national morale, but they were nevertheless keen to win: the Ibrox side totally dominated football during those years of war. In the seven years of the conflict, they won 25 of the 30 major competitions they entered. They won all seven championships, losing only 26 games of the 211 League matches they played. While wartime competitions are often excluded from the official records, these seven championships were part of a winning sequence of nine consecutive titles that Struth won over the period.

It was not all joy for the manager, however. The war years brought sadness with the death of his wife in 1941. He became closer to the Dallas family which by now were a rock to him. With no one else at home at 193 Copland Road, Struth had little reason to leave the stadium, other than to sleep. Rangers and Ibrox absorbed more and more of his time.

Ibrox had a major morale-boosting role to play in wartime, as the stadium was used for a variety of sports designed to lift the spirits of the Glasgow public. But it was put to one of its strangest uses late in the war when it was used as a transit camp for prisoners-of-war. The captured enemy soldiers were marched from Bella-houston army camp down Edmiston Drive and into the stadium. They were deloused in the showers and then camped overnight under guard as they slept on the pitch and under the enclosure. The Army Catering Corps served them with food from large drums that were sited under the stand. The soldiers may have known where they were, but any invading armies may not have recognised the ground – the 'RANGERS FC' sign above the stand was blacked out throughout the conflict.

One evening as the war neared a conclusion, Struth sat in his chair by the fire chatting with Charlie Dallas as the latter's wife tidily completed the day's paperwork and their young daughter Alison busied herself with homework. They were startled by a pounding on the great oak door of the main entrance. Struth and Dallas made their way downstairs and opened the door to find two Canadian servicemen. They were stationed at nearby Bellahouston army camp. They explained that they had heard all about Rangers and wondered if they could have a look around. From the army activity in Glasgow and the huge number of barrage balloons that seemed to be holding up Scotland, the servicemen knew that something was about to happen on the front-line, but they were uncertain what. They were due to leave Glasgow, however.

Struth, who was particularly courteous and respectful towards servicemen, invited them in for a browse around Ibrox's inner sanctum. He showed them the beautiful Art Deco mirror that hung behind the cocktail bar and offered them a drink. He invited them down to view the famous turf. As they stood on the touch-line, one of the young servicemen bent down to pick some of the grass which he then tucked inside his tunic pocket. He explained to Struth that where they were going they may not see grass for a long time. 'Let us know how you get on, then, and make sure you bring that grass back,' replied the manager. They left, never to return. A few weeks later, Struth enquired of the men and their destination. He was told they were part of the first assault on Omaha Beach on D-Day. Their regiment suffered heavy losses.

Just after the war, in November 1945, Rangers played one of the most famous matches in their history when the Russian side Moscow Dynamo came to Ibrox on a tour. It was the last in a four-match series of games for the Russians against British opposition, a series which was organised more for political reasons than any interest the Soviets had in broadening their knowledge of the game. It was also the first all-ticket match at Ibrox and it was a case of all hands on deck as manager, players, trainers and even Mr and Mrs Dallas checked every ticket when they arrived from the printer. Even then, there were concerns over forgeries!

On the field, Struth had other difficulties. The Russians, chastened by their match against Arsenal in which the Highbury side had featured some guests, demanded that Rangers exclude new signing Jimmy Caskie. They saw it as an attempt by Rangers to bolster their team for the match – even though Caskie had been acquired with the future in mind, rather than as a short-term stop-gap as implied by the Russians. Nevertheless, they insisted, 'If Caskie plays, we go home.' It was hardly an international incident, but Struth bowed to their demands.

Absenteeism reached unprecedented levels on match day and some schools bowed to the inevitable. A crowd of around 90,000 saw the game on a Wednesday when it has often been said that more grannies died than at any other time!

Rangers and Moscow Dynamo served up a football feast that is still recalled by many old timers. Rangers went on to gain a 2–2 draw after having gone behind by 2–0, and the Russians were fulsome in their praise of a side they considered to be the fittest that they had faced on the tour. The Scottish team needed more than fitness – some mathematical skills were also necessary as the Russians ended up with an extra man on the field! They would have finished that way had it not been for the eagle eye of Torry Gillick.

INTERNAL STRIFE AND BLOOD-LETTING

Rangers emerged from the war stronger than ever. Attendances at Ibrox had continued at a high level through the war years, with gates averaging around 17,000, but by 1946 crowds had risen to around 25,000, and a massive 135,000 watched Aberdeen beat Rangers in the Southern League Cup as wartime football wound up. The Glasgow side won the championship and in 1947 were on course for their ninth successive title. With attendance figures now at around 32,000, a new and formidable side in harness, and declared record profits of £12,000, the club had every reason to feel content. But trouble was brewing behind the scenes.

Sensing that the pressures of the job were getting to Struth, now of pensionable age, James Bowie, the chairman, suggested to him that there might be a position on the board of directors if he were to resign. Bowie also suggested to the manager that it would be better if he could find an assistant who could take over the reins when Struth moved into the boardroom. Asked if he had anyone in mind for the job, Struth replied that the one man he would charge with the responsibility of running the club had since taken up an 'important job in football'.

It is almost certain that the man he had in mind was Scot Symon, who had taken up the job of manager at East Fife just a few months earlier. Ironically, Struth would eventually pass over the keys of the manager's office to Symon some seven years later.

On the face of it Bowie's suggestion seemed reasonable, but the move disguised a deep split in the management of Rangers. The club secretary, J. Rogers Simpson, was a close ally of Struth, and the three-man board of Bowie, Alan Morton and George Brown were increasingly concerned about the division between them and the men who were involved in the day-to-day running of the club. Simpson was later to claim that the directors had gone on record as stating that he would never attain directorship 'at any cost'. Simpson saw the offer to Struth of a seat on the board as a deliberate attempt to split the bond between secretary and manager.

Whatever the truth of the politics, Struth clearly fancied a place on the board, but he was not prepared to sacrifice his position as manager to attain it. He had a fundamental problem to overcome if he was to fulfil his ambition – Article 74. It stated that no director could hold any other office within the club. If he was to take the available position on the board, he would have to resign as manager – unless Article 74 could be changed.

Bringing their strength to bear on the beleaguered board, Struth and Simpson orchestrated an EGM to alter Article 74 and allow them to take up directorships. The constitution was also changed to allow the board to be expanded from three to five, accommodating both Struth and Simpson – or so the existing board members thought.

Three days before the EGM, the board sensationally called a press conference. They announced that they had learned from a casual comment that proxy voting cards had been issued to some members along with a letter signed by Struth and Simpson. The letter, which sought proxy voting on behalf of Struth, Simpson and J.F. Wilson, referred to proposed changes in the directors, adding 'they are needed'. The inference was that Bowie, whose position was up for election, would be ousted.

Bowie announced that the board would be calling on all shareholders to attend a meeting at the stadium on 11 June, just 24 hours before the EGM. Bowie called the meeting 'one of the most important in the history of the club'.

Struth, in response to press enquiries for a statement, said that the whole affair would be 'a matter for the shareholders', adding that he and Mr Simpson had 'never let the club down' and would continue to be 'good and faithful servants'. The next day he and Simpson were forthright in their condemnation of the board for 'making public the domestic affairs of the club'. There seemed no way back for either faction.

When the board met the shareholders inside Ibrox, Bowie led an impassioned defence of his role in what he called 'this deplorable story' and which Brown termed a 'crisis'. Bowie stated that the shareholders 'would be confronted by an issue which amounted to control by block financial interests as against an administration solely concerned with maintaining the high sporting traditions of the club. He was aware that the consortium which Struth had assembled would, in effect, control the club, overriding the influence of the ordinary shareholder.

Many of the shareholders in the 150-strong meeting rallied behind the board as Bowie introduced an amendment that would block the coup. On a show of hands, his amendment was carried by 84 votes to 31. Simpson then called for a poll vote calling up the respective shareholdings of his and Struth's supporters. The amendment was defeated by 13,286 votes to 3,787. Struth and Simpson were appointed directors. The battle was lost for Bowie.

At the AGM the following evening, Bowie sought re-election to the seat vacated by his retiral. He stood against John F. Wilson. Again, on a show of hands, Bowie took the vote by 45 to 27, but he stood no chance when Simpson called on the poll vote once again. Bowie was finally ousted. It is doubtful if he ever set foot inside Ibrox again.

Though the boardroom battle was of intense interest to the Scottish press, that fascination was not generally shared by the fans. On the evening of 12 June 1947, when, according to the Bowie camp, the very future of the club would seemingly be decided, not a single fan waited outside the stadium for news of the crucial vote. One newspaper correspondent mused that there would be 30,000 gathered if the team was playing a practice session. For all the machinations of the skulduggery behind the scenes the supporters were only interested in how the team performed. In that respect, with the championship flag flying over Ibrox and the new League Cup on the cabinet they had every reason to be satisfied – especially with Struth.

Struth's transition to the boardroom and his new title as director-manager was seamless. On the field, the championship was lost in season 1947–48 to new post-war challengers Hibernian, but the Scottish Cup was captured for the eleventh time after a thrilling replayed final against Morton. The final and the replay attracted a total crowd of 265,725 over the space of just five days, with the 129,176 who turned up at the replay a midweek record.

The following season Struth led his boys to the first ever treble of the Scottish League championship, the Scottish Cup and the

League Cup. To many, it was a victory for the 'Iron Curtain' defence of Rangers over the 'Famous Five' forwards of Hibernian. The Rangers defence of Brown, Young, Shaw, McColl, Woodburn and Cox were in place throughout almost the entire campaign, conceding just 32 league goals compared to the 48 their nearest challengers lost. They rightly received the plaudits, but the contribution of the forwards, including the prolific Willie Thornton and Willie Waddell, could not be underestimated. As Thornton often said, 'We scored a few goals too.'

The team of the post-war era was the third or fourth great side that Struth had assembled. He had a keen eye for a good player, but he looked for more than just ability in his acquisitions. Rangers players had to have the right mental make-up, an in-built desire to be the best. Importantly, they had to understand the demands placed on a Rangers player in maintaining discipline and upholding the traditions of the club. In all of this Struth relied heavily on his captains. He expected his captain to gather the players and make them 'Rangers-minded'. The captain would invariably be steeped in the traditions of the club. He was expected to carry Struth's philosophies and aspirations for the side on to the field. There was no place for tactics – the manager expected the captain to sort things out on the pitch. The players were expected to do the rest.

During his tenure as captain up to 1936, Davie Meiklejohn was called to the ground each Sunday to discuss the performance of the previous day. He and Struth would walk around the pitch endlessly assessing every moment and every player's contribution. George Young was another in later years who had the manager's ear.

Although he left much of the co-ordination of the players to the captain, Struth's hand was very much in evidence in guiding them to the standards he expected of a Rangers player. A ruthless disciplinarian at times, he was always fair – and respected. He always put the club first and expected his boys to do likewise. Ian McColl found this to his cost as he neared completion of college studies that would qualify him as a civil engineer. With his final exams pending, McColl asked Struth if he could miss training on the Friday to allow him to finalise his preparations. 'Do what you have to do, my boy,' was the reply. McColl duly took the time out to study, then turned up on Saturday afternoon for the match. Walking straight to his peg, McColl was then directed to the team list on the noticeboard in the dressing-room. He saw that he was excluded. The puzzled wing-half asked Struth why he had been dropped. 'If you don't train on a Friday, you don't play on the Saturday', the manager replied.

Struth had no favourites, seeing all of his players as one team. Contract negotiations were always straightforward. If any player looked for more money, he considered the situation, but his philosophy was simple. He would often tell them, 'You are one of a team – only one of eleven.' They all had a role to play and he had no time for anyone who felt that they were above this attitude. If a player had a grievance or even any domestic trouble that interfered with his game, the matter was dealt with swiftly in a transfer. But there were never any arguments, dressing-room gossip or newspaper revelations. Everything was kept discreet and private. Struth expected a lot of his players but he gave them much in return. To him, they were Rangers players – a badge that set them apart from the rest.

His insistence on smartness was legendary and if anyone failed to meet the standards he set he took firm action. One youngster spotted leaning against one of the pillars inside the main hallway at Ibrox was sternly rebuked for his slovenly attitude. No one dared be seen with their hands in their pockets. Rangers players had to be tidy at all times.

On one occasion, a newly signed young player turned up for his first night's training dressed rather shabbily. Struth despatched him to the club outfitters with instructions that he be properly attired. The cost of the outfit was drawn over several weeks from the player's wages. Torry Gillick also saw his wages systematically docked by the manager, but in quite different circumstances. Aware that his star forward had caught the eye of a young girl and that the relationship was serious, Struth called Gillick to his office.

'I've heard that you've got yourself a girl, Torry,' he said.

'Aye, that's right sir,' replied Gillick.

'Is it serious?' asked Struth.

'I think so,' said Gillick.

'Well, I suppose you'll be thinking of a ring some time. Tell me when and I'll give you the money and we can draw it out through your wages in the meantime,' said the manager, knowing that Gillick was unlikely ever to be able to save the money himself. Struth saw the situation from two perspectives. He wanted to help the player accumulate the money for the ring, but there was also a moral issue. If he was going out seriously with the girl, Struth felt it only right that they should be engaged.

So, a few weeks later, Gillick got the ring and Struth managed his finances accordingly. This was a typical gesture from a man who genuinely had the interests of his boys at heart. If they committed themselves to Rangers, and to him, they could expect the attention to be reciprocated.

Struth was everything to his players. He was their guiding hand, their mentor and even their personal physician at times – or so it seemed. One young player was concerned with a knee injury and a build-up of fluid that he was sure would keep him out of an forthcoming important fixture. Struth called the youngster to his office. He examined the injury and did not consider it serious, although the player was clearly anxious.

Without revealing his true views on the injury, he applied some lotion and asked the player to return next day to see if the medication had had any affect. Struth knew that it would cause blistering. When the youngster returned with a large water-blister, the manager called for a needle and hot water. Bursting the blister he explained that the fluid was now draining from the knee! The youngster was satisfied that the treatment was effective and played the match without further care. When reminded of the story some years later, Struth called it 'a little bit of mental massage'.

Torry Gillick was subject to rather sterner treatment when he announced his lack of fitness prior to one match. Hobbling into the dressing-room, he told the trainer Jimmy Smith that he was 'crippled' and would be unable to play. Smith told him to report to Bill Struth upstairs. Gillick replied that he 'couldnae crawl up the stairs' let alone walk. Smith was adamant that he should see the boss. A few minutes later he returned to the dressing-room saying, 'That auld _____ would have you playin' unless the bones were sticking oot yir stockings!' Gillick played and scored the winning goal.

If Struth's assessment of injuries seemed potentially dangerous, it is important to recall that he had attained qualifications in physiotherapy during the First World War and had gained ample experience of dealing with sports injuries, even if it seemed that he sometimes stole crutches away from the players. George Young recalled one incident when Willie Findlay, recuperating from a broken leg, hobbled on crutches into Ibrox and upstairs to the manager's office. He came back down with only a walking-stick and claimed to feel the better for it. Struth's reasoning was that Findlay needed to strengthen the leg – a sensible decision in the rehabilitation process even if it looked rather strange to the uninformed.

While Struth had the health and well-being of his players at the forefront of his mind, he also had to contend with his own failing strength. From 1949 onwards he was hit by a succession of ill-nesses, including haemorrhaging in his stomach, that increasingly limited his capacity to serve the club. By then, however, his disciplined approach was well ingrained in the hallways of Ibrox and there were several prepared and willing to assist in sharing the managerial burden. Transfer negotiations were handled in Struth's absence by directors Brown and Simpson. George Young, the captain, continued to direct operations on the field as he had always done. Struth had also installed Bob McPhail, a former Ranger, in the backroom team as reserve coach; he knew enough about Ibrox to ensure that things continued just as Struth would want.

In 1950 the manager suffered gangrene in one of his toes. The condition threatened to spread and he was rushed to hospital. Dr Alexander Miller, an orthopaedic surgeon who had treated many of the players in Struth's care, was the man who would operate. As he was about to be whipped off into the theatre, Struth looked down at his leg which by now was shaved and covered in iodine. Showing remarkable courage, he instructed the surgeon: 'Help yourself, Sandy.'

Struth lost his leg just below the knee. When he returned to Ibrox a few months later he displayed phenomenal spirit and character. 'Look what they've done to me', he said to Tommy Muirhead. 'Aye', replied Muirhead, 'and I mind the time when you would have kidded us into going out and playing like that.' The manager laughed, saying, 'So I would, and ye always came back.' Later, he acknowledged the difficulties that his disability pre-sented, saying, 'We've had many a joke with an injured player, offering to knock them [crutches] away, but it's different when you really have to use them yourself.'

Struth may have been disabled but he was unbowed. He had a job to do and was unstinting in his determination to continue. The marble staircase that he climbed thousands of times was a real obstacle. Loyal servants Jimmy Smith and Joe Craven were to carry him up many times after the operation.

If his hold on the reins at Ibrox was slackened, the sheer aura of his presence engulfed the stadium. When Irishman Billy Simpson came to Ibrox for signing talks in October 1950, his lasting impression was of 'meeting Mr Struth'. Simpson joined up and went on to become one of the greatest Rangers players.

The increasing difficulties Struth had in contending with his disability forced him to leave the two-storey flat in Copland Road. The Dallas family gave up their home to join him in his new place at Dalkeith Avenue in Dumbreck. There, they cared for him, virtually assimilating him into their own family in a remarkable display of devotion. Mrs Dallas continued to work at Ibrox while Charlie Dallas worked at the turnstiles on Saturdays.

Despite being increasingly debilitated by illness, Struth's enthusiasm for his work was unbridled. In the weeks leading up to the end of the season, he set out to procure the world's best athletes for the Ibrox Sports, which was still one of the most significant sports meetings in the calendar. The Sports were also important to Rangers, generating summer income for the club. Struth was always keen to highlight the benefits of his efforts in bringing the best athletes from around the world to Glasgow, but his interest was not just financial. It was borne of his early career. He was part of the world athletics scene and Rangers benefited from the esteem in which he was held.

Among the great athletes who came to Ibrox were Sydney Wooderson, the great English runner who held the world record for the mile and dominated middle-distance running through the late 1930s and early '40s; John Lovelock, the New Zealander who was a double Olympic gold medal-winner; and the legendary Finn, Paavo Nurmi, who won nine Olympic golds and three silvers. Records were regularly broken at the stadium as the best that athletics could provide came to Ibrox. The famous black athlete MacDonald Bailey, who was the world record-holder over 100 yards was another who visited the ground and built up a close friendship with the Rangers boss. *Chariots of Fire* athlete Eric

Liddell also ran at the stadium and had strong associations with Rangers during the period. He was offered training facilities by Struth. He and Harold Abrahams were regular visitors.

The Ibrox Sports day was an important event in the Scottish calendar and Struth's contribution to athletics in Scotland during this period is immeasurable.

On the football field, the early '50s brought disappointment for Rangers as they suffered barren seasons in the first two years of the decade. They did come back with a double in 1952–53 but it was a short-lived revival. By season 1953–54 the side was slipping and Struth was ailing. By now the manager was taking a reduced role in the club affairs as it became obvious that he would have to be replaced. If the pressures of his illness were not enough, discontent was growing among the supporters at the failure of the team to match the standards they had reached a few years earlier.

The bells that rang in the New Year of 1954 failed to bring good fortune to Bill Struth. At the end of the Ne'erday fixture against Stirling Albion, he slipped and tumbled down the stairway leading from the directors' box to the main hallway inside Ibrox. He was rushed to hospital. It was clear that the time had come for him to vacate the manager's room that had been his home for 26 years of the 34 he had spent at Rangers.

In 1951 he had written to the board seeking an assistant, but his fellow directors resolved to continue with things as they were. Struth wrote to them again on 26 January, 1954. The letter read:

> Mr Chairman and Gentlemen,
>
> I would like once again to bring to your notice the fact that the time has come when I feel I will have to take things easier.
>
> Could we not appoint an assistant as soon as possible, with a view to his taking over the position as manager at the end of the season?

On Struth's advice, moves were made to lure East Fife's boss, the former Ranger Scot Symon, to Ibrox. William Struth resigned from the position of manager of Rangers on 30 April, 1954. He left office with long testaments to his contribution to the game from everyone in football.

He battled unrelenting illness to participate in club affairs but by the summer of 1956 he was confined to bed for many months. The Dallases looked after him. Many considered that he would never return to the stadium but, dragging himself from bed, he made an unexpected appearance at the Ibrox Sports. It was one of his last appearances at Ibrox. On 21 September 1956, William Struth died at home at 27 Dalkeith Avenue, Dumbreck, aged 81.

His death came on the eve of an Old Firm game at Parkhead, and such was the respect that this great figure commanded on both sides of the Glasgow divide that not a sound could be heard in the ground when the teams, wearing black armbands, their heads bowed for a one-minute silence, lined up before kick-off. At the funeral at Craigton Cemetery, his coffin was carried by six of his boys.

Struth was a colossus of a man in every sense. Introduced to the club by William Wilton, he shared many of his predecessor's ideals. Indeed, so similar were they in their attitudes that it is often difficult to pinpoint the origin of some of the Ibrox traditions. While Wilton was an undoubted stickler for smartness, and is generally attributed with the Rangers affiliation to the bowler hat, Struth was the Beau Brummel of football. Willie Thornton used to tell of one encounter with Struth early in his career. Impressed by the shine on the young Thornton's boots, the manager added another shilling to his pay. Thornton never told him that it was his mother who cleaned his boots each day!

But while Wilton was undoubtedly at the centre of most things that happened at Ibrox through the early part of the century, Struth was an altogether more imposing character. He ruled Ibrox with firmness but always with fairness – the proverbial iron fist inside a velvet glove. He was well respected by his players and they would often take their troubles to him, domestic or otherwise. He regarded all who came under him as his boys and would do anything for them. If they served Rangers well, the club would look after them. It was a philosophy that Struth held true and one that has remained to the present day.

On his desk he had a small sign that was strategically turned towards all who faced him across the table. It read: 'The club is greater than the man.' At Ibrox, Struth *was* Rangers for much of his time there – a colossus in every sense.

SCOT SYMON

James Scotland Symon walked into Ibrox Stadium on 15 June 1954 with the glowing testimony of his former boss, William Struth, ringing in his ears: 'On behalf of those who cherish the good name of Rangers – a sacred trust given to so few – I extend the hand of welcome to this young man. I came to know and admire the qualities of Scot Symon when he joined us from Portsmouth. He was a man of indomitable courage, of unbreakable devotion to purpose, a man, indeed, who became a true Ranger, and no more imposing accolade could be given to anyone.'

These were no false platitudes – Struth knew Symon well. He had signed the Perthshire-born wing-half 16 years earlier and guided him through nine successful years at Ibrox. To Struth, he was the archetypal Rangers player: determined and spirited. When he finally hung up his boots and turned to management with East Fife and then Preston North End, Symon showed that his ability and knowledge of the game extended beyond the field of play. As one of Struth's boys, Symon was the only realistic candidate when the legendary manager decided to relinquish the office he had held for more than three decades.

When Struth announced his successor there was no surprise expressed by either the press or the massed ranks of the Ibrox support. The appointment was welcomed not just because it signalled the return of an old Ibrox favourite, but because the club was in turmoil. Bill Struth's power had waned in tandem with his health and the Light Blues' support had become disenchanted in the final years of his stewardship. A side that had dominated Scottish football for so long had slipped from the high standards they once enjoyed under Struth's leadership. The team was ageing and there were rumours of discontent in the dressing-room. Symon offered the opportunity of a fresh start. Importantly, he was reared in the Ibrox traditions and he was the natural heir to take Rangers into a new era.

SYMON THE PLAYER

Symon was a draughtsman by trade but showed an aptitude for sports that would set him on another career. Educated at Perth Academy, where the oval ball was preferred to the round variety, he revealed a footballing talent that would initially take him through the junior ranks to Dundee FC, his first senior club. Football did not command Symon's entire sporting interest, however. He was also a keen cricketer who went on to represent Scotland.

He joined Rangers from Portsmouth in August 1938, the same month that another legend (and future manager), Willie Waddell, made his début for the club. Symon stepped into the left-half position previously held by George Brown, and capably fitted in with the likes of Thornton, Gray, Shaw, Venters, McPhail and a succession of other greats who would carve their names in Rangers folklore. Symon made an immediate impact on the side in his first season as the club surged to the championship, but his career was to be marked by more than the glittering silverware and cascading cheers that his peers had enjoyed in previous years.

Shortly after his arrival at Ibrox, the growing concerns that conflict in continental Europe would draw Britain into the global theatre of war were realised. A country obsessed with football turned its attention to defeating the Third Reich and the game took second place.

The league structure was regionalised and teams changed to accommodate fluctuating personnel. While the core of the team that had graced Ibrox prior to the outbreak of war remained, many other players joined the services. Just as football had served to maintain the spirit of the people in the First World War, so it became a focus of apparent normality during the Second World War. The competitive element of the league system remained, although the results were generally considered of little consequence in comparison to the peacetime records. Interestingly, although some allowance should be made in relation to the alteration of the league structure during the war years, Rangers won nine successive championships, with Symon a key figure in every season. He also played in the Rangers side that trounced Celtic 8–1 in the New Year League fixture of 1943, a result often lost deep in the archives but occasionally trawled out by loyal Light Blue fans. Despite these glorious years on the field of play, there is little doubt that the reduced credibility of the league structure robbed Symon and his team-mates of the opportunity to demonstrate their true potential.

SYMON'S MANAGERIAL APPRENTICESHIP

Shortly after the restoration of peace, Symon retired as a player at the age of 35 to take up the manager's position at East Fife. It may not have appeared the most auspicious of clubs at which to make a mark, but Symon made an immediate impact, propelling the Methil side to promotion in their first season under his stewardship.

Next season, in the top flight, Symon's side continued their remarkable progress, finishing in fourth place behind the champions, Rangers. Any suspicions that this East Fife side were one-season wonders were emphatically dispelled the following year when Symon took his unfashionable team to two Cup finals. Significantly, they ousted Rangers at the semi-final stage of the League Cup before going on to lift the trophy, to the amazement of Scottish football.

They returned to Hampden for the Scottish Cup final a few months later, but on this occasion their opponents, Rangers again, exacted revenge by comfortably lifting the trophy to complete the League and Cup double. East Fife emphasised their quality by once again securing fourth position in the championship.

Symon, his stature as a manager soaring, maintained East Fife at their newly found position in the upper echelons of Scottish football through the next few years. Inevitably he was lured to newer, more lucrative pastures, and when Preston North End moved to secure his services in 1953, few would have expected to see Symon back north of the border for many years. They certainly would not have anticipated his return in just over a year.

RETURN TO IBROX

Symon had given England a taste of his capabilities when he took his Lancashire side to the FA Cup final at Wembley, but the call of Rangers was far too strong to hold Symon in the south. Although he was desperate to manage Rangers, it was a role that filled him with trepidation. There is little doubt, however, that the club was equally keen to see Symon succeed Struth.

Symon's appointment was universally applauded. Fans, newspaper columnists and directors for once were united in their view that 'Symon was the man', but there was also a realisation that the new boss had a mountain to climb. While no one would deny that Struth's contribution to Rangers in his forty years of service was immeasurable, the club needed a new stimulus as it stuttered through the legendary boss's final term. At the end of the 1953–54 season, only the Glasgow Cup sat on the boardroom cabinet. The side had slumped to fourth in the championship, lost out in the semi-final of the League Cup to Partick Thistle, and then succumbed embarrassingly (6–0) to Aberdeen at the same stage of the Scottish Cup.

Many people considered the Rangers job as the biggest in football. Struth handed Symon the keys to his kingdom. Many also felt that he had passed over a poisoned chalice. Sceptics mused that the new boss had a mammoth task on his hands, such was the air of disenchantment that had descended upon Ibrox as the ailing Struth slipped from office.

Symon recognised that he would need to rebuild the side as he surveyed a squad more than half of whom were on the wrong side of 30. Some of the key members of Struth's side, including Waddell, Young, Woodburn, Paton, Cox and Prentice, had few years left in them. There was a general awareness that European competition would soon beckon, but Symon knew that he would have a hard task in lifting Rangers to the top of Scottish football let alone succeeding beyond these shores. He was not lacking in resolve, however, showing a determination that Struth had seen in him as a player sixteen years earlier.

As Symon stepped into the role that Struth had filled for 34 years, he paid tribute to his former boss in the *Supporters Association Annual* with a pledge of devotion to Rangers: 'It shall be my endeavour to keep up the standard which [Struth] has set and as in the past I shall do my utmost to maintain the high traditions of the club and to add to its records.'

The traditions of Ibrox were in safe custody. Symon shared the Struth philosophy of what would be expected of Rangers and the players. He also maintained a distance from them, just as his former boss had done. No one would be allowed up the marble staircase unless it was for good reason, disciplinary or otherwise.

But if Symon could slip into the manager's chair without any obvious change to the fabric of the institution that Struth held so sacred, the playing field presented quite different problems in the beginning.

Training would continue to be taken by the trainers, with Symon making observations from the touchline. He was a familiar figure at the side of the pitch in his coat, hat and galoshes, sometimes shouting instructions, though discussions with players were largely left until matchdays. The tried-and-tested methods of management that Symon had experienced and seen succeed would prevail. Training would be routine – rarely varying throughout the season, or, indeed, from year to year.

The challenges of Symon's first full season proved insurmountable as the side made an early exit in both of the major Cup competitions and finished a poor third in the championship. The manager's problems were compounded by the loss of defender Willie Woodburn, exiled from the game in a savage SFA *sine die* suspension following repeated ordering-off offences.

By the start of the following season, 1955–56, however, a new side had taken shape with young full-backs Bobby Shearer and Eric Caldow alongside the experienced George Young. Struth's side had been built upon his defence, but Symon adopted a more attacking perspective with two out-and-out wingers. On the right he had the young Alex Scott with old war-horse Johnny Hubbard, a South African, on the left flank. Sammy Baird was hailed as 'the new Bob McPhail' at inside-forward, and the number 9 jersey was given to another South African import, Don Kichenbrand. 'The Rhino', as he was affectionately known to the fans, was far from a stylish centre-forward, but he was effective. Sports journalist Hugh Taylor related a conversation with Scot Symon years later, when the question of Kichenbrand's propensity to miss numerous chances was raised. 'I know he misses a lot but what impresses me is that he is usually in the right position to miss them,' Symon remarked. In fact 'Kitch' got in the right position to score 24 times in 25 League appearances that season.

After an indifferent start to that season, the side embarked upon a 23-game unbeaten run, which included 20 wins, to secure Symon's first championship as Rangers manager. It was a vital success for him – he was desperate to prove that he could fulfil the hopes that had carried him into the manager's chair.

The following season Rangers built on their success but Symon faced the new challenge of European competition. It was a challenge that Symon relished, and one that would forever more set new standards for the club to attain, but defeat in the first round of the European Cup at the hands of Nice left a sour taste in the manager's mouth.

It was a valiant Rangers side that took the French to a replay in Paris after the two-legged tie failed to separate the teams. The clashes with the French champions were bad-tempered and tiring. Rangers' form suffered and Symon admitted that there were times in the aftermath when he doubted whether European competition was worth all of the problems it brought with it. He observed, reflecting on his men's tiredness, that 'all the travelling and the strain of rough play by opponents abroad had a serious effect on the players'.

Their European excursions may have proved a distraction, but Rangers managed to regain the championship with a side that included five of Symon's new recruits, though the team that Struth built remained at the heart of the side.

By 1958, four years after Symon had taken over at Ibrox, however, only goalkeeper George Niven and defender Eric Caldow still survived from the Struth era to claim a regular place in the side. Caldow believed that Symon wanted to rebuild completely the side to the exclusion of the men he had inherited from Struth.

While there may have been an element of truth in that, and Caldow was clearly echoing the thoughts of some in the dressing-room, Symon was conscious of the advancing age of his predecessor's squad. Whatever the motives, Symon's side, playing with an attacking flair, won the championship again in 1958–59. The team that would go on to dominate Scottish football through the early 1960s had begun to take shape. By the end of the year a new forward line of Scott, McMillan, Millar, Brand and Wilson had emerged.

The following season, the championship eluded Rangers, but they won the Scottish Cup for the fifteenth time in their history, with a 2–0 win against Kilmarnock, giving Scot Symon his first Cup success as Rangers manager. He took the side to the semi-final of the European Cup before falling heavily to Eintracht

Frankfurt, who themselves were on the receiving end of a comprehensive defeat from Real Madrid in a memorable final played at Hampden.

The club had enjoyed domestic success in the early years of Symon's era, but despite progressing to the last four in the competition, the Eintracht result showed how far Rangers still had to go. But the players had had a taste for the glamour of European competition and they wanted more. So did the fans – the four European ties played at Ibrox that year attracted crowds averaging around 80,000.

THE GLORIOUS 1960s

By 1960, six years into his reign, Symon had at last moulded the team he wanted and was achieving an almost unprecedented consistency of selection. In comparison with the 1959–60 season, in which he used 24 players in 34 League matches, he used only thirteen players in the opening 21 matches of season 1960–61. Remarkably, he fielded the same eleven players in sixteen successive matches over a twelve-week spell from November to January. One of these players was the elegant left-half Jim Baxter whom Symon signed from Raith Rovers for the princely sum of £17,500.

Many still consider Baxter to be the finest player ever to wear the Rangers jersey, and Symon deserves immense credit for bringing him into a side which provided the perfect platform on which the Fifer could display his talents. It would be wrong, however, to deduce that the Rangers boss scoured the country looking for the missing ingredient for his 'dream team'. Symon had a real tactical awareness and knew what he wanted from his side, but his philosophy of team selection was much simpler than that which drives the modern-day coach. He had a fundamental belief that if you had good players and played them in their best positions, the quality of the team would be assured.

For that reason, many of the players who served Rangers during the Symon era mock the very suggestion that the Rangers boss ever dwelled on tactics in his rare team-talks, but they had the utmost respect for his judgement in team selection. He knew what they could do – he just wanted them to get on with it! Colin Jackson, who went on to play over five hundred games for Rangers, under five different managers, made his début in a light blue jersey under Symon in January 1966. 'Symon had a brief chat with me before the game about how I should play but it was really down to the players to organise themselves,' he recalled. 'They did that well because they were a good team at that time although things were beginning to wane. There was no tactical preparation for the match because, quite simply, tactics weren't considered so important in those days.'

Even if Symon bothered little about tactics, his knowledge of the game was undeniable. John Greig, in his autobiography, recalled that the boss was generally a quiet man, but that he would open up when he talked about football. Greig had little doubt that Symon was in tune with modern ideas, although he seemed reluctant to adopt the new systems that would eventually sweep the game in the 1960s. Greig believed that Symon adhered to his traditional methods simply because he believed they worked. These were based on the conventional 2–3–5 system where every player had a well-defined role.

Symon relied on the players' ability, believing they could respond to circumstances as a match developed. It was a trust and belief that the men never abused, and they would often work outwith normal training hours to improve their skills. Jimmy Miller and Ralph Brand in particular worked diligently on the field, perfecting a partnership that would become feared throughout the country. The players had a job to do and they had to fulfil the manager's expectations on a Saturday. Moreover, they invariably had a deep respect and love for the club, an affection that Symon fostered from their first introduction to the stadium. He once wrote, 'We don't have to tell our players what we expect. The new boys at once sense our traditions and follow the example without being coerced.'

If the grand edifice that is Ibrox Stadium was not in itself enough to impress upon new players the greatness of Rangers, there were enough people behind the scenes who could relate the club's history. Symon had retained most of Struth's backroom staff of former players. These included trainer Davie Kinnear and his assistant Joe Craven, Jimmy Smith (chief scout), Bob McPhail (youth coach) and Jock Shaw (youth coach).

Rangers marched through season 1960–61 triumphantly, winning the championship and the League Cup. They also maintained their progress in adapting to the European game by reaching the final of the Cup-Winners' Cup, only to go out to Fiorentina. Even though a European trophy would continue to elude them for several years, Rangers dominated the domestic scene through the early years of the decade. In that period, the Ibrox trophy-room – conceived and established by Symon in 1959 – was never empty. If the championship flag were not fluttering triumphantly over the north enclosure, which invariably it was, the Scottish Cup and League Cup would make regular appearances at the stadium.

By 1962–63 Symon had put together a side that combined youth and experience, strength and subtlety. Youngsters Willie Henderson, Ronnie McKinnon and John Greig came in to the team, providing vitality and adding flair. Shearer, Caldow and McMillan added maturity to a side that won the League and Cup double. A year later the team went on to sweep the board of domestic honours, achieving the second treble in the club's history. 'There's not a team like the Glasgow Rangers,' the fans sang, and no one could doubt them. Rangers were on a high and Symon enjoyed the fruits of ten years of labour in a role he had initially taken up with some trepidation. The success prompted new chairman John Lawrence to announce in March 1964 that: 'Mr Symon will be our manager as long as he wants to stay.'

Where would it all end? Inevitably the team would need to change further as some key players neared the end of their careers. Shearer, Millar, Caldow, McMillan and Wilson began to drift out of the scene during 1964–65 as Symon struggled to maintain the consistency of selection he had previously enjoyed. The League Cup was retained, but the fans watched with disappointment as their side slid to fifth position in the title race as former Rangers player Willie Waddell took Kilmarnock to the championship in a thrilling last-day clincher against Hearts at Tynecastle.

If the Light Blue legions were disappointed in 1965, they were to become even more disillusioned in the following season when the team lost out in the championship once again, this time to their resurgent Old Firm rivals Celtic. The Parkhead men had already won the League Cup with a victory over Rangers in the final, and only a dramatic goal from Kai Johansen in a replayed Scottish Cup final dashed Celtic's hopes of a treble and salvaged the season for the Ibrox side. That famous Hampden victory provided welcome

respite for the Rangers fans in a disappointing season, but the outlook was ominous as Celtic, under Jock Stein, impressed with a
free-flowing attacking style.

It has always been the case that the fortunes of the Old Firm are
polarised. In the classic 'see-saw' of Scottish football, the two clubs
never enjoy an elevated position side by side. When one is up the
other is inevitably in the depths of despair, because there is no
achievement in second place.

In a city where the two giants are constantly being compared,
their managers themselves become a focus of attention for their
contrasting styles. The 55-year-old Symon, a quiet man in a dapper
suit and often wearing galoshes, shunned publicity. He was from
the old school of football managers, keeping himself aloof from
the rigours of the training-ground where he would stand by the
touchline but leave the organisation to physiotherapist/trainer
Davie Kinnear. The new Parkhead boss, Jock Stein, was a younger
man, who captured the media's and the public's imagination as a
'tracksuit manager'. He had earlier enjoyed success at Dunfermline
Athletic, bringing the Pars their first Scottish Cup win in 1961, and
in 1965 he had broken Rangers' three-year monopoly of the trophy
to give the Celts their first Cup in seven years.

Stein's management style was seen as comparable with the
famed European coaches who had taken football on the continent
to a higher level. From his earliest days in management Stein
showed a keenness to learn more about the tactical side of the
game, even travelling to Italy to learn the methods of Inter Milan
coach Helenio Herrera.

Symon, despite the increasing respect given to the European
style, had his own methods. To many, though, the Ibrox boss was
symbolic of a past era from which Rangers had to emerge. John
Greig recalled telling Symon that he believed in the 'tracksuit
manager' and that when the opportunity came for him to move
into management he would never be a 'desk man'. Symon replied
that there were too many administrative duties for a manager to
attend to at a club like Rangers. It wasn't a situation that Symon
was inclined to change. Greig believed that the boss felt no need
to change the set-up. He was simply following in the traditions
that had been laid down before him. In many respects Symon
would have found it hard to see the need for change – the methods

that he had used had generally been fruitful, winning him a steady stream of silverware, particularly in the 1960s.

It was an attitude that would leave Symon terribly exposed to doubters and critics. He was also vulnerable because of his lack of rapport with the press. Quiet and reserved, he shunned publicity and rarely sought to justify himself. He would be an easy target for the newspapers whenever things went wrong.

Over on the other side of the city, Stein had brought a new enthusiasm to a Celtic side dispirited by years of subordinance to Symon's victorious Rangers. Their march to dominance seemed unrelenting. In August 1966 Symon, determined to redress the balance and conscious of the growing unrest among the fans, went into the transfer market, bringing Dave Smith from Aberdeen for £45,000 and Alec Smith from Dunfermline for £35,000. The new signings did little to alter the trend, though. Successive defeats from Celtic in the Glasgow Cup, the opening League fixture and the League Cup final further agitated the supporters and by the turn of the year Stein's side had a clear lead in the championship.

The Scottish Cup had provided the club's solitary moment of glory in the previous season, and the first-round pairing with Second Division Berwick Rangers looked certain to provide some respite from the rigours of the title race.

BERWICK: THE 'WORST RESULT IN OUR HISTORY'

While there were no illusions that the fixture at the small Shielfield Park would be easy, everyone expected the Light Blues to progress. Berwick had shown some recent form under new player-manager Jock Wallace and the big goalkeeper had some inside information on Rangers – Scot Symon had invited him to watch the side in pre-season training. After attending an endless number of coaching courses in England, Wallace brought new training methods to Berwick which many considered had 'speeded' his players and 'improved their stamina'.

The match would certainly be a big day for the 'Wee Rangers', but their more illustrious opponents had their eyes on a return to Hampden in May to regain the trophy they had won with Kai Johansen's memorable goal eight months earlier. On 28 January 1967 Rangers took the field against a spirited Berwick side. Ninety minutes later they trudged off the park reeling from one of the biggest shocks in Scottish football history. A second-half goal from a former Motherwell player, Sammy Reid, had been enough to see off a desperately disappointing Rangers.

As the stunned players sat in the tiny and antiquated Shielfield Park dressing-room, a shaken Scot Symon paced the room with some anxiety. As he nervously fingered his cigar, occasionally drawing on it, only his mumbles and words of despair broke the deathly silence: 'There will be hell to pay for this. This is terrible. There will be hell to pay.' He was speaking not only of the fortunes of his players, but also of himself. The tide of discontent would flow unrelentingly towards the manager.

On the long bus journey back to Glasgow scarcely a word was heard. Players such as George McLean and Willie Henderson, normally at the centre of the hilarity, sat stunned – to some extent in shock. As whispers emerged from the small band of directors at the front of the bus, some players strained to hear while others turned away, not daring to catch the words that would condemn them.

As the press sharks swarmed around Ibrox, Symon left them in no doubt of his opinion of the game and those responsible for what he called 'the worst result in the club's history'. He reflected: 'It's there now in the history books and these players took part in the game. That cannot be forgotten . . . The major blame lies in the fact that we could not score.'

While Symon faced the torture of the 'humiliation', Berwick boss Jock Wallace talked of his philosophy in management. 'Everything is done in spirit – I believe in them [his players] and they believe in me,' he said.

Symon was under the spotlight, but he found some public backing from his chairman, John Lawrence. 'There is no doubt in my mind that the only people who can be blamed for this defeat are the ones on the field – the players!' said Lawrence in a long speech peppered with words such as 'unforgivable' and 'made me sick', delivering a damning viewpoint from the upper echelons.

'We will be having a full discussion at our weekly board meeting about this humiliating result,' he stated ominously. The message was clear: things would have to change.

The scapegoats for the Berwick defeat were forwards Jim Forrest and George McLean. Neither was given the opportunity to play competitively for Rangers again, although Forrest did appear as a substitute in a friendly against Leicester as Rangers tried to orchestrate his transfer to the Filbert Street club. Forrest eventually went to Preston North End for £38,000 and McLean was transferred to Dundee as part of the deal that took Andy Penman to Ibrox.

Scot Symon was generally considered to be a fair man but the treatment of 22-year-old Forrest was unduly harsh, irrespective of the enormity of the disappointment surrounding Berwick. The young striker had a remarkable scoring record for Rangers. In 164 first-class games he scored 145 goals, an average unrivalled since by any Rangers striker. Few players break through and make such an impact by their early twenties, but here was a youngster singled out among a team of seasoned internationals for his failure to find the net in one 90-minute spell of play. He left to carve out a good career at Aberdeen and Preston North End before travelling abroad. There is little doubt that he could have served Rangers well for many years, having benefited from the experience of Berwick, but it was not to be.

It has often been suggested that John Lawrence had an over-riding influence in the decision to dispense with both Forrest and McLean after Berwick. Indeed, it is commonly believed that the late chairman dictated that neither player would kick a ball for the club again. Even if this were the case, Symon could have made a stand if he felt there was an injustice. The fact that he didn't, together with his veiled criticism of his strikers in the post-match interviews, suggests that he was at least party to the decision. It was one that would haunt him to the end of his days at Ibrox.

On the Monday after Berwick, Symon told youngsters Colin Jackson and Sandy Jardine to move their gear from the Away dressing-room to the Home dressing-room, traditionally reserved for the first-team squad. Alex Willoughby recalled that the team would normally be announced on the Friday before a game and that generally no one knew whether they would feature until then, but Symon pulled Willoughby aside at the beginning of the week to inform him that he would be in the side for that weekend's fixture against Hearts. Jardine was also called into the side.

In a strange irony Sandy Jardine had missed the Rangers Reserves game through injury on the day of the Berwick defeat and had instead joined his father at Tynecastle to watch Hearts in their Scottish Cup tie. Little did he expect that a week later he would make his début against the Edinburgh side in the aftermath of that infamous Scottish Cup defeat. Jardine and his young team-mates performed well and Rangers trounced Hearts 5–1 in front of 33,000 fans at Ibrox, with Willoughby scoring three.

The Berwick defeat stung Rangers into action and triggered a run of nine successive League victories. The side edged within striking distance of Celtic at the top of the table, only to suffer a lapse in the closing stages before losing out by three points to their rivals. The championship was important to Rangers but it had gone and Celtic completed the treble with victory in the Scottish Cup final. By this time the relationship between the board and Scot Symon had become increasingly strained. The situation was exacerbated by John Lawrence's courting of the press, something that Symon abhorred.

THE DISAPPOINTMENT OF NUREMBERG

It was a desperate season but Rangers had one remaining chance of silverware – in the final of the European Cup-Winners' Cup. Ordinarily, to reach the final of a European competition was (and still is – even more so now) a great achievement, but that sense of achievement was somewhat diminished by Celtic's drive to the final of the European Cup, a tournament widely considered to be of higher standing.

Celtic played their match in Lisbon less than a week before Rangers' final and emerged with a win over Inter Milan that carved the names of Stein and his players in the British football history. Rangers went into their game against Bayern Munich at Nurem-berg facing an uphill task. The Germans were playing on home soil and would have a huge support – the final was played in a stadium less than a hundred miles from Munich. Perhaps of more signifi-cance, however, was the enormous psychological burden on the players, who knew that Celtic had already succeeded in the Euro-pean Cup and were being lauded around the continent. Cruelly, even victory in the Cup-Winners' Cup would be diminished in the light of Celtic's Lisbon triumph.

Incredibly, on the eve of what was perhaps the biggest game in Rangers' history, Lawrence publicly condemned the players and

Symon, sacked the chief scout and proclaimed that Celtic were the yardstick against which Rangers' achievements had to be measured. It was hardly the vote of confidence that Symon and his players could have hoped for on the eve of such a big match in their history. The players later claimed that they had not heard the chairman's comments until they returned from Nuremberg, but the manager would undoubtedly have been informed of Lawrence's views by the press pack prior to the match. (Sandy Jardine, who played in Nuremberg, recalled that 'It was only after the game, when we got back to the hotel and were having a few beers to commiserate, that someone got hold of the newspaper from back home. Some of the more experienced players were a bit upset and annoyed about the chairman's comments.')

Putting Lawrence's remarks out of his mind, Symon set about preparing his men for the match based on good, sound scouting. Ironically, as the pressure mounted, Symon dispensed with his tried-and-trusted method of simply putting his best eleven out on the field and instead embraced tactical analysis. He had awakened to the modern ideas. The manager and his coach Bobby Seith had watched their German opponents before the final and identified their strengths and weaknesses. Seith had joined Rangers from Dundee six months earlier to ease the burdens on Symon and, perhaps, eventually succeed him. He ran a check on all opposing sides and assisted the boss with the pre-match preparations.

Symon felt that his men could win the match on the wings with Henderson on the right flank and Willie Johnston on the left. It was a tactical acumen that the manager had rarely revealed to the players in the past as he carefully ran through the dossier with his team the day before the game. Bayern were led by Franz Beckenbauer, the great German captain who would later go on to lead his national side to the World Cup as both player and manager. Symon noted that the elegant German star played a deep sweeper role with Bayern and he needed a bustling Rangers centre-forward who could unsettle the normally unflappable 'Kaiser'.

In reality, Symon had few options for the number 9 jersey. When he dismissed his two recognised strikers in the aftermath of the Berwick defeat he had reduced his strike force to just two players – inside-forwards Alex Willoughby and Alex Smith. Willoughby's introduction to the side after Berwick had been fruitful, producing sixteen goals in eleven League appearances. The youngster had also scored in an earlier European tie, against Real Saragossa. Smith was not a striker as such. He had played throughout the season in the inside-right berth with some success but he was not the out-and-out goalscorer Rangers needed. Strangely, though, and without any justification, Symon dropped Willoughby from the sixteen-man pool for Germany despite the youngster's scoring form. It was a controversial decision.

The manager opted instead for centre-half Roger Hynd, who had played only three games that season, but who had performed reasonably well in the games leading up to the final. Hynd was a tall, solid defender who occasionally played as a forward in training. Symon had thrown him into the centre-forward role in the semi-final against Slavia Sofia and, a few days later, he held his place for the concluding Old Firm match of the season. Hynd justified his position against Celtic by grabbing the equaliser in a 2–2 draw with only nine minutes remaining. Stunned at being left behind without reason, the devastated Willoughby immediately requested a transfer.

Rangers took the Germans to extra-time and created enough chances to win the game but they could not breach the barrier erected by Beckenbauer in front of keeper Sepp Maier. Late in the closing period Franz Roth, who had been identified by Symon in his pre-match talk as one of the Bayern danger men, burst into the box to slam the ball high past Rangers' keeper Norrie Martin. It was the only goal of the game. Symon's plan to win the contest on the flanks was thwarted when the German full-backs adopted tight man-for-man marking. Hynd made little impact on Beckenbauer.

John Greig recalled afterwards that the result meant more than simply losing a trophy. To him and everyone else who sported the light blue colours, the game was a disaster. In his autobiography, *A Captain's Part*, he wrote: 'They [Celtic] had won everything they had played for . . . we had won nothing.'

When the sad group returned to their hotel, Scot Symon went straight to his room and locked the door behind him. He was not seen again until the following morning. It was a further devastating defeat just four months after that dreadful day at Berwick. Then the manager had received some backing from the chairman while the critics had rounded on the team. The manager had survived

the Berwick result although the ranks of the dissenters were growing and now included members of the board.

When the team returned to Glasgow they faced an Ibrox support that was completely disenchanted and crestfallen. Celebrations at the other side of the city, meanwhile, proclaimed Celtic
the champions of Europe. While Rangers and Symon should have
received credit for reaching a European final for the second time,
they faced only condemnation for failure. In reality, Celtic's victory
over Inter Milan at Lisbon had already undermined that achievement before a ball was kicked in Nuremberg.

While in Germany, Symon invited the Clyde boss Davie White
to join him at Rangers as assistant manager for the new season.
The young manager had impressed in just over a year in the Shawfield job and was part of the gradual evolution to a more modern
approach in the club backrooms which the fans, encouraged by the
press, so craved. White was to be groomed to become Symon's
successor, an arrangement that was commonly known but not
publicly acknowledged by the club. Certainly the players were told
that White would be their boss in the future, but it was expected
that the transition would take a few years.

White, with his varied training régimes which focused on
increased ballwork, was a welcome addition to the backroom. He
was accepted quickly by the players.

In a desperate bid to regain the ascendancy in Scotland, the
board sanctioned some major spending for the new season. Rangers
returned from the close season with new players Alex Ferguson,
Eric Sorensen and Orjan Persson in their ranks. Old stalwarts
Jimmy Millar and Davie Wilson departed. Significantly, none of
the players who had taken Symon to his first championship in the
1960s now remained in the first-team squad. The new side had
largely been assembled by spending on some big-money transfers,
rather than through the promotion of young players from the
ranks. Ferguson's deal alone cost the club £65,000, a Scottish
record at the time.

While Rangers reached for the chequebook every time they
faced trouble, Celtic were reaping the rewards of a good youth
policy. When Stein did occasionally venture into the transfer
market it was invariably with great success, turning low-budget
players into stars. One man signed by Celtic – to the agitation of

many of the Light Blues' fans – was Willie Wallace, a player who had never hidden his admiration for Rangers. Stein signed Wallace from Hearts and he became a key member of the Lisbon Lions side who won the European Cup.

The unsound practice of attempting to buy success was one that would haunt Rangers for many years. The arrival of every player who came with a price tag was heralded as the defining moment when a change of fortunes would be experienced. In reality, this rarely occurred. Symon sought to bring the best to Rangers, but the strategy was fundamentally flawed in that most of the best players were already in Stein's Celtic squad and acquiring any of the Parkhead players was unthinkable. The situation was compounded by an unprecedented flow of talent from the Celtic youth sides. While Stein could easily feed youngsters into a side that had a solid and successful base, Symon looked for players who could turn around the club's fortunes. It was a bridge too far for many of the new signings.

Rangers kicked off the 1967–68 season in a League Cup section that included Aberdeen, Dundee United and Celtic. It was a cruel twist of fate for Symon that he should be drawn against the side that had caused him so much anguish in recent years. Now he would have to face them twice in two weeks before the League even kicked off. In the first match, in front of 95,000 fans at Ibrox, Rangers grabbed an equaliser in the final minutes to turn all eyes towards the outcome of the Parkhead fixture scheduled for a fortnight later. In that match, with Rangers leading 1–0, Kai Johansen missed a penalty with only fourteen minutes remaining. A Rangers goal at that point would almost certainly have killed the tie, but instead the miss threw Celtic an unexpected lifeline and, to the utter dismay of the Rangers contingent, they went on to score three times.

Celtic progressed to lift the trophy, as Rangers steadily eased themselves to the front in the championship race. By the end of October they had played eight League games, winning six and drawing two. That run included a much-needed win over Celtic at Ibrox, and helped Symon's side to a one-point lead over Dundee at the top of the table. The Parkhead side were three points adrift in third place, with a game in hand. This was hardly a free-scoring Rangers side – the four teams behind them had all scored more goals – but the defence was resolute, having conceded only two goals in these eight League games.

On Saturday, 28 October 1967, as the side trudged off the field after a 0–0 draw with Dunfermline, the frustrated Ibrox crowd turned to berate Scot Symon and the board as they sat in the directors' box. Later that evening, as Symon joined one of the directors for dinner, there was no hint of the ensuing trouble.

Three days later, Jock Stein and his players arrived in South America to take part in the World Club Championship. That same night, Symon had joined some of his players at the BBC television studios in Glasgow as they filmed *Quiz Ball*, a novelty TV sports challenge between the top sides in the country. After the show, the Rangers boss drove skipper John Greig to Queen Street station to catch the last train to Edinburgh. Meanwhile, in Room 230 of the St Enoch Hotel, the directors were deep in discussion.

The following day, Scottish football was rocked by the news that Scot Symon had resigned as manager of Rangers. Symon himself announced the decision to the press with the following statement: 'I was informed by a Glasgow businessman at his home that at a meeting of the directors of Rangers Football Club it was decided to terminate my appointment as manager forthwith. I am awaiting confirmation of this.' Alex McBain, an accountant who had no formal connection with the club, had summoned Symon to his home. The club claimed that McBain's profession best suited him to negotiate the terms of the manager's resignation. Symon was devastated as much by the manner of his dismissal as by the actual events themselves.

The club released a statement through its PR officer, Willie Allison, the next evening confirming that Symon's appointment had been terminated. John Lawrence later attempted to justify the move with reference to the team's poor scoring record. Ironically, the knee-jerk decision to off-load the two prime strikers after Berwick could only have contributed to the side's lack of finishing power. If, as is generally accepted, Lawrence and his co-directors were the instigators of the dismissal of Forrest and McLean ten months earlier, the statement citing a lack of goals as a major factor behind the sacking of Symon must have been particularly galling to the manager.

Whatever was behind it, the timing of the events was hardly

appropriate. The team were at the top of the table, had negotiated a potentially difficult opening tie in Europe, and had shown they could defeat Celtic by winning the opening League encounter. They lost their assistant manager too. Immediately after the announcement of Symon's departure, coach Bobby Seith resigned, saying, 'I no longer want to be part of an organisation which can treat a loyal servant so badly.'

Davie White conveyed the news of Symon's departure to the players in the morning at training. There were no goodbyes from Symon, who didn't even have the chance to empty his desk. Indeed, in recent times, during some refurbishment of the office, the contractors employed to polish the great desk that has been used by all of the club's managers found a secret drawer containing cigars and photographs of key squad players. From the age of the contents it has been assumed they were Symon's.

John Greig recalled that everyone around Ibrox was stunned by the loss of the manager, not least of all the players, most of whom had been signed by Symon. His departure felt like a bereavement to many of them. Greig spoke of looking to the touchline during training, expecting to see Symon standing in the place where he always watched proceedings.

Symon was deeply hurt by what had happened, so much so that he only ever went back to Ibrox in an official capacity, as manager of Partick Thistle whom he later joined. Sandy Jardine recalled that whenever Rangers visited Firhill, the players always made a point of seeking out their former boss.

The departure of Symon marked the end of an era. Gone were the days of the old-style manager who was aloof from the players, remaining in the sanctuary of the old office at the top of the marble staircase. The traditions that had been established by Wilton and Struth and continued by Symon seemed unwanted as Rangers embraced a desire for a new era, a fresh approach to management, and a longing for a return to the dominance they had enjoyed in the earlier years of Symon's reign.

For Symon, the manner of his departure cast an enormous shadow over a great career on the field and in management. It is an eternal indictment of the club that such a great servant should have drifted into virtual obscurity when all he had done was be in charge at a time when Celtic had the greatest team in their history.

Symon paid the price of Jock Stein's success more than he paid for Rangers' failure.

What kind of man do the players remember? Willie Henderson recalls Symon as 'a very straight man and a manager who allowed players to express themselves individually'. Sandy Jardine said that the boss was 'the perfect gentleman'. He remembered Symon swearing only once, at half-time inside Tynecastle Park, after a defender had carelessly conceded a penalty. The curse sent genuine shock throughout the dressing-room. Eric Caldow's views were somewhat coloured by his losing the captaincy to Bobby Shearer as a result of Symon's determination to shape his own side, recalling the manager as rude and unapproachable.

On balance, it is clear that Symon was heavily influenced by the managerial style of Bill Struth. He was undoubtedly from an earlier era in terms of his approach, but who could deny that his methods had been successful for Rangers? He could well have continued that success but for the emergence of Stein's side. The statistics show that he served Rangers as manager for just over thirteen seasons during which time he won fifteen out of the forty domestic trophies he competed for, with twelve of these coming in the glorious years of the early 1960s.

It is doubtful whether Symon could have halted the green tide that would sweep over Rangers in the latter part of that decade, but he had already left his mark on the club. He took the side to two European finals, six championships and their second treble. He also introduced players such as Greig, Baxter, Henderson, Millar, Brand, Jardine, Johnston and an endless list of Ibrox heroes who would themselves carve their own place in Rangers folklore.

Symon was a good manager with a good record and was the last link with the old traditions that had developed through Wilton and Struth. But Rangers were ready for a new era.

DAVIE WHITE

Davie White climbed the marble staircase, paused for a minute at the top and then entered the manager's office which Scot Symon had vacated a day earlier. It was a moment of solitude away from the bustling media corps who had feverishly pursued every angle of the story of the demise of Symon and White's appointment to the biggest job in football. White stared, almost transfixed, at the great oak desk from which Symon and the legendary William Struth had steered the club to countless memorable victories and trophies.

White had confidence in his own ability, but at that moment he vowed that he would not sit behind the desk until he had earned the right to do so. It was a reticence born out of an acknowledgement that he came into the position without the credentials of his predecessor. Unlike Symon, he had never worn the light blue jersey and he had little intimate experience of the club's traditions. But he did offer a break from the old ideas that had ultimately been the ruin of his predecessor. No more would a Rangers manager stand aloof from the training field. Directors, fans and the press alike had longed for a tracksuited figure who could take the challenge to Stein's all-conquering Celtic. Now they had him: Davie White was the man.

As Scot Symon retired from the glare of the media spotlight, he offered words of support to the new boss: 'Davie is a very fine man. I wish him all the best. He is with a wonderful club.' Ironically, it was Symon who had introduced Davie White to Rangers with his appointment to the position of assistant manager just five months earlier. White was a keen student of the game and the move was first suggested when the young Clyde manager had attended Rangers' European Cup-Winners' Cup final clash in Nuremberg. A few days earlier he had returned from Lisbon where he had watched Celtic win the European Cup.

At that stage, White topped up his part-time earnings as Clyde boss with his day-to-day job as a draughtsman in Motherwell. In fact, the useful left-half had never really seen football as providing a career for him when he hung up his boots after serving the Shawfield club as captain for six years. He even looked into the possibility of emigrating to Canada and had already completed the preliminary enquiries when former Ranger John Prentice resigned as Clyde boss to take over as Scotland manager in 1966. White was offered the opportunity to fill the Shawfield vacancy and he did so with remarkable success. In his one year in charge – during which training was restricted to just three evenings a week – he took Clyde to third place in the championship behind the Old Firm. In fact, his side held Rangers to a draw at Ibrox with only two games remaining, a result which ultimately cost the Light Blues the title and gave Celtic the second of their nine successive championships.

When White joined Rangers in June 1967, his role as assistant to Symon consisted mainly of coaching the reserves. (Bobby Seith, himself only recently appointed, handled the first-team coaching at that time.) The reserves enjoyed White's varied training techniques and his popularity with the fringe players would be an important factor in his acceptance by the squad as manager. In his autobiography, John Greig talked of the 'dressing-room grapevine' which carried good reports from the reserves of White's work with the side.

Seith resigned 24 hours after the departure of Symon, leaving White a solitary figure at the helm with Rangers in turmoil. Any chance that he had of succeeding in the hottest seat in football would be dependent on his ability to rally the players and the fans behind him, and he knew it.

The players were comfortable with their new boss, and it was fitting that he was the one to announce the departure of Scot Symon in a solemn gathering of the players at Ibrox the morning before the news was banner headlines in every newspaper. He instructed them to offer no comment to the press, conscious that there was enough controversy enveloping the club without the added problems of the players becoming involved.

White was aware that his appointment didn't meet with universal approval. Many felt that he didn't have the credentials or the experience to manage Rangers. He had no trouble with that attitude, because he had an unshakeable belief in his own ability. What he didn't have, however, was control over the co-operation from the players and, in particular, the response of the stars at Ibrox to his appointment. In fact, in the early stages he was to find that the strongest bonds came from the senior players, and John Greig, especially, eased the new boss into a good relationship with the players. The squad had respected Scot Symon and was solidly behind him right up until the end of his stewardship, but White too commanded the respect of the players from an early stage.

In reality, the players depended on White perhaps more than he needed their commitment. Their performance had clearly dipped, precipitating Symon's departure, and many of them questioned there own long-term future at a club desperate to return to the glory days.

White worked at building his relationship with the squad and the players were generally receptive to him. They found the new manager to be quite different from the reserved, stoical Symon. After a good result one Saturday the team travelled to their Largs base in preparation for a midweek European tie. White astounded them as they sat in the hotel bar by coming in and buying them a few beers. They had never known anything like it before. Mirroring times past, White referred to the team as 'my boys', echoing the term of endearment used by Struth.

The players were encouraged to mix freely with their new boss, but White did not blindly dispense with the traditions upon which the club had successfully negotiated itself to the highest standing within the game. He may have been a tracksuit manager, but off the field he insisted that the standards of dress for all officials and players that had prevailed since Wilton's days be maintained and the players had to wear club blazers and flannels when travelling to away matches.

White would join the men for practice games in training but although he courted their affections, he also instilled discipline. He was approachable but they knew that they dare not step out of line. One of the players felt that he was a little overawed by some of the experienced squad members, a situation that was perhaps understandable given that he came from little Clyde.

SUCCESS SO CLOSE, YET SO FAR

While White worked hard to create a good atmosphere within the dressing-room, he knew that he would be judged not on his rapport with the players but on the side's performance on the field of play. The manager was bursting with ideas on how to shape the side but he was reluctant to make too many changes in the early stages. There seemed little need – he had inherited a side that Symon had taken to the top of the League.

The chairman had cited the lack of goals as a key reason for Symon's dismissal. Centre-forward Alex Ferguson had scored just six times in sixteen games, but the goals weren't exactly flowing freely from other parts of the team. White knew that this matter would have to be addressed immediately, at the very least to demonstrate some improvement to the board.

His first match as Rangers boss came at St Johnstone's Muirton Park. The manager reorganised his front line in a bid to increase the penetration that had been lacking in previous games. He reintroduced Willie Henderson to the wing and shifted winger Willie Johnston to inside-forward. The switch paid off. Johnston scored the opener and White had a winning start to his Ibrox managerial career.

He needed it. In his first few weeks in charge he steered the side through a perilous tie in the Inter Cities Fairs Cup (later renamed the UEFA Cup) with Cologne and then saw his men string nine successive League wins together, maintaining Rangers' position as leaders in the title race. Despite that flawless run, they couldn't shake off the challenge of Celtic and White took his boys to Parkhead for the New Year fixture knowing that defeat would knock his team off the top of the table.

It was to be a good day for White. A stirring fightback from the Ibrox side produced an equaliser from Kai Johansen with just two minutes to go after Celtic's Bobby Murdoch had shot his team into a 2–1 lead. When the manager returned to his Ibrox office, relieved and elated that he had negotiated his first Old Firm tester, he took his place behind the desk – which he had refused to do until, in his own words, he 'had earned the right'.

Davie White was under no illusions that a favourable result at Parkhead would be enough to earn acceptance at Ibrox. 'You have to win one of the major honours for this club before the fans and the people in football think of you as successful,' he acknowledged. He was only partly correct. The fans expected the side to deliver a Cup, but it was the championship flag that they craved.

Unable to extend the lead over Celtic despite the continuation of their 100 per cent record, Rangers realised that the title might ultimately be decided on goal average. White instructed his players to go out and score as many as they could. By the end of March they had extended their winning run to eighteen League victories, interrupted only by that Ne'er Day draw with Celtic. They had scored a remarkable ten goals against Raith Rovers, six against St Johnstone, five over Partick Thistle and Stirling Albion, and four in as many other fixtures. They still remained behind Celtic's strike rate of three goals per game, though. White's hunch that goals would be crucial in determining the destination of the flag proved to be correct.

In the closing run, Rangers dropped valuable points in draws at Tannadice and Cappielow, leaving Celtic top on goal average with two games remaining. Both sides won their penultimate game and the championship went to the final game with Celtic still holding a vastly superior goal average. Rangers travelled to Aberdeen more in hope than in expectation that Celtic might slip up. It would become academic, however, if the Light Blues did not win their match. It wasn't to be the dream outcome that White so desired. A last-minute goal at Pittodrie saw Aberdeen win 3–2 and seal Rangers' fate. Remarkably, they were only 60 seconds away from completing their League schedule without defeat. It would have been of little consequence if they had held out, however: by that stage the title was already on its way to Celtic Park.

White shared the frustration of the fans, and the players were desperately disappointed they didn't win the title for a manager whom they regarded as a friend. He had avoided wholesale change as he tried to guide the club to the championship using the men who Symon had signed. They had failed. Now was the time for White to introduce the sweeping ideas he felt could break Celtic's dominance.

He entered the new season, his first full term in charge, with no new personnel, although he had tried unsuccessfully to add to his squad. He did, however, give youngsters Colin Jackson and Sandy Jardine a run, albeit in different positions from those that would eventually earn them places among the Rangers greats. He also appointed Willie Thornton as his assistant manager, a move which appeased some who felt that the club was losing touch with its traditions. Thornton offered some tangible connection with the great days of Struth and his experience of Rangers and Ibrox bolstered White's eroding credibility as the manager of the biggest club in the land.

The season opened with the League Cup sectional ties. Ideally, the Rangers boss would have liked to ease his team into the campaign with a comfortable draw. Fate dealt him a cruel hand, however, when the draw placed Rangers in the same section as Celtic, alongside Partick Thistle and Morton. It was almost a boom or bust scenario for White and Rangers at the earliest stage of what would be a long season: victory could launch the side into a good League challenge. Defeat, coming on the back of the disappointments of the previous season, would be too much for many to bear. White's worst fears were realised. Celtic won at both Ibrox and Parkhead and saw Rangers off to a dismal start to the season as they exited from the Cup.

They regained some pride with a win in their first League clash with their Old Firm rivals, at Parkhead (4–2), but the fans were unimpressed by a start to the campaign that showed little sign of matching the consistency of the previous season. By the end of October 1968, the side had slid to fifth place in the League table, although they were just two points behind leaders, Celtic. The Light Blue legions called for the board to pull out the chequebook once again. It was painfully apparent that the squad could not sustain a challenge to Celtic without an injection of new blood.

White responded by bringing a new striker to Ibrox in the first six-figure transfer in Scottish football. The loyal Rangers support had a new hero: Colin Stein. He burst on to the scene in a manner that surely exceeded even his wildest dreams. He scored a hat-trick on his début at Arbroath's Gayfield Park, then followed it up with another in the next match, his first at Ibrox, in a 6–1 win over his former club, Hibernian. Two more goals followed in his next game, an Inter Cities Fairs Cup tie against Dundalk. Stein seemed to be the answer to the scoring problems that had afflicted the side since the golden days of the early 1960s, when Millar and Brand caused every net in the country to bulge.

Rangers had not completed their spending as White still strove to improve the team. Less than three weeks after Stein's arrival, Alex MacDonald was signed from St Johnstone for a fee of around

£50,000 but in his early days at Ibrox he failed to find the form that had attracted Rangers' interest. 'I was overawed with the place when I arrived,' he recalled. 'I used to live just down the road and as a youngster I used to sneak into the ground at night to act out my dreams of wearing a Rangers jersey and scoring at Ibrox. I played on the field with my pals and when I scored I would run to the Rangers end to take the imaginary cheers. At the Celtic end I made some gestures. The games ended with old caretaker Bobby Moffat hounding us out of the ground. I was a Rangers boy through and through and when the opportunity did come to play for the club I found it quite overwhelming.' MacDonald did eventually come to terms with his achievement and went on to become one of the Rangers greats.

Despite MacDonald's slow start to his career, he and Stein boosted the team, but the side could not shake off the inconsistency that had marred the early-season performances. By the turn of the year, Rangers had slipped five points behind Celtic, closed the gap to three with victory in the Ne'er Day fixture, but surrendered another point at Rugby Park a week later.

Colin Stein did not maintain the free-scoring form that signalled his arrival at Ibrox, although his enthusiasm and effort were vital to the side. It was not Stein's failure to hit the score sheet on a regular basis that was the biggest worry for White, though. The striker had a fiery temperament and frequently found himself in trouble with referees, generally for retaliation. As the season neared its conclusion, Stein's onfield misdemeanours caught up with him. Following two ordering-off offences within the space of ten weeks, on top of previous incidents during his spell at Easter Road, he was called before the SFA and punished with a five-week suspension. He would be out for the remainder of the campaign, missing seven League matches. It was a major blow to the team's title ambitions and White knew it would now be very difficult to overcome Celtic.

Disabled by the loss of their star striker, the side won only three of these matches and dropped six points in the other four games. Celtic won the championship while Rangers languished five points behind.

The torment for White had not ended. His men had surged impressively into the Scottish Cup final after a crushing 6–1 win over Aberdeen and were destined to face old rivals Celtic. Alex Ferguson regained the number 9 jersey, as the suspended Stein sat disconsolately in the Hampden stand. Rangers had not won a major honour for three years and the fans' patience was wearing thin. Defeat at any time was hard for the legions to tolerate, but a Cup final failure at the hands of a Celtic side looking to complete the domestic treble would be unbearable after three long seasons in the wilderness.

The players were unbowed, showing a confidence in the pre-match preparations that convinced their manager that the time had come for his side to capture some of the glory that had eluded them. It was not to be. An early goal from Celtic skipper Billy McNeill set the pattern for the game, and a series of defensive blunders handed Jock Stein's men a 4–0 victory, one of their most convincing Cup final wins over Rangers. It was Rangers' first defeat in a Scottish Cup final for forty years, and their biggest Scottish Cup loss to the Parkhead side.

Celtic's keeper, Fallon, who played out of his skin, thwarted any chance that Rangers had of hauling themselves back into the game. White had meticulously planned for a Rangers win, resting key men in the weeks leading up to the match. As the disconsolate players returned to Ibrox, White refused to berate them publicly, although they all knew that their basic errors had destroyed his plans.

He had spent around £400,000 strengthening the squad and, no matter the paucity of luck that marked his tenure in the Ibrox hot-seat, the growing discontent on the terracings and in the board-room placed a question mark over his long-term future at Rangers.

THE MISERY OF NEWCASTLE

With all hope of domestic success in season 1968–69 gone, White turned his attention to the Inter Cities Fairs Cup, a tournament that provided Rangers with some respite from the imposing, ever-present shadow of Celtic. They had gamely fought their way through to the semi-final, where Newcastle United awaited. Like a couple of trumped-up boxers at a weigh-in, the two clubs exchanged contemptuous comments in a pre-match build-up that agitated White and his players. The manager was undaunted, believing that his side was more than a match for the Geordies and their band of exiled Scots.

The pre-match hype helped swell the crowd to over 75,000 for the first-leg tie at Ibrox. Unfortunately, White's plans were savaged by the loss of two key defenders, Mathieson and McKinnon, on the eve of the game, compounding the selection problems already imposed by the suspension of the incisive Willie Johnston.

White had every reason to believe that Lady Luck was conspiring against him when keeper Ian McFaul dived full stretch to his right to save an Andy Penman penalty in a sorry first half against the St James' Park outfit. As Rangers piled forward looking for the break, the young Belfast-born keeper, who supported the Ibrox side as a boy, piled on the agony for Penman with a wonderful save from a 30-yard shot that streaked through the embattled Newcastle goal area.

In the second half Rangers continued to dominate but, try as they might, they could not breach the resolute Tynesiders' defence. When the final whistle sounded, most agreed that Newcastle were fortunate to leave Ibrox with a 0–0 draw, but there was little point in White dwelling on his ill-fortune. He had a second leg to face, one in which Rangers quite simply would have to score if they were to continue to harbour dreams of success in the tournament.

White welcomed back his three absentees for the return tie at Newcastle, and he had an air of confidence borne out of his assertion that the side was more suited to attack than defence. He didn't consider the match at St James' Park as a typical European tie where the away side would be expected to tighten the defence. His policy would be attack and he made no secret of the fact in press briefings.

Another large crowd, over 60,000 this time, were attracted to the game, including a large contingent in light blue. The first half was goalless, but two Newcastle strikes in the second period sealed Rangers' fate. The night's agony was compounded when their fans invaded the pitch in a vain effort to cause a postponement. The players looked a shadow of themselves as they trudged dejectedly from the field.

White's spending had brought no tangible rewards to adorn the trophy-room and he was becoming increasingly isolated. He had already lost much of the confidence of the boardroom before the

Newcastle tie, and the discontent on the terracings had reached epidemic proportions. White knew that he needed to inject some inspiration into his jaded players, and was aware that it was unlikely that the board would sanction any big-money transfers on the scale of Colin Stein. Just a few days after the heartbreak of Newcastle, the manager finally had a stroke of luck: Rangers' long-lost prodigal son, Jim Baxter, had become available with Nottingham Forest placing a value of £15,000 on on his head.

White moved quickly and, on 28 May 1969, the supporters received the news that would help dispel the disappointments of the season past – Jim Baxter, 'The King', would return to Ibrox. White insisted that Baxter would have to earn his place like anyone else on the staff, but no one was under any illusions that this was a final throw of the dice for the manager. Quite simply, he would rely on Baxter to resurrect the ailing fortunes of the club – and save his own job.

In an interview after the formalities of his signing had been completed, Baxter said: 'I know that I have got to be a success here. There is no room for failure at Ibrox . . . there never has been.' It was a realisation with which White himself was familiar.

NEWCASTLE TO GORNIK

After just 21 months in the Ibrox hot-seat, Davie White entered a critical phase in his managership. By the start of the 1969–70 season, he had failed to capture any of the six domestic competitions the team had played for – and he had watched as Stein's Celtic won five of them. Europe had offered little respite. More importantly, there seemed little obvious sign that Rangers were likely to wrest the championship from Celtic and regain the dominance that they had once exercised on the Scottish game.

Once again, White was dealt a cruel hand with the League Cup sections draw, which placed the Old Firm together for the third time in succession. The Light Blues won the first game at Ibrox but a blunder by goalkeeper Gerry Neef in the second cost them the match at Parkhead. The result in itself was not fatal but Rangers' fate was sealed a few days later when they failed to beat Raith Rovers at Ibrox and tumbled out of the Cup. The club had been eliminated at the sectional stage of the Cup for the third year in succession – and each time Celtic had progressed.

With little support for him now on the terracings and the boardroom also disenchanted, a dispirited but unabashed White continued his quest for success. The League campaign opened disappointingly with a draw at Tannadice and, by the beginning of November, Rangers were in a lowly sixth place in the table, although only two points separated them from leaders Dundee United. However, they had lost the first Old Firm game of the championship as Celtic celebrated their first League win at Ibrox in twelve years.

White's reliance on the old guard that had served Symon well in the early 1960s was misplaced. There was talk of growing indiscipline in the ranks and the portly Baxter was no longer the 'Slim Jim' the fans remembered. The manager entrusted his future to players who were patently past their best and rarely gave young talent a chance. Ironically, when he did, they failed him. Stung by calls to introduce youngsters to show that Ibrox had its own nursery to contend with Celtic's famed youth policy, he brought in Brian Heron, a winger who had been converted to a full-back. Introduced to the side in October, Heron was pitched in against Polish side Gornik Zabrze in a Cup-Winners' Cup tie that Rangers were expected to win. The youngster had a nightmare of a match, but he was not alone as the Light Blues failed to contend with the pace and artistry of the Poles.

Stirred by the performance of Lubanski, their star player, Gornik won the first leg in Poland by three goals to one. Defensive frailties that had been obvious throughout the early part of the season were highlighted a few days later when Rangers conceded three goals to Kilmarnock – but scored five times to seal victory. A few days later they lost another two goals as the side slipped to a 2–2 draw against Morton at Greenock.

White knew that Rangers would have to keep things tight at the back if they were to overcome the two-goal deficit in the return match against Gornik. Heron was pitched in again for a game that was vital to Rangers – and White. Jim Baxter scored the opening goal early in the first half, raising the Ibrox crowd's hopes of a fine European victory as the team reached half-time with just one more goal needed.

The darting runs of the speedy Polish forwards were dangerous, however, and increased in the last half hour as Rangers pushed forward. Olek grabbed an equaliser from a tight angle and twelve minutes later Lubanski picked up the ball on the halfway mark before waltzing past the labouring Ibrox defence to hit a second. By now, the dispirited Scots, needing four goals to win, were in disarray. In the last fifteen minutes, Gornik totally dominated and added a third. The Ibrox crowd rose to applaud them off the field. Quite different sentiments were reserved for White on Edmiston Drive outside Ibrox. On 27 March 1969 he was dismissed from his post as manager of Rangers.

The Gornik result compounded the growing concerns that the Rangers boss had let standards slip inside Ibrox. Even one of the players who was in the squad at the time conceded that for a club built on tradition, 'many things did slip and there was a lack of professionalism from some players that went unheeded'. One of White's fiercest critics had been Willie Waddell, who was at that time a writer with the *Scottish Daily Express*. Along with some other former Ibrox stalwarts, Waddell launched a bitter attack on the Rangers boss that left White isolated from the old school of former Rangers, as far as many fans were concerned.

To the end, however, the players were supportive of Davie White. They knew that he was going through a hard time, as they were, but they expected him to ride the storm, 'because they were not far away from Celtic'. When the manager was dismissed, there was shock in the dressing-room.

Reflecting on White's sacking, Sandy Jardine felt that the boss was unlucky. 'He was unfortunate with the circumstances that pitched him into the job at the start of Celtic's "Nine in a Row",' he said. 'Jock Stein had assembled a magnificent team and Rangers did get close, taking them to the last game of the season. So when you consider that Celtic had their best ever team, it was hard for White inheriting the team at a time when the fans had become used to them being top dogs although the mantle had slipped.

'In fairness, he was very good tactically, but the job came too early for him and I think he would concede that,' ventured Jardine.

Davie White left Ibrox as the only manager of Rangers never to have won a major domestic trophy. He had failings that contributed to his downfall, but his greatest problem was in the timing of his appointment. He didn't receive the guidance he needed to ease him into the Ibrox hot-seat, an apprenticeship that was expected, but which never materialised. His greatest difficulty was down to the events at Celtic Park when Jock Stein enjoyed the greatest spell in Rangers' rivals' history. Arguably, White could have done more to halt the advance of the green machine, but he did get so close in his first season. Ultimately, the manager was only as good as the players he had assembled, and in that respect Rangers needed to rebuild. The reconstruction of the side would take several years but White had run out of time.

WILLIE WADDELL

Dejection, desperation, anger and frustration were worn alongside the scarves which proclaimed Cup victories of a seemingly bygone era by the Light Blue legions. The defeat by Gornik had not only sent Rangers tumbling out of Europe, but had also plunged the club into an abyss from which there seemed no escape.

Reacting to the cruel chants of 'White Must Go!' which echoed around Edmiston Drive late into the evening, the Ibrox board summarily dismissed the manager. The fans had got their scape-goat, but they knew that the removal of the unfortunate Davie White would not in itself signal a change in Rangers' fortunes. They desperately needed hope and a leader around whom the club could rally. There seemed only one man with the experience and understanding of the role necessary to lead Rangers from the wilderness – Willie Waddell.

Waddell was fondly remembered for his prowess as a wonderful winger who served the club in a golden spell from 1938 to 1955. Introduced to the side at the tender age of fifteen by the legendary Bill Struth, he played 558 matches for Rangers, scoring 143 goals and earning a stream of honours for the club. 'How can you buy Willie Waddell?' the fans would sing in celebration of a man who, with determination and grit, was the epitome of a true Ranger.

Waddell also packed nineteen international caps into his career, but his success in the game did not end when he packed away his boots. In 1957 he had become the manager of Kilmarnock and celebrated eight good years at the Ayrshire club, taking them to a remarkable championship victory in his final term, 1965. As the Rugby Park side celebrated, Waddell bade farewell and took up a job in the the newspaper industry. It seemed that he had finally called time on football, preferring to observe and comment on the game rather than dictate the action. He had a young family to support, after all, and Waddell was determined that he would spend his time with them, away from the pressures of management that had become all-consuming at Kilmarnock. Nothing, it seemed, would lure Waddell back to the game.

As speculation mounted about who would succeed White, Waddell's name was one of those linked with a possible return to the stadium that held so many happy memories for him. He seemed like the logical choice. He had been openly critical of White's methods in a series of damning articles in his newspaper column – he felt that Rangers had fallen below the standards expected of the great club, both off and on the field, and saw no sign that White could lead the Rangers to glory. Many fans, remembering Waddell's standing in the game, respected his judgement and endorsed his views. As a former Ranger, he had the credentials for the vacant position and quickly became the fans' choice. They saw him as the only man capable of challenging Jock Stein. The Celtic boss had become a statesmanlike figurehead to the Parkhead club – Waddell seemed to offer the same to Rangers.

One week after the turmoil and anguish of the Gornik defeat, Rangers released the press statement that every fan wanted to hear: Willie Waddell would be the new manager. On Monday, 8 December 1969, the new boss was introduced to the hacks who, only a few days earlier, had been press colleagues, as the club chairman, John Lawrence, proudly announced: 'This is one of the greatest moments of my life – the moment I welcome Willie Waddell back as manager of the club. He returns to us and we have every confidence that he will put Rangers back where they should be. He will be given all the support possible by his directors. He knows that a formidable task lies ahead of him – but he will have all the help we can give.'

With the optimistic, almost grateful tones of the board ringing in his ears, Waddell set to work, outlining his plans to the fans. In a quite unprecedented move, he called for a face-to-face meeting with the supporters at the stadium. Delegates from the Supporters Association and elsewhere were invited, and so many wanted to come that two sittings were arranged.

Waddell's address to them was straight, hard-hitting, but with no little humour. He spoke of his hopes and ambitions for the future, but warned them that success could not be guaranteed to be immediate. What he could promise them, however, was that he would put everything he had into the job, 24 hours a day if neces-

TOP: RANGERS' FIRST MANAGER, WILLIAM WILTON

INSET: THE PIER AT GOUROCK WHERE
WILTON SLIPPED TO HIS DEATH

ABOVE: THE TERRACING COLLAPSE AT THE
DISASTER SCENE – IBROX STADIUM, 1902

TOP LEFT: WILLIAM STRUTH

TOP RIGHT: WILLIAM STRUTH, THE 'BEAU BRUMMEL OF FOOTBALL', ON BOARD A LINER TO NORTH AMERICA

ABOVE: SANDY ARCHIBALD TURNS AWAY TO CELEBRATE RANGERS' FOURTH GOAL IN THE 1928 SCOTTISH CUP FINAL

OLD FIRM
CAPTAINS DAVIE
MEIKLEJOHN
(RANGERS) AND
WILLIAM McSTAY
(CELTIC) BEFORE
THE 1928 SCOTTISH
CUP FINAL

STRUTH

ABOVE: WILLIAM
STRUTH (SEATED) AND
HIS CAPTAIN, GEORGE
YOUNG, INSIDE THE
MANAGER'S OFFICE

LEFT: WILLIAM STRUTH
IN UNIFORM DURING
HIS TENURE AT
BELLAHOUSTON ARMY
HOSPITAL

RIGHT: SCOT
SYMON

BELOW: CAPTAIN
ERIC CALDOW
BEING CARRIED
ALOFT AS SCOT
SYMON'S SIDE
CELEBRATES THE
1962 SCOTTISH
CUP WIN

SYMON

DAVIE WHITE

WHITE

RIGHT: WILLIE
WADDELL

INSET: THE NEW
BROOMLOAN
STAND UNDER
CONSTRUCTION

WADDELL

ABOVE: THE VICTORIOUS 1972 CUP-WINNERS' CUP
SQUAD INSIDE THE BLUE ROOM AT IBROX BEFORE
THE 25TH ANNIVERSARY CELEBRATIONS

TOP: A DEJECTED JOCK WALLACE LEAVES IBROX AFTER HIS
DISMISSAL

ABOVE: WALLACE CELEBRATES THE SKOL CUP WIN DURING HIS
SECOND TERM AS MANAGER

JOHN GREIG

GREIG

THE ENIGMATIC BUT
OFTEN BRILLIANT DAVIE
COOPER

sary. The response was overwhelming. One fan commented: 'Not a man will leave this place tonight without the conviction that a new hope exists without stupid promises. We ask for nothing more.'

Waddell also called a meeting with the players and announced that they would be treated on an equal footing whether they were big-name stars or youngsters. All first-team players would be on a wage structure, with none earning any more than the other. Turning to the young players, he highlighted the rewards that they could expect if they performed well. He told them that they were the future of Rangers and they would get their chance. It was up to them to grasp the opportunity.

He also emphasised the importance of discipline. The players were left in no doubt that he expected them to act like Rangers players both on and off the field and carry themselves accordingly. There would be no long hair and no facial hair. In reality, he needn't have mentioned his desire for the 'clean-cut' look. His views on these issues had already filtered through to the players before he officially took up office and both Jim Baxter and Willie Henderson attended the meeting already shorn of their 'Gringo' moustaches.

Waddell outlined his mission for Rangers in a series of one-to-one conversations with the assembled press pack. He told them his aim was to restore the image of the club not only on the field, but also off it. He wanted to make Rangers the most respected club in the land and he would give every player a chance to make a success of his football career. It was clear, however, that things would be done his way and that anyone who had trouble conforming would find that Ibrox was no longer welcoming.

The talking was over, the spirits were revived, but now Waddell had to deliver.

THE START OF THE REVIVAL

Concerned at the poor level of fitness, the new boss immediately instigated double training, with shifts in the morning and afternoon. He watched as trainers Harold Davis and Lawrie Reilly put the squad through their paces but was quick to refute any suggestion that he would be a tracksuit manager. 'I don't want to be known as one,' he would reply sternly, pointing out that he would play the situation as it came. In essence, despite the fashionable ideas of the merits of the 'tracksuit boss', Waddell was very much his own man and would remain that way. Ironically, his ideas were more in tune with those of Scot Symon, who had lost his position at Ibrox as the fans and directors clamoured for a manager with more up-to-date methods.

Davie White had opened the 1969–70 season with a core pool of nineteen players, although his regular side was drawn from just thirteen. When Waddell took over, he extended the opportunity of a place in the first team to a further twelve players, many of whom were youngsters who had been on the fringes. Jim Baxter, the legendary star of the 1960s, who had failed to produce the flashes of brilliance which characterised his initial term at Ibrox, was discarded by Waddell within a matter of weeks. Orjan Persson also found his appearances limited as the new manager shifted the emphasis to youth. Davie Provan also drifted out of the picture as did Bobby Watson, who joined Motherwell alongside Brian Herron in the deal that brought Peter McCloy to Ibrox. By the end of the season, Kai Johansen was also on his way.

Among those who immediately benefited from the rejuvenation of the side were Alex MacDonald, Sandy Jardine and Alfie Conn, all under 23, and the 24-year-old Colin Jackson.

Waddell's arrival stimulated a twelve-match unbeaten run in the League, punctuated only by a controversial League Cup quarter-final defeat from Celtic. By April, however, the title was well beyond Rangers' reach after a miserable series of defeats and just two wins out of seven in March. Waddell by this time had had the opportunity to assess his entire playing resources as the task of restoring the club's lost pride gained momentum.

Everyone recognised that there would be casualties when the new boss took over, but most were unprepared for the clear-out of the backroom that Waddell announced in mid-April. Davie Kinnear, Harold Davis and Lawrie Smith were all shown the door as the last remnants of the White era disappeared. Old-time play-ing partner Willie Thornton remained and in came Jock Wallace, who relinquished his role as assistant manager at Hearts to take up the position of Rangers' chief trainer and coach. Waddell would later add assistant trainer Stan Anderson to his backroom team, whose remit was to improve the flow of talent from the youth ranks.

One of Waddell's criticisms of Rangers under White had been that the side was patently unfit. He set to work on the players' fitness levels with heavy training. He wanted them to work hard during the week so that they were better prepared for the rigours of matchday. His idea was they *worked* during the week so that they could *play* on the Saturday. In some ways the reverse had been true under the White era.

Sandy Jardine recalled the impact Waddell made: 'He was in many ways a bully, goading players into response through his strong personality. You had to be a strong person to stand up to "Deedle". He had been brought up under Struth and he knew what it meant to be a Ranger and he ensured that everybody else knew too. He wouldn't stand any nonsense. The players were slightly afraid of him, but full of respect.'

Rangers recaptured something reminiscent of the Struth era as Waddell took a step back from the closer contact that White enjoyed, but he was still part of everything that happened with the team. He performed all team talks and watched from the sidelines as Wallace took the training.

Wallace was the ideal trainer to fulfil Waddell's expectations. He was famed as a fitness fanatic. He had an interest in body conditioning gained during a period of active service in Malaysia, and his tough training schedules were legendary throughout the game. There was an irony in his appointment, though: Wallace was the architect of Rangers' disastrous defeat at Berwick three years earlier as both the goalkeeper and manager of the Shielfield Park side. Willie Johnson, at least, had some unhappy memories of the formidable Wallace – it was in a clash with the new trainer that he broke his ankle on that sad day in Berwick.

TRAINING

Shortly after assuming his duties, the enthusiastic Wallace introduced the players to the kind of intense training that they had never experienced under White. On his first session with the players at Ibrox, under the watchful eye of Willie Waddell, the entire playing staff of around 46 men embarked on what Wallace called '40 minutes'. The players ran constantly, doing lifts, 200-yard sprints, lung-bursting 440-yard dashes, and hikes up and down the steep terraces – all without a break for 40 tortuous minutes. With physiotherapists strategically placed around the track and oxygen available for those who required resuscitation (three needed it), he drove the players to the point of collapse. By the end of the session only six remained standing, with the rest hanging exhausted over the track wall, lying spent on the turf or squatting reddened and exhausted on the pitch.

The players faced that routine every Tuesday, unless there was the mercy of a midweek game. Extreme, yes, and there was a general feeling among the players that the training was too hard, often leaving them weary and lacking that vital edge on matchdays.

I asked Sandy Jardine of the players' reaction to Wallace's training. His answer was short. 'We were sick,' he laughed. It was, however, Wallace's way and no one could deny that Rangers had the fittest team in the League.

The players settled into the new regime without difficulty, enjoying the stiff but varied training schedules that Wallace instigated. Apart from the torture of a Tuesday, a typical day for a Rangers player in those days would see him appear at Ibrox around ten in the morning and begin the session with jogging, followed by six successive 220-yard sprints, with the aim of improving the speed each time. That would be followed by short sprints, or 'shuttle runs', before the squad moved inside to the gym where Wallace had devised circuit training, incorporating weights. The final part of the session was devoted to ball-work with the focus on the basic skills of passing, shooting and heading. Many of the players would return for afternoon sessions when they would concentrate on specific problem areas of their game.

Of all the training methods that have been used through the years at Ibrox, none has received the attention that Wallace's trips to the sand dunes at Gullane got. Once a week he would take the players for a very strenuous session running up and down the ash-white sands of the East Lothian town. The demands of the training were such that players were frequently physically sick, but they had no quibble about following Wallace's commands – invariably he joined them and they respected him for that.

While the players suffered to the point of exhaustion, there is little doubt the stern training methods proved beneficial to most. A number of them found that they attained fitness levels that saw them able to continue their playing careers well into their thirties.

A MANAGEMENT PARTNERSHIP

Waddell would often stand on the sidelines during training, but he never took part in the sessions, preferring to leave the rigours of the Albion training ground to his younger coach. The Rangers boss devolved much of his authority to Wallace even in those early days. In fact, Waddell and Wallace evolved a managerial partnership that was innovative for the period. Waddell's day-to-day concerns extended to administrative matters as well as the management of the team, while Wallace relieved him of the daily routine of the training ground. It is a model that many clubs now use in what some have described as a new style of management.

Although he had few dealings with the players each day, Waddell always had the final say on team matters. On some occasions, Wallace disagreed and the pair had many heated discussions as they debated team selection. These conflicts were often obvious to the players and they, too, were encouraged to express their views to the manager. Several of the players of that era recalled arguments with Waddell when ideas were exchanged in heated debate. Some reckoned he enjoyed a good argument, but all agreed that he rarely held grudges.

Colin Jackson remembered an incident that took place on a pre-season tour some time after Waddell had given up the manager's job. Several players joined the ex-boss in his room for a drink after a hard day of training. Waddell soon became embroiled in an exchange with newly signed defender Tom Forsyth. Unwilling to take any more, Forsyth stood up angrily, stating that he had 'had enough', then promptly walked out and closed the door – of a cupboard! It was an embarrassed if not disorientated Forsyth that emerged a few seconds later from behind the door. The atmosphere was broken, though, and Waddell and the others laughed.

Such camaraderie was typical of the team that Waddell moulded and he took great pleasure from seeing his players mix well, although he always maintained a distance from them. Jock Wallace, on the other hand, was with the players night and day, providing a 'buffer' between the manager and his men. Waddell knew they were in good hands because Wallace shared his belief that 'the club was greater than the man' – the famous William Struth doctrine. They were representing the Rangers Football

Club and Waddell could not have picked a better 'minder' than Wallace.

While Wallace cared for the players on a day-to-day basis, Waddell was always there to ensure that they were treated in a manner befitting their position as Rangers players. Nothing was too good for them in travel, accommodation and general well-being while representing the club. On many a trip he would be seen at hotel receptions loudly demanding improvements to the arrangements where he felt they had slipped below the standards he expected.

SILVERWARE RETURNS TO IBROX

With his new backroom staff in place, Waddell embarked on his first full season as manager of Rangers, determined to give youth a chance. Davie White's team was hardly elderly – the average age was around 27 – but Waddell's ruthless clearout of the old stars and introduction of new blood lowered the average age to just 24.

His preparations for the new season began in a pre-season tour of Germany, a favourite testing ground for the manager. He saw little point in testing his side against weak opposition, preferring to introduce them to the tougher, disciplined sides of the German leagues. The matches against Hamburg and Kaiserslautern were anything but friendly, though. Colin Stein was despatched for an early bath in the first match and Kenny Watson saw red in the second as the games turned into a rough-house. Waddell, while unhappy at the dismissals, took a lot from the tour and was sure that his young team had gained invaluable experience. He could see that Jardine was maturing into a fine full-back and Alfie Conn was good enough to command a regular place in the side. He had, in just a few months, put together a team that looked fresh and exuberant, if not experienced enough to provide a sustained challenge to Stein's formidable Celtic.

Rangers opened their campaign with a series of confident and impressive displays in League Cup sectional ties against Dunfermline, Morton and Motherwell. Sixteen goals registered with just one conceded sealed qualification for the quarter-final and raised the fans' hopes of attaining the first trophy in over four years. This optimism was somewhat dispelled as the League season got under way. Defeat at Celtic Park (0–2) and then by Aberdeen at Ibrox left Rangers in fifth place and adrift by October.

The side's cup form was better. Although their interest in the Inter Cities Fairs Cup ended in September at the first stage with defeat from old foes Bayern Munich, Rangers fought their way to a League Cup final showdown with Celtic. Waddell believed they could win the trophy and give the fans something to cheer after a long time in the shadow of their rivals from the east of the city. The supporters themselves, buoyed up by the sense of belief and optimism installed by Waddell, shared the manager's confidence, but it was not a conviction that was held by many others. On the morning of the match the *Daily Record*'s poll of First Division skippers found few predicting a Rangers win. In fact, those who did feel that Waddell could bring the silverware back to Ibrox based their views more on statistics than anything that they had seen in the respective abilities of the two sides.

Waddell was undeterred. He had already formed some reservations about the team's capability to sustain a consistent League challenge, but he had little doubt that they were a match for anyone in the head-to-head challenge of cup competition. The side had, after all, a sprinkling of international players with experience at the highest level. The team appeared to pick itself – or so it seemed. The manager, however, had other ideas.

It was always Waddell's philosophy that if a player was good enough, he was old enough. He had never hesitated to introduce youngsters to the fray and had even taken 15-year-old George Donaldson on the pre-season tour of Germany. On the eve of the Cup final, the players trooped back to the dressing-room at the end of their morning session. Waddell pulled 16-year-old Derek Johnstone aside and gave him quite stunning news. He would line up against Celtic in the number 9 jersey!

It was an amazing gamble by Waddell, although the precocious teenager had shown an eye for goal with a brace against Cowdenbeath on his début less than four weeks earlier. Johnstone displayed an aerial strength that belied his tender years and Waddell felt that the enthusiasm of the youngster could unsettle Celtic's solid defence.

Johnstone's inclusion was not the only shock to greet the fans as the teams were announced minutes before the start. John Greig, the captain, had failed to shake off the effects of flu that had savaged his preparations in the run-up to the match and he finally conceded defeat just an hour before kick-off. Waddell remained confident and fired up his players in the Hampden dressing-room while 106,000 fans gathered inside the old arena that had seen many historic encounters. It was prepared for another.

Straight from the kick-off, Rangers impressed with an urgency that dispelled the pre-match nerves of their fans. Surging runs and sharp tackling unsettled Jock Stein's side as Rangers poured forward, the pace of Willie Johnston causing havoc as he switched flanks from left to right and back again. Five minutes before the break, he broke away on the right, steadied himself near the touch-line and then swept a cross deep into the Celtic area. Derek John-stone rose between the despairing leap of Celtic's Billy McNeill and Jim Craig to send the ball past the outstretched hand of Evan Williams and into the net.

Hampden erupted and, as Rangers closed out the game, there was a realisation amongst the fans that the significance of the victory extended beyond the merits of a Cup win. Waddell had raised Rangers from the depths of despair they had been in just eleven months earlier as the side drifted aimlessly with seemingly no end to Celtic's dominance in sight. The win brought silverware back to the Ibrox trophy-room, but Waddell had achieved much more. He had created the foundations of a team that could re-establish Rangers as the premier team in Scotland. It was clear to all that the side was raw with many rough edges, but it had time on its side.

As he left Hampden, Waddell paid tribute to his young stars and offered them as inspiration to those in the lower ranks looking for the chance to break through. In less than a year he had trans-formed the side. Only four of the players who had succumbed to Gornik on that sad night at Ibrox were in the victorious Hampden team. More significantly, the team included five youngsters who had grasped the opportunity promised by Waddell.

As the fans rejoiced long into the night, the manager remained philosophical. He had achieved success earlier than he had expec-ted, but his target remained the championship. This was only the beginning, but his players had tasted the sweetness of victory, many for the first time. The work would continue.

FROM TRIUMPH TO TRAGEDY

The League Cup win failed to ignite a title challenge for Rangers as the inconsistency of the season persisted. Lost points to lowly Ayr United, Hibernian and Dunfermline put paid to any serious challenge as Celtic and Aberdeen contested the top spot. The customary New Year fixture was always a trial of strength and Rangers welcomed Celtic to Ibrox on 2 January 1971, determined to dent their rivals' title aspirations even if victory in the League race seemed beyond their own reach.

A crowd of around 80,000 gathered inside the stadium, boisterous and vocal but not unruly. In truth, the match hardly provided the excitement normally expected of an Old Firm clash, until the closing moments. With just over a minute left on the clock, and the tie goalless, the diminutive Jimmy Johnstone headed Celtic into the lead. The goal signalled an exodus of despondent fans from the east terracing, Rangers' end of the ground.

With only seconds remaining, Rangers launched a last-gasp attack. Colin Stein latched on to the ball inside the area and slammed it into the Celtic net for the most dramatic of equalisers. As the roar went up from the Rangers contingent, a number of fans on their way out of the ground tried to return up the steep stairway exits to take part in the celebrations. The final whistle had sounded, however, and the masses were already pouring out of the exit at the top of Stairway 13. Five minutes later the stairway was the scene of devastation, with a tangled mass of bodies strewn around the area and buckled metal barriers lying in shocking testimony to the crushing pressures of the cascading crowd.

An eyewitness claimed that two youths being carried shoulder-high at the top of the stairway fell and caused a tumble of bodies behind them. Many suggested that the exiting fans were toppled as others returned up the stairs to catch the celebrations in the wake of Colin Stein's equaliser.

While the exact details of the events have never been completely clarified, the result made headline news around the world. The commotion on Stairway 13 left 66 dead and over 140 injured. It was the blackest day in the club's history. The emergency services rushed to the scene and worked late into the night to relieve the suffering of the injured and comfort the bereaved. As a line of bodies, shrouded in simple white sheets, lay on the Ibrox turf, from the corner flag to the goalpost, a young nurse stood in tears, regretting that she 'felt so helpless'.

The players knew little of the tragedy as they left the stadium. They were aware that there had been some disturbance and saw some of the injured carried inside to a small room adjacent to their dressing-room. In fact, the ambulance room and many adjoining areas resembled a scene from the battlefields.

As the players departed, Willie Waddell and Celtic boss Jock Stein helped direct stretcher-bearers to the dressing-rooms which by that time had been set up as casualty stations. Ironically, the match itself had been a good-natured affair with little of the hostility that traditionally marred the fixture. These were not casualties of war, but fans attending a football match to support the team they loved.

As telegrams of condolence arrived at Ibrox and everyone from the highest level of government to the shocked local community visited the stadium to view the terrible scenes, Waddell and several capable members of staff worked feverishly to attend to the varied demands of the aftermath. With chairman John Lawrence debilitated by illness, Waddell took the lead in most of the press enquiries. Indeed, he virtually held the club together during these fraught weeks of January 1971. It was he who faced the cameras, sullen-faced outside the ground as the morning broke and the sheer magnitude of the events was exposed to the cold January light. He read the club's statement on the tragedy to a press corps at fever pitch.

Aside from the dealings with the media and the constant enquiries from officialdom, Waddell turned to the personal needs of the bereaved and injured. He organised representation from the players and directors at 65 of the 66 funerals (one preferred a private ceremony). On some days, the players attended several funerals, an inevitable consequence of the internment of the large number of dead. The players also visited the injured in the nearby Southern General Hospital and elsewhere.

The players performed their public duties with great dignity and were a credit to the club, but behind the scenes many of the Ibrox staff endured great anguish in carrying out their various new responsibilities – many who were unsung heroes in the aftermath. Through it all, however, Waddell was the rock, the inspiration around which everyone could rally. When he was appointed manager just over a year earlier, the club needed him. With football far from the minds of everyone connected with the club there was a realisation that Rangers needed Waddell more in the darkest days of the tragedy than they could ever have imagined. Quite simply, he was the embodiment of strength as the club faced its most difficult moments. He had reconstructed the team – now he would face the rebuilding of the stadium.

A NEW DAWN OVER IBROX

Tortured by the tragedy of what became known as 'The Ibrox Disaster', the Rangers directors resolved to ensure that the stadium would never again witness scenes resembling the dark days of January 1971. They recognised that, in the interests of safety, the steep stairways that led from the end terracings would have to go and that such modifications would inevitably mean a complete reshaping of the ground. More importantly, they realised that there would have to be more consideration given to the comfort of fans attending the stadium. In Europe, and particularly in Germany, which was preparing to host the World Cup finals, the trend in stadium construction was towards all-seated accommodation.

It was decided that the old terracings should be replaced, but the practicalities of embarking on a redevelopment scheme would need detailed research and scrutiny. Later that year, following the opening of Rangers' new social club on Edmiston Drive, director David Hope spoke of his hopes for the future: 'It's no longer enough for the fans to stand on bare terracings in all kinds of weather.' He outlined plans for more covering and a greater proportion of seats. 'The fans today want a bit of comfort. More and more women are going to games . . . we want facilities that will keep them coming.'

Although the details of the plans were still being evolved and were being kept quite secret, it was clear that the club had decided to embark on a major programme of change, financed by the supremely successful Rangers Pools. Waddell was charged with the responsibility of overseeing the work, but such a transformation could not be expected to happen overnight.

With their interest in the League championship effectively over,

Rangers looked to finish the season on a high with a Scottish Cup win. Waddell had considered his men to be a 'Cup team' and they had justified that tag with a determined campaign that took them to a final against Celtic. For Rangers it was an opportunity to add another trophy to the League Cup won in such thrilling circumstances in November. Celtic, who had cruised to a sixth successive championship, were determined to complete the double.

Preparations in the lead-up to the match were hardly ideal for Rangers. The influential sweeper, Dave Smith, broke his ankle in training six weeks before the final. Their problems were compounded when Sandy Jardine suffered a hairline fracture in his leg during a match with Cowdenbeath just three weeks from the Hampden showdown, and then, with only seven days to the kick-off, young Alfie Conn collapsed with a serious knee injury in a Glasgow Cup match.

If that wasn't difficult enough for Waddell to contend with, he also had to endure the uncertainty of the availability of Mathieson, Jackson and Henderson, who were on the treatment table. Stein, in contrast, had a full squad available to him.

Rangers' injured trio were cleared for the match just before kick-off, but the side was undoubtedly weakened and morale among the fans was not high. A crowd of around 120,000 watched a dour encounter with Celtic opening the scoring late in the first half through Lennox, before substitute Derek Johnstone repeated his Cup-final heroics by snatching an equaliser with just three minutes remaining. It was a game that Rangers should have won, but by the end they were just pleased to have a second opportunity. There were further injury woes for the Ibrox side, however, with the loss of Alex Miller, who broke a cheekbone.

With his defensive resources stretched and his options severely limited, Waddell once again turned to youth for the replay. He introduced Jim Denny at right back, a 21-year-old who had signed from the Junior ranks just four months earlier. Denny did all that was asked of him, but Rangers failed to revive their sparkle of the previous match and Stein's men ran out comfortable 2–1 winners.

It had been a long and eventful season. Waddell, for one, was glad to see the end of it and looked forward to the new campaign. His team had matured a lot both as players and men in the past twelve months. Now was the time for them to deliver greater consistency to an Ibrox support desperate for success.

Waddell went into the 1971–72 season with one major new signing – Tommy McLean. The diminutive winger was acquired from Kilmarnock for a fee of around £60,000, reuniting him with the man who guided his early career at Rugby Park. Waddell had in fact captured McLean for Killie from under the nose of Rangers boss Scot Symon nine years earlier, and had nurtured his early development at Rugby Park.

Rangers had a tough start to the new season with a League Cup sectional tie against Celtic at Parkhead. Remarkably, the Old Firm had been drawn together in the sections for the fourth time in five years. Ominously, Rangers had failed to progress on all four of the previous occasions. True to form, Celtic won the opener 2–0 with youngster Kenny Dalglish, playing in his first Old Firm match, getting the second from the penalty spot. He scored again a fortnight later when the sides met for the return match at Ibrox as Celtic clinched their place in the quarter-final with a 3–0 win.

It was hardly the start that Waddell wanted or expected, and the League Cup setback affected the side's form as the players embarked on the long League campaign a week later. Defeat in the opening game from Partick Thistle was followed by another Old Firm loss at Ibrox. Rangers' miserable form continued through September and, with only five League games gone, they had lost four with a solitary win registered on the table. It was Rangers' worst-ever start to the championship. By the New Year they were seven points adrift of Celtic and defeat at Parkhead through a last-minute goal from Jim Brogan all but ended any hopes that Willie Waddell had of bringing the championship back to Ibrox.

THE ROAD TO BARCELONA

Rangers put aside their erratic League form to add credence to Waddell's claim that he had a Cup team by confidently progressing in the European Cup-Winners' competition. The manager studied European opposition with such intensity that it suggested a strong desire to elevate Rangers' standing across the continent. Players would be given photographs of their opponents and a detailed breakdown of their strengths and weaknesses. Both Wallace and Waddell compiled such dossiers after a series of scouting missions.

For Waddell, European competition was an opportunity to test the methods and tactics he had evolved in pre-season fixtures. After his first tour as Rangers manager, he spoke of the lessons the players had learned in countering the style of continental teams playing in their own stadium. He knew that for any team to be successful in Europe it would need to be able to show resilience in the away leg. Bayern had rapidly quenched any hope that Waddell had of making an impact in Europe in the previous season, but the manager was determined that this season would be different.

After victory over top French side Rennes in the first round, Rangers faced Sporting Lisbon, with the first leg to be held in early November at Ibrox. In a convincing first-half display, the Light Blues had a 3–0 lead at the interval. The Portuguese side rallied and, after some slack defensive play, Rangers conceded two goals.

In front of 60,000 spectators in Lisbon, Rangers stoutly defended their one-goal advantage, even coping with the loss of Ronnie McKinnon who broke his leg, until a goal seven minutes from time reversed the Ibrox scoreline (2–3) and pushed the game into extra-time. Willie Henderson shot Rangers into the lead once again, but the Portuguese replied with a goal four minutes later taking the score to 3–4, with the aggregate level at 6–6. On the final whistle the Rangers were convinced that they had triumphed on the away-goals rule, but the Dutch referee caused confusion when he ordered a penalty shoot-out.

With havoc in the press-box where some were in little doubt that Rangers had gone through, the team proceeded to miss four of their five kicks while the ecstatic Portuguese celebrated victory. Some of the journalists rushed to the Rangers dressing-room to alert Waddell to the UEFA ruling. It stated quite clearly that away goals scored in extra-time counted double in the event of a tie. Rangers were through.

Waddell grabbed the rulebook and dashed along the corridor to find the UEFA observer. He sat in conference for some time with the official representative of European football's governing body, before emerging with the news that Rangers were indeed on their way to the quarter-final. It was a tense night for the Scots, but Waddell was proud of his players and their commitment. They had shown that they were a force to be reckoned with, and the manager knew he had a squad capable of taking the club all the way to the final.

Rangers' reward was a clash with Torino in March. It would give Waddell time to smooth the rough edges of the team. With the dismal form of the early stages of the season behind them, Rangers went into the quarter-final with greater consistency, having won five and drawn one of their previous seven matches.

Waddell's reconnaissance missions to the city of Turin indicated that the Italians were an aggressive side who would undoubtedly fly at Rangers from the kick-off. Showing cute tactical awareness, he decided to adopt the typical Italian *catenaccio* system of defence he had studied on a visit to Inter Milan coach Helenio Herrera several years earlier. He knew the system could frustrate the Italian strikers who would be driven forward by a large, excited crowd. Dave Smith was assigned the sweeper role alongside Colin Jackson and young Derek Johnstone, whom Waddell had converted into a fine central defender.

The tactics worked perfectly, with the game finishing all-square at 1–1, although the Light Blue defensive line was under siege for most of the match. Back at Ibrox, Rangers adopted their more conventional attacking style to hustle the Italians out of the tournament with a solitary goal from MacDonald.

With their minds now very much focused on the real possibility of European success, Rangers eagerly awaited the draw and were delighted with the outcome – a semi-final tie with Bayern Munich. The Germans' stature in the game was beyond doubt and they boasted six members of their sensational international side, including the great Franz Beckenbauer and Gerd Muller.

In the first-leg tie in Munich, the Germans were superbly drilled but they met a Rangers side equally well organised. In one of the club's most convincing away performances in Europe, Rangers emerged with a 1–1 draw that left everything neatly balanced for the return leg at Ibrox a fortnight later. A crowd of 80,000 gathered inside the stadium with an air of great expectancy, although there was gloom over the loss of the injured captain, John Greig.

Greig had missed the League Cup final eighteen months earlier, when Waddell introduced young Derek Johnstone and the youngster created history by scoring the winner. With Greig again missing, it seemed unlikely that there would be a further shock team selection because the manager had built a more versatile pool from which he had any number of options. Even young Derek Parlane's father never expected his son to feature as he stood on the steps of the Ibrox enclosure waiting for the teams to come out.

Sure enough, and as if to emphasise that he was very much his own man when it came to team selection, Waddell thrust Parlane into the biggest match of his young life – after only two League appearances. Parlane's father was stunned to see his son emerge from the tunnel with the number 4 jersey! The youngster had no time for nerves – he had learned of his selection just minutes earlier.

In a night that will remain vivid in the memories of all who witnessed it, Jardine grabbed a first-minute opening goal and Parlane justified his inclusion with the second in 23 minutes. As the game moved into the closing stages, the normally unflappable Germans began arguing among themselves. On the final whistle, with the scoreline at 2–0, Ibrox erupted in celebration. Waddell had taken the club to its third European final. Would it be third time lucky?

THE TRIUMPH AND DISGRACE OF BARCELONA

Before the cheers at Ibrox had subsided, Rangers learned that they would meet Moscow Dynamo in the final of the European Cup-Winners' Cup, to be held in Barcelona's Nou Camp Stadium. Having despatched the Germans, the Light Blues found themselves favourites for the trophy, which introduced unwelcome pressures but was flattering nonetheless.

The scheduling of the Scottish fixtures saw the season end a full three weeks before Rangers were due to depart for Spain, which gave Waddell a chance to nurse his players through to the final, although they would perhaps enter the match with their competitive edge slightly dulled. The manager arranged friendly fixtures away to Inverness Select and St Mirren, which the side strolled through, scoring five times on each occasion.

These games honed the fitness of the team and also gave John Greig a chance to get some match fitness after being out for a couple of weeks with a bad ankle injury. The captain came through the matches unscathed, but in the week before the side travelled to Barcelona the skipper damaged his ligaments once again. He was joined on the doubtful list by Colin Jackson, who had missed the final match of the season through injury and had not recovered sufficiently to take part in the friendlies. A decision on their fitness would be left until the last possible moment.

Both travelled to Spain with the rest of the squad two days before the match and settled into the hilltop hotel that Waddell had selected away from the bustle and noise of the city. The Russians, in contrast, found themselves in a beach hotel in the heart of the tourist area, with no privacy or seclusion. It was further evidence of the Rangers manager's attention to the needs of his players. He also brought along food to ensure that there were no upsets that would disrupt his plans.

The players were forbidden to sunbathe in case the hot Spanish sun had an ill effect on them. Waddell insisted that they wear tracksuits at all times when they ventured outdoors. It was certainly uncomfortable for the players and the stay at the hotel became tedious in the run-up to the match, but Waddell was determined that they should enter the game in perfect physical condition.

Waddell's teams were always well prepared going into Europe and despite the difficulties of getting access to the Dynamo side, every Rangers player was given a photograph of the man he would face and a dossier on his opponent. They were instructed how to play the match and how their opponents would set about the game. It was invaluable.

The doubts over Greig and Jackson remained. On the day before the game both players appeared to have won their fitness battle, but Jackson broke down in a training match as he moved in to tackle Tommy McLean. Greig was declared fit, but Jackson had to be replaced. As he had done before, Waddell turned to youth in adversity. Derek Johnstone slipped back to take the position vacated by Jackson and the manager threw one of the eleven starting jerseys to young Alfie Conn.

With the kick-off only a couple of hours away, the Rangers contingent headed for the coach that would take them to the giant Nou Camp Stadium. Only as they neared the ground did the players realise the magnitude of the support that had travelled from Scotland to back them. The bus was silent as the players looked out on the thousands of fans bedecked in blue marching to the stadium in a scene more reminiscent of Paisley Road West on matchday than a Spanish street. That sight formed the basis for

Waddell's team-talk as the men prepared to take to the field. 'Look how much it means to these people,' he said, before urging them to do their best for the Rangers Football Club.

The players were focused. They were eager to get out on to the pitch to put behind them the boredom of the two days they had spent at the hotel. Waddell had ensured that his players were free from distractions and they were now ready. The Russians were far from satisfied with their preparations, but they did not have the meticulous pre-planning of Rangers.

As the matched kicked off Rangers displayed real urgency and a tenacity that dispelled any fears that they may approach the game tentatively. John Greig set the pattern in the first few seconds, launching into a tackle that removed any doubts that his ankle would not stand up to the rigours of the 90 minutes. Midway through the first half, Colin Stein got the vital opening goal and Willie Johnston added a second just before the break. Within four minutes of the restart, Johnston latched on to a long clearance from goalkeeper Peter McCloy to put the Light Blues 3–0 ahead. The Russians fought back in the closing stages and scored twice, but Rangers held out for a famous victory.

The pitch invasion which ensued on the final whistle saw the Rangers players run to the dressing-room for cover, while the Spanish police misjudged the situation and engaged in a battle with the over-exuberant Light Blue legions. While mayhem broke loose on the pitch, John Greig was led to a small room deep inside the stadium where he received the Cup in an inauspicious cere-mony. Waddell joined in the celebrations, but his mind was else-where. He knew that the club would suffer when UEFA heard about the post-match disturbances.

As the players returned to the hotel to join their families for the partying that continued long into the night, UEFA was already in session, debating the events. An enquiry would be held and Moscow Dynamo would vainly submit a protest seeking a replay, but Rangers were determined to put the controversy behind them to celebrate the greatest result in their history. Waddell hailed his players and called them 'Ibrox Immortals'. He saluted 'a tremen-dous win, the final effort in a wonderful European run by a team which had to battle through against some of the best club sides on the continent'.

Two weeks after the triumph in Barcelona, Waddell called a press conference to make a dramatic announcement: 'From now on, Jock Wallace will be known as team manager of Rangers and he will be totally responsible for all matters concerning the team and players, including team selections.'

Waddell went on to explain that, although the team matters would now effectively transfer to his assistant, he would retain the number-one position. He explained his reasons: 'I have never made any secret of the fact that in my opinion team management is a young man's game and it becomes more and more difficult these days for one man to run the entire show.' He added, 'Our organisation must be streamlined. It is too much for one man to handle all the details in League and European football.' Waddell paid tribute to Wallace, affirming his confidence that the coach would be a success. 'Jock Wallace has made a terrific impact since I brought him here,' he said. 'You only have to look at the number of times he is invited to lecture at European coaching sessions to get an idea of that.'

Just as he had done at Kilmarnock, Waddell relinquished the reins at the height of his success. That was his way: he felt the best time for change came when there were choices rather than when troubles forced change.

As Wallace settled into his new role, Willie Waddell faced his first challenge in his newly created position of general manager. UEFA cracked down on the club for the Barcelona disturbances, barring Rangers from European competition for two years. It was a penalty the club scarcely deserved when they had little control over the behaviour of their fans and, more importantly, over the Spanish authorities. Waddell appealed to UEFA and successfully achieved a halving of the sentence. This was Waddell at his best.

The circumstances surrounding this appeal to UEFA have never been well documented. Waddell did, in fact, threaten to resign from Rangers if the club did not appeal the ban. His wife Hilda told me, 'We were in Sitges, near Barcelona, on holiday, when news of the ban was communicated to us. In a few phone calls from our hotel to Ibrox, my husband urged the board to proceed with an appeal. They told him they were reluctant because they were afraid that the club might suffer repercussions if it appealed. They had a board meeting and came back to confirm that they would not appeal. My husband told the chairman that unless they appealed he would resign. The chairman went back to the boardroom. He called back a few hours later to say that they would back an appeal.'

Mrs Waddell was in no doubt that her husband would have resigned, such was the strength of his feeling of injustice.

He would continue to campaign for an elimination of the hooligan element that tarnished the club's reputation through the early 1970s, to protect 'the good name of Rangers Football Club'. He would also pursue that other great dream – to turn Ibrox into the most modern and best-equipped stadium in the land. With Wallace in command of team affairs, Waddell turned his energies to the reconstruction of Ibrox.

Within nine years the fruits of his labour were there to see. The old terracings began to disappear in 1978 to be replaced by massive new stands providing seating for almost 40,000. The new stadium, with the Copland, Broomloan and Govan stands, was opened in 1981 at a cost of around £10 million. It was evidence of Waddell's vision and determination that the bright new Ibrox should emerge a decade after its darkest moment. The ground was a monument to those who had perished in the Ibrox Disaster. 'Only the best is good enough for Rangers' was an axiom that Waddell held true.

Waddell had lifted Rangers when the club was on its knees. Ruling with a rod of iron, he smacked the players into shape, completely overhauling the backroom in one of the biggest staff turnovers in history. He reinstated the belief that only the best was good enough. 'You are playing for the Rangers,' he would tell them. 'Remember what it means.' For those who knew, the words were inspirational. For those who didn't, they dared not defy him.

The manager established a good base for the future prosperity of the club on the field and off it. The management game that he had always claimed was for young men would be passed over to his heir apparent. Waddell had been lured into management not out of desire but through a belief that he was needed by the club he loved. There were other pressing duties. Jock Wallace's time had come.

JOCK WALLACE

If Willie Waddell had been schooled in the life of a Ranger by the greatest of mentors, Bill Struth, Jock Wallace was born to assume the role. Unlike Waddell, who had earned the adulation of the Ibrox supporters in a glittering career, Wallace's football education was less glamorous. The son of a miner, he was born in the Midlothian town of Wallyford on 6 September 1937. Always interested in football and a fervent supporter of Rangers as a youngster, he showed some aptitude for the game at an early age. He signed for Workington in 1952 as a handy but by no means outstanding goalkeeper. A year later he was freed after breaking his right hand in a match against Tranmere Rovers. He joined Lancashire non-league side Ashton before National Service took him into the King's Own Scottish Borderers, where he served for three years.

On his exit from the services, Wallace broke through to the Senior ranks at Airdrie and in 1959 he was transferred to West Bromwich Albion for £8,000. Showing strong will and determination, he walked out on the club after they transfer-listed him at £10,000. He joined Bedford, where he remained for a couple of years before moving on to Hereford. He returned north to the border town of Berwick in 1966 as player-manager of the local Rangers at Shielfield Park.

Wallace made a reasonable impact at Berwick Rangers, taking them to the upper echelons of the Second Division, although they were unlikely to offer a decent challenge to the bigger clubs of the top flight – or so it seemed.

Wallace was already familiar with his opponents when the Ibrox side came out of the hat paired with little Berwick Rangers in the first round of the Scottish Cup in 1967. He had been invited by Symon to watch the Glasgow giants in pre-season training, continuing an interest in coaching methods that had taken him to a number of clubs in the south. Wallace was a keen student of the game, and when he sent his young Berwick side out at Shielfield Park on 28 January 1967 to meet the mighty Rangers, he knew that his players could not compete on skill alone with a side of seasoned internationals. What they could not offer in the fine arts of the game, however, they could compensate for in terms of sheer effort, a defining characteristic of the teams reared by Wallace. He had honed a side that was not short of stamina or determination.

As the 90 minutes unfolded, Berwick forward Sammy Reid scored the only goal of the game in one of the biggest shocks in Scottish football history. A tale of two Rangers became a tale of two managers – a defining moment for both Symon and Wallace. In Symon's case, it was the beginning of the end of an era, a period when the traditional grey-suited boss would be replaced by the manager who would put his tracksuit on and join the players in training. The future looked dim for the Rangers boss. For Wallace, appearing every bit the modern coach, the future couldn't have looked brighter. 'Everything is done in spirit,' he said of his players, as every club in the land took note.

A year later, he was snapped up by Hearts boss John Harvey, who was looking for an inspirational assistant to help drive the capital side to success. It was in some respects a return home for Wallace, although Rangers had always been his team as a youngster.

THE WADDELL–WALLACE PARTNERSHIP

Wallace's training methods at Tynecastle were strict and regimented, a reflection of his period of active service with the King's Own Scottish Borderers with whom he served initially in Northern Ireland, then confronted communist insurgents in the jungles of Malaysia. 'Jungle-fighter' became a clichéd nickname for Wallace, which remained with him all his days, but it was a description that summed up his character and one he revelled in. He had learned in the services that intensive training produced men who were supremely fit and capably suited to the type of endurance test successful football sides faced with a long arduous season. That simple philosophy formed the basis of the Wallace training ideals and methods.

Wallace had taken the Hearts players to the sand dunes of Gullane and, if they weren't quite equipped to make a serious impact on the stranglehold of the Old Firm in terms of sheer quality, they more than matched them in fitness and endeavour. Fitness became the mark of the Wallace side.

When Willie Waddell took over at Ibrox in 1969, he set about sweeping the club clean from top to bottom. The malaise which he considered to have enveloped the club in the White era needed the sternest of treatment and, after the dismissal of the entire backroom training staff, the way was clear for Waddell to introduce his own men. Jock Wallace was identified as the ideal coach to improve the fitness of the squad and offer a strong broad shoulder to share the great load of responsibility that Waddell had assumed.

In tandem with Waddell's determination to reinvigorate Ibrox, Wallace introduced the Rangers players to the dunes of Gullane. Pounding up and down the sands of the East Lothian coast was hardly relished by the players, but they undoubtedly reaped the benefit long into their careers.

The sweat was not confined to the sands of Gullane. The arduous '40 minutes' training sessions every Tuesday pushed the players to their limits and Sandy Jardine reckoned that the new trainer was too hard on them in the beginning. 'I don't think the balance was quite right at first. We were tired on a Saturday, but Jock was learning and eventually he knew how to adjust the training so that we peaked for games. When he eventually got it right, we found that we were full of running late in games, while the other side would generally be wilting. When we played, there wasn't a team fitter than us.'

As if to illustrate his own fitness and to show the players that he asked no more of them than he himself could endure, Wallace would often initiate the training with a gruelling personal routine of press-ups in the dressing-room.

The Waddell–Wallace partnership enjoyed success, culminating in that famous win in Barcelona, but Waddell's decision to give up management to concentrate on the wider affairs of the stadium reconstruction created the vacancy that Wallace longed for. Not since he marshalled Berwick Rangers to victory over the Light Blues had he had sole control of a football team. Now he was to be in charge of the biggest club in the country. When he took over on 7 June 1972 he said that Rangers, as Cup-Winners' Cup holders, earned universal respect, but they would not be considered the premier side in the country until they dislodged Jock Stein's Celtic, who were now on an apparently unending sequence of titles.

Wallace's target was clear. Despite his protestations that there were other teams in the League that Rangers had to overcome, he knew that only the Parkhead men stood between the Light Blues and their return to the top in Scotland. Wallace believed that he had a side capable of wresting the title from Celtic, but there would be no championship flag flying over Ibrox until the side could attain some of the consistency that had eluded them in the Waddell years and before. Rangers were acutely aware that they were labelled a 'good Cup side' and little more.

In their first tilt at the title, Wallace's men failed to make any real impact after a disastrous opening. After six games Rangers had gained only five points, but Wallace had other troubles.

He was unhappy with the attitude of Barcelona heroes Willie Johnston and Colin Stein, whom he called 'prima donnas', and it became obvious that Wallace would not allow any deviation from his own ideas of how Rangers should progress. Despite their prominence in the club's finest success just a few months earlier, the two players would find their prospects at Ibrox already curtailed by Wallace. As the manager sought to impose himself on the squad and deny any suggestion that he was anything other than his own man, Stein and Johnston prepared to exit. The message was clear: it would be the Wallace way, or no way at all.

Although Wallace publicly criticised the players' attitude, Sandy Jardine reckoned that the problems the boss faced over Johnston and Stein were quite different. Johnston was being suspended more and more often by the SFA following his indiscipline on the field. Stein was finding it harder to secure a place in the side with Derek Johnstone in the wings and Coventry were keen to sign him.

When Johnston made a gesture to the fans at Ayr and then was ordered off against Partick Thistle in September, leading to a nine-week suspension, he all but blew any hopes of a future at Ibrox. While the ban delayed Johnston's exit, Stein was moved quickly to Coventry in a £90,000 deal that also saw Cutty Young come to Rangers. Johnston joined West Brom three months later.

The team's poor start to the season sealed any realistic chance of the title in 1972–73, but a run of 16 consecutive League victories which began in December, including an Old Firm win, almost snatched it for Wallace. In the end, they lost out by a solitary point.

Wallace had inherited a good pool of players and continued with the youth policy that his predecessor had initiated, but he knew that he would have to add to the squad. Displaying some prudence in the transfer market, he added Tom Forsyth (Motherwell), Stewart Kennedy (Stenhousemuir), Doug Houston (Dundee), Ally Scott (Queen's Park) and Johnny Hamilton (Hibernian) for a total of just £105,000. The revenue from the Stein and Johnston deals more than financed the new arrivals, leaving some money in the Ibrox coffers. But if the transfer merry-go-round saw the departure of two Ibrox heroes, some of the new recruits were destined to make their own inimitable mark on the fans.

Forsyth, in particular, was revered by the supporters and carved out his own little piece of history with the winning goal in Rangers' Centenary Cup final win over Celtic. Introduced to Ibrox initially as a midfielder, Forsyth was a rather unlikely goal hero. His exploits more often featured saving tackles, but he popped up this time with as vital a goal as any scored by a Rangers player – even if the strike came from all of 18 inches! It was a memorable goal for Forsyth – and for Wallace, celebrating his first success as Rangers manager.

Ironically, the Cup that Wallace carried back to Ibrox was the very same trophy that he had contested in 1967 when he first made his mark on Rangers. Then it was sadness for the club and Scot Symon as the Ibrox men trooped wearily home from Berwick. Six years later, the victory – significantly against old rivals Celtic – gave Wallace a taste of success at Ibrox. He and the fans wanted more.

If 1972–73 was filled with promise, the following season provided little to suggest that better times lay ahead. A dismal start to the League campaign saw the side slide to seventh place after just six games with just five points – matching the same poor start they had made just twelve months earlier. The Scottish Cup offered no solace as the Light Blues tumbled out of the competition in a shock 3–0 home defeat at the hands of Dundee. The disappointment was not confined to the domestic scene. The side tumbled out of the Cup-Winners' Cup on their return to Europe after the ban that followed the fan troubles in the aftermath of the Barcelona win.

Wallace could do nothing to arrest Celtic's march to a ninth successful title. The pressure built on the boss as the Ibrox side suffered taunts of being more brawn than brain, the Gullane sessions considered more gimmick than a serious system of training. In two seasons he had delivered just one trophy out of six. It was hardly enough to appease the fans who had suffered so long and so wearily under Celtic's dominance.

Wallace did not turn to the chequebook in this period of discontent. Indeed, more players were shipped out of Ibrox than were bought as he turned to some of his young aspiring stars from the youth and reserves ranks. An increasingly dissatisfied Alfie Conn moved to Tottenham Hotspur for £140,000, and another of the Barcelona heroes, Dave Smith, left to join Arbroath for £10,000, leaving just seven of the side that lifted the Cup-Winners' Cup eighteen months earlier. The main acquisition was Bobby McKean, who joined the club from St Mirren for £40,000.

Wallace's rehabilitated side got off to their best start in the championship in years, despite an opening-day draw at Ayr United's Somerset Park. A 2–1 win secured Rangers' first success in an opening Old Firm league fixture in six years and they completed the double over their Glasgow rivals in the New Year clash with a comprehensive 3–0 victory.

Despite disappointment in the third round of the Scottish Cup, where they exited to Aberdeen, the optimism of the Ibrox support grew as Rangers moved clear in the title race by the turn of the year. At last it seemed that Wallace had broken the Parkhead stranglehold as Celtic went into freefall in the closing stages of the season, leaving Hibernian as Rangers' main challengers. The side received an unexpected boost in the crucial latter stages of the League race with the return of Colin Stein. The move was not precipitated by a change of heart by the manager on the striker but by Coventry's failure to fulfil the transfer terms. Stein's return, at a cost of £80,000, proved timely – despite a flash of his old discipline problems when he saw red in just his second match back. He was more often the hero, though, his moment of glory coming at Easter Road where Rangers, needing just a point to secure the championship, faced Hibernian. Rangers went behind early in the game, but Stein lunged with a header, with less than half an hour to go, to propel the ball into the net and send the Rangers contingent into delirium. They knew they could hold on and so did Wallace. In the final moments, the compassionate

Rangers boss threw his captain into the fray. Greig was unfit and patently unable to compete, but Wallace gave him a chance to savour the moment.

More than any other player in the club's history, Greig deserved that title success, having battled gamely through Celtic's great years. Wallace was determined that Greig should experience the occasion, even if his debilitated captain's inclusion on the bench could have been risky.

Afterwards, the captain paid tribute to the men who had given him a chance to take part in the game. 'It had all been pre-arranged by Jock Wallace and Sandy Jardine. I didn't know a thing about it until Sandy was coming off the park. It was a gesture I really appreciated.'

Wallace said, 'His inclusion was not about sentiment, it was about respect – respect for a great Rangers player.'

Inspired by their title win, the new champions confidently beat Celtic 2–1 on the opening day of the new League race and continued the torment of their Old Firm rivals by taking the League Cup with an Alex MacDonald goal. With only young striker Martin Henderson added to the ranks, Rangers put together a run of 21 games without defeat from December. It was enough to ensure that Rangers retained the championship as Wallace turned his attention towards the Scottish Cup final and the Treble.

Any doubts that Rangers could go on and secure their third domestic trophy that season in the final against Hearts vanished moments after kick-off when Derek Johnstone headed the opening goal in just 42 seconds. Rangers were 1–0 ahead before the scheduled kick-off time! The clock had yet to reach 3 p.m. Hearts never recovered and Rangers went on to win 3–1.

If the 1975–76 season was one of outstanding success, the following term brought disappointment in equal measure. The side that had won Wallace the treble was barely changed but the players themselves never recaptured the form and consistency that had swept all before them in the year past. In attack, the strike partnership of Johnstone and Parlane proved as potent as in the previous season, but defensively the Ibrox side was poor. Over the League season they lost 39 goals compared to the previous year when they conceded just 24 League goals. One of the main reasons for the failure was an inconsistency in the selection of the back four. The regular partnership of Miller, Forsyth, Jackson and Greig played together in 17 of the 36 League games in the treble season. The following season, with Jardine largely restored in place of Miller, the original back four only appeared together in eleven games as Wallace juggled his defensive options. His biggest headache was caused by Forsyth, who was becoming a regular fixture in the treatment-room.

The side's defensive frailties were obvious in the opening games of the campaign when, after just eight League matches, they had just eight points and lay sixth in the table, conceding a goal per game on average. Wallace looked to strengthen his defence with the introduction of Jim Steele for a short-term loan in the absence of Tom Forsyth and he also made an unsuccessful move for Motherwell centre-half Willie McVie.

Rangers' disappointing performance in the League extended into the League Cup. Clydebank's Davie Cooper scored three times in four matches against the Ibrox side in a marathon quarter-final tie. Wallace took note of the winger's outstanding contribution to the Bankies' bid. Rangers made it through to the semi-final but tumbled out after a 5–1 drubbing from Aberdeen.

After their dismal start to the League, Rangers made no real challenge for the title and surrendered the championship to Celtic. They also meekly exited the European Cup in the first round to FC Zurich. Lack of success on the continent was very disappointing for Rangers, especially after the sweet taste of the triumph in Barcelona. In the four years since, Rangers had failed to qualify once and they had not survived past the second round in any of the other seasons.

The team reached the Scottish Cup final in May but there was little solace here. A disputed penalty gave Celtic the double and only served to increase the pressure on Wallace. The Rangers boss found that the fans had short memories. Once he had been a hero; now there was growing concern that Wallace was not the answer at Ibrox. He had won the treble, but the barren season that followed raised doubts about whether he could bring sustained success to Rangers in Scotland let alone make any impact on Europe.

Wallace answered his critics in the most emphatic way possible – with another treble. The 1977–78 season was everything that the previous term had not been. Despite the customary miserable start to the campaign, when the side lost the opening two games, the manager achieved consistency in selection and good results followed. Where he had used 25 players in the League championship challenge of the previous year, Wallace settled to a pool of twenty players of which just fourteen played most of the campaign.

He settled into a 4–2–4 system with McLean and Davie Cooper, signed from Clydebank for a fee of £100,000, providing width on each flank. Wallace added Gordon Smith of Kilmarnock early in the season for a fee of around £65,000. Smith was to be converted from a left-winger into a potent strike partner for Derek Johnstone. They proved a deadly combination, scoring 45 League goals between them.

Rangers' form continued to improve throughout the season as champions Celtic slumped to one of their worst seasons in years. In fact it was Billy McNeill's Aberdeen who provided the main challenge to Wallace's men. Rangers emerged winners in the League Cup final against Celtic when Gordon Smith scored in the last minute of extra time. Victory against Motherwell at Ibrox in the final match of the League race was enough to seal the title for Wallace.

The Scottish Cup competition (which, incidentally, had taken Wallace and Rangers to Berwick's Shielfield Park in the third round) completed a memorable season for the Ibrox boss. In a thrilling final against Aberdeen, Rangers completed the sweep of domestic trophies with a 2–1 win.

As John Greig hailed what he considered the 'best football-playing Rangers team for years', and Jock Wallace applauded the 'magnificent' performance of a side he proudly proclaimed had 'played the way the script was written', little did they realise what the coming weeks held for both of them. As Scotland prepared to embark on their fateful journey to the 1978 World Cup, problems were afoot for Rangers and Wallace. Just 17 days after revelling in a Scottish Cup win that sealed a second treble in three years, the boss announced that he was quitting the club he loved.

After a stormy boardroom meeting, an ashen-faced Wallace emerged to reveal that he had resigned and was now looking for another job. Surprisingly, he told of how he had been 'unsettled and unhappy for some time' at Ibrox. The players and others close to him had seen no obvious signs of discontent. Club secretary Frank King confirmed in a press statement that Wallace's decision was accepted by the board with regret, before adding, 'The board are grateful for all he has done for the club and wish him well in his future career.'

It seemed a very abrupt ending to the Ibrox career of a manager who was revered by fans and players alike. Twenty-four hours later, John Greig, whom Wallace acknowledged as his 'obvious successor', was appointed to a role he dreamed of, but did not expect to get so soon. Wallace, meanwhile, considered the many offers he had been made before opting for Leicester City, who had just parted company with their boss, Frank McLintock, after being relegated from the English First Division.

Wallace left Ibrox without disclosing the true reasons for his shock departure, generating a great deal of speculation. Some suggested that the manager had been irked by Waddell's reluctance to release the purse strings for new players. Indeed, the general press view was that Rangers would have to add to their squad if they were to make any impact on Europe.

The financial budget that Wallace worked to was tight, but the club generated some money through the careful trading of players under the control of Willie Waddell. Ian McDougall, Alex O'Hara and Martin Henderson left for modest fees and Stein and Hamilton went on free transfers, but there were signs that the manager had access to funds that many reckoned were needed to improve the side. Rumours were rife of a proposed bid for Leeds United's Gordon McQueen, said to be worth around £400,000, in a deal that would have taken Derek Parlane to Elland Road. If Jock Wallace did have some money available to improve the side for Europe, he used it sparingly. In his five years in charge, he spent just over £350,000 in improving the squad. His return on players sold amounted to close to £450,000. The manager had delivered two trebles and three championships in five years and still showed a profit on transfers.

The speculation continued but Wallace maintained his silence for many years, as did Willie Waddell, considered to be the other key party in the dispute. I was privileged to have been given an insight into the real reason for Wallace's departure by the man himself. It came in a chance meeting I had with Wallace following a testimonial dinner held in his honour in Glasgow's Thistle Hotel in 1995.

As I stood outside the main banqueting hall, an emotional Wallace confided that his discontent was of a financial nature but was not related to funding for the improvement of the squad. Quite simply, he was discontented with his own remuneration. Wallace's salary was generally believed to be around £12,000. Alex Ferguson was reputed to be on similar terms at St Mirren, while Jock Stein commanded over £15,000 at Celtic Park. The players of the Waddell–Wallace era were no better off. Derek Johnstone recalls being paid £350 per week at that time and being offered an increase of £10 per week, which he duly accepted without complaint.

The comparatively poor wages in Scotland were in stark contrast to those available in England. Liverpool boss Bob Paisley earned around £20,000 at Anfield, but it was generally believed that Wallace had a number of offers in excess of this. Among them was the offer from Leicester City, said to be £25,000. Wallace told me that he considered it quite ridiculous that he could earn more than twice his wages with a side that had just been relegated in England, while the Scottish treble winners offered what he considered a paltry sum in comparison. Wallace felt undervalued at Ibrox. He was also stung by the criticism that he had suffered following the barren season of a year earlier. There was some suggestion that he took the blame for a poor season while Willie Waddell took the credit when the side enjoyed success.

Whether there was any justification for that belief is almost irrelevant because it was not the reason for Wallace's departure. He had a number of stormy meetings with Waddell, but that was the relationship both men enjoyed. The failure of Rangers to pay what Wallace considered top dollar was not compatible with his views on the importance of the job. Waddell felt otherwise, as did the remainder of the Ibrox board. In what became clearly a battle of wills, the message to Jock Wallace was clear: take it or leave it.

The two men who had helped restore respectability to Ibrox after the lean years had gone down a road from which neither could easily return. The Ibrox board and Waddell would have the final word. There would be no capitulation from Rangers or Wallace. The Rangers boss walked out on arguably the biggest job in football, quite simply because the terms were not anywhere near commensurate with the position.

Waddell's perspective on the situation is unknown, but he would almost certainly have argued that he shared Wallace's burdens on the more general management matters, leaving the coach to attend to the footballing side. In typical Struth fashion, he probably also considered that to manage Rangers was in itself an honour that could never be matched by money.

For these reasons it may have been overly simplistic to compare the terms available at Ibrox with those at other clubs. However, the pressures on the manager of Rangers (as indeed it is for the other half of the Old Firm, where success means one thing only – the championship) are hardly comparable with the stresses at most other clubs.

The situation was borne out of intransigence on both sides and it is puzzling that a solution could not have been found to meet the demands of the two parties. However, stubbornness was a trait that was an integral element in the characters of Wallace and Waddell. The latter certainly had an interest in maintaining some control on expenditure as he was faced with the mammoth task of rebuilding Ibrox – though even doubling the manager's salary would not have emptied the coffers.

Ultimately Wallace and Waddell leapt over the precipice like a couple of lemmings. They only knew one way forward and it was *their* way. They went headlong over a cliff with only uncertainty at the bottom. For Wallace, it would be a life without Rangers. For Waddell, it was a step into the unknown with a new manager.

Why did Wallace never publicly discuss the facts surrounding his departure? I believe that it was his love for Rangers and his great respect for Waddell that kept his lips sealed. He didn't wish the club's name to be besmirched by any scandal, and the dispute about remuneration would not have cast a favourable light on Rangers. Waddell was his mentor and, for all their differences, the men were close and it was not in Wallace's nature to air what he considered a private matter.

It is to Waddell's credit, too, that he never discussed the background to Wallace's departure, particularly as he was often cast as the villain of the piece. Waddell never sought to justify his or the board's position. The matter was concluded with some dignity, despite the circumstances and given that the timing of the events was somewhat irrational with the treble nestling in the trophy-room.

ABOVE: THE
INSPIRATIONAL RANGERS
AND ENGLAND CAPTAIN,
TERRY BUTCHER

RIGHT: THE
CONTROVERSIAL MAURICE
JOHNSTON

ABOVE: A SOMBRE-LOOKING GRAEME SOUNESS AND DAVID MURRAY AT THE PRESS CONFERENCE INSIDE IBROX FOLLOWING THE ANNOUNCEMENT OF THE MANAGER'S DEPARTURE

RIGHT: SOUNESS SURVEYS THE SCENE AT TRAINING

SMITH

TOP: WALTER SMITH AND ASSISTANT, ARCHIE KNOX, PROUDLY
DISPLAY THE 'TREBLE'

ABOVE: MARK HATELEY SCORES THE VITAL OPENING GOAL IN
THE CRUCIAL 1991 LEAGUE CHAMPIONSHIP 'DECIDER' WITH
ABERDEEN

PAUL GASCOIGNE

SMITH

BRIAN LAUDRUP SCORES THE GOAL THAT
SEALS 'NINE-IN-A-ROW' IN A 1–0 WIN
OVER DUNDEE UNITED AT TANNADICE

ALLY McCOIST SCORES AGAINST LEEDS UNITED AT IBROX IN THE FAMOUS 1993 'BATTLE OF BRITAIN' CHAMPIONS LEAGUE CLASH

DICK ADVOCAAT

JORG ALBERTZ, WHO SET ASIDE EARLY
DISAFFECTION WITH HIS ROLE ON THE SIDELINES TO
BECOME A VITAL MEMBER OF ADVOCAAT'S SIDE

ADVOCAAT

BARRY FERGUSON, WHO WAS PERSUADED BY ADVOCAAT THAT
HE HAD A GREAT FUTURE AT IBROX AND REMAINED TO SHOW
GREAT MATURITY IN THE RANGERS MIDFIELD

RONALD DE BOER, WHO WAS LURED TO RANGERS FROM
BARCELONA BY ADVOCAAT
IN AUGUST 2000, SCORING AGAINST STURM GRAZ IN THE
CHAMPIONS LEAGUE FOR
SEASON 2000–01

A few days later, Wallace joined Leicester, saying, 'This city needed something to believe in – so I gave them me.' But his love for Rangers never left him, and it was an affection he displayed quite openly. In his new manager's office he hung a picture of the Ibrox treble-winning side on the wall behind him. Every player who entered his room and saw the picture was reminded of the standards that they had to attain. Wallace would tell them that the photograph showed a real football team.

Wallace saw real success in his first season at Filbert Street, introducing a lot of fresh young talent, including a young Gary Lineker, and leading the side to their sixth Second Division title and a place in the semi-final of the FA Cup. In the summer of 1982 he returned to Scotland, taking up the reins at Motherwell with a ten-year contract. Forever a lively and imposing character, Wallace had no trouble fitting back into the Scottish scene. John Greig, meanwhile, toiled under increasing pressure as the spotlight fell full square on events at Ibrox. Eighteen months after joining the Fir Park side, Wallace's world was about to turn full circle.

THE RETURN TO IBROX

The chapter that closed when Wallace walked out of Ibrox in 1978 was reopened in 1983 when a crisis-torn Rangers turned to the man they had felt they could do without five years earlier. In turmoil following a troubled spell that saw the departure of John Greig, Rangers found that filling the vacancy that Wallace once called 'the greatest job in football', hardly created a rush of applicants.

In fact, Wallace was not the first or even the second choice of the Ibrox directors. The fans and the media were pressing for the men who had introduced the challenge of the New Firm clubs of Aberdeen and Dundee United. Their approach for Aberdeen's Alex Ferguson was dismissed as the former Rangers star rejected the move in favour of a new five-year contract at Pittodrie, reputedly worth £250,000. Rangers then turned to the Dundee United manager, Jim McLean, whose brother Tommy was in temporary charge at Ibrox. McLean too turned down Rangers, the prospect of managing such a large but potentially unwieldy institution clearly not attractive.

The situation seemed quite incredible to Rangers and the faithful but bewildered Light Blues followers. With Ferguson and

McLean ruled out, there was only one other realistic candidate for the position: Jock Wallace.

Rangers made a tentative approach to Wallace who, by now, had settled into a comfortable role at Motherwell. He accepted. He was third choice and he knew it, but he was undeterred: 'I'm not in the slightest bit worried about the fact that anybody thinks I'm third choice. As far as I'm concerned, I'm not.'

If the fans were not entirely overjoyed by the appointment of Wallace, they at least welcomed the prospect of change in the wake of a dismal period in the latter stages of Greig's management. While Wallace was perceived by many as yesterday's man, he still exuded an infectious enthusiasm and determination that raised Ibrox hopes. He rekindled the memories of the treble years and fired the optimism of the fans.

There was one crucial difference in his appointment this time compared with his last glorious period, however. When he had first stepped into the role almost twelve years previously, he inherited a side that had just won the club's greatest honour – the European Cup-Winners' Cup. It is undeniable that he was taking on some great players who were to be the backbone of his success. This time, though, the squad he found was a mere shadow of the team he had taken to two treble successes in four years. Wallace needed to do more than mould the side: a complete restructuring of the team was required.

It is also worth noting that he took over when a quarter of the League season had passed and the club were languishing in sixth place in the table with just seven points from ten games. 'My immediate aims are to restore morale and discipline within the club,' he said. 'I think that has slipped.'

Talking about how every player would be given a chance despite there being money available to improve the squad, he spoke of his expectations of the players. 'If my players don't have the character or the commitment, they are not much good to Rangers. I want players playing for the jersey every time they wear it.'

Ironically, Wallace was reputedly paid a salary of £60,000 – five times what the board had valued him at five years earlier.

With the full support of the directors and money available for transfers, Wallace moved to secure Bobby Williamson from Clyde-bank for £100,000 and Nicky Walker from Motherwell in a deal

which cost around £50,000 and included the transfer of Kenny
Black and Kenny Lyall.

Just two months after rejoining the club, Wallace told the *Daily
Record* of 'The Wallace Way' in management. Denying that he was
a 'blood-and-guts man', he explained that his secret of management lay in communicating with players, insisting that he never
raised his voice to motivate them. 'My methods are about talking
to players, getting them thinking about the game, and getting
them working as a unit. If they are fit and the spirit is right, you
have no problem.'

Telling them that he would sign new players if they become
available, he explained that: 'My first duty is to Rangers Football
Club, because I'm the best fan they have.'

True to his word, the new manager gave the players a chance,
making few changes to the side in that first season; but he did
reinvigorate the side, improving fitness and introducing some self-
belief. He was rewarded with a League Cup win over Celtic just
four months after his appointment, when Ally McCoist scored a
hat-trick, finally showing signs of the predatory skills that would
eventually take him to a series of goalscoring records in his Ibrox
career.

Although they failed to impress in Europe, or make any progress
in the Scottish Cup, Wallace's side did have a 15-game undefeated
League run that augured well for the future.

As the season drew to a close, Wallace moved once again into
the transfer market to secure Iain Ferguson and Cammy Fraser
from Dundee, their fees decided by a tribunal and amounting to
around £365,000. In just seven months Wallace had spent over
£500,000 and had brought in just £25,000 through the transfer of
Gordon Dalziel to Manchester City. The Ibrox board had backed
him financially. The League Cup was gladly received, but the club
and the fans wanted more. They wanted the championship. The
fact that Celtic had lost out to Aberdeen in the title race hardly
appeased them. Rangers had not seen the League flag fly over
Ibrox since Wallace first departed in 1978. With crowds dwindling,
Rangers, who always seemed to be just a few games away from
crisis, appeared perilously close to failure.

At the end of October 1984 Wallace added Ted McMinn to his
squad for a fee of £100,000, assisted by some of the money from

a jersey sponsorship that the Old Firm had jointly signed with a double-glazing manufacturer. Rangers also regained the League Cup with Iain Ferguson repaying some of his fee with the only goal against Dundee United. However, there were also some troubles for Wallace with his skipper, John McLelland. The Irish centre-back could not accept the terms offered within the Ibrox wage structure. Rangers had never before broken the structure and they refused to do so now. The player lost out and was transferred to Watford for £265,000, much to the dismay of many of the fans.

Just seven wins in the 25 League games from the beginning of November destroyed any hopes that Wallace might have harboured of another title success. The Scottish Cup also proved disappointing, with Dundee winning at Ibrox in the fourth round. A spirited second-leg performance against Inter Milan in the UEFA Cup was insufficient to change Rangers' dismal fortunes as the pressure increased on Wallace. He had spent more money than any other manager before him in such a short period, with no tangible return. Although much of his expenditure was recouped in the McLelland transfer, that particular move was seen by many as weakening the side.

Wallace was under fire from all sides as he took his men into the 1985–86 season. He had used 28 players in the League as he tried to find a successful blend. While he achieved greater consistency in selection the following season, choosing his side from a regular pool of just sixteen players, a miserable spell through September and October saw the side earn just seven points from a possible sixteen. Three League defeats before the turn of the year, followed by a 2–0 reverse at the hands of Celtic in the New Year fixture left Rangers trailing badly.

Beaten in the semi-final of the League Cup by Hibernian in October, and losing 3–2 to Hearts, led by Alex MacDonald and Sandy Jardine, in a stunning third-round game of the Scottish Cup in January, Rangers' season was virtually over with four months still to go. It was clear that Wallace had little more to offer. He had brought some silverware back to Ibrox, but the two League Cups were not the return that the fans and the board had sought when he was appointed.

Off the field, Rangers were in the throes of revolution. In February 1986 Lawrence Marlborough, who had a controlling interest in the club, arranged the removal of three directors. Dismayed by the failure of the club to make progress, he began the reshaping of the boardroom, as his business organisation, the Lawrence Group, increased its hold and control of Rangers. Marlborough lived in California and David Holmes managed his business interests in the Lawrence Group. Marlborough installed Holmes on the Ibrox board with a remit to carry out the changes that were required within the club. Holmes instigated a greater commercial awareness within Rangers as the club moved to embrace the trend towards corporate entertainment, increasing revenue from off-field sources.

Throughout the boardroom upheaval, Wallace stood quietly on the sidelines wondering what effect the changes would have in his fortunes with Rangers. When pressed to clarify the position of Wallace, Holmes refused to be drawn, other than to highlight that, 'The manager's contract runs to the end of the year,' adding that the board had 'not even discussed it'.

A few weeks later, Wallace bowed to the inevitable. On 7 April 1986, he was sacked. The previous day the side had lost dismally in a friendly against Tottenham Hotspur at Ibrox. But Wallace's departure was unrelated to the result. His future had been decided behind the scenes several weeks earlier. He told the assembled press that he was leaving with 'honour on both sides', and that he wished 'the next guy' good luck. 'I did the job to the best of my ability,' he added. Finally, in the moments of his deepest despair, he found time to offer hope to the fans. 'Rangers will be back, there is no fear of that,' he proclaimed.

Jock Wallace took a well-deserved break from the game he loved but was soon lured back to football with an exciting coaching role at Spanish side Seville. Later, he returned to Britain, taking up a management position at Colchester United who then gave him a directorship. It was while he was in Colchester that he received the devastating news that he was suffering from Parkinson's Disease. Unbowed, he tried to live his life to the full and latterly made regular trips back to Glasgow and Ibrox.

On one trip north for an Old Firm game, he went to a Glasgow nightclub when one of the Celtic players, Polish international Dariusz Dziekanowski, turned up. A friend of Wallace at the time, Willie Goodfellow, recalled: 'Jock was introduced to the player and complimented him on his performance that afternoon. The Pole launched into some heavy criticism of Celtic and the management team. Jock just lost it. He angrily told Dziekanowski that Celtic were a great club and that he had no right to criticise them. Even though he was a Rangers man through and through, he respected Celtic and wouldn't hear of any foreign player coming in to offer criticism. The player was stunned.'

Wallace received huge support at his testimonial functions as his illness became increasingly debilitating. He was remembered for the successes that brought the trebles, not for the comparative failure of his final years at Ibrox. Watching the Rangers stage play, *Follow, Follow*, he became so engrossed in the video sequences played out on a large screen behind the stage that he was heard to say: 'Go on, wee man!' as McLean burst through on the Celtic defence. 'Up, big man!' he muttered, as Johnstone rose for a header. He relived those moments in the Ibrox dugout, playing out memories of happy times.

He died on 24 July 1996. At his funeral, the minister said that he was 'the epitome of a Ranger'. Nothing more was said or needed to be. It summed him up.

JOHN GREIG

From the chairman David Murray to the faithful ladies of the Ibrox kitchens, he is known simply as 'Legend' or 'Ledge' for short. It is not an idle platitude or some kind of colloquial triviality. It is an epithet borne of a genuine respect for the achievements of a man for whom the word 'loyal' is hardly adequate to describe the commitment he has shown to Rangers Football Club. He is a true Ranger, the archetypal Ranger: John Greig. It was no surprise when he was honoured in a recent poll of fans who selected their choice of the best Rangers players of all time. Greig came out top – 'the Greatest Ranger'. As former club-mate and friend Sandy Jardine said, 'He wasn't given the title for nothing. He has been immense to this club and has great pride in it.'

Through thick and thin he led them as a player. He was the veritable rock around which the team rallied in the lean years of Celtic's dominance of the late 1960s and early 1970s, and the foundation of the revival that saw Rangers enjoy the treble years and the Barcelona success.

Strangely, when he joined Rangers back in 1960, they were not his first love; his affections lay along Gorgie Road at the Tynecastle home of Heart of Midlothian. Indeed, it took the stern instructions of his father for him to put pen to paper, when a Rangers scout turned up pleading with the youngster to sign for the Light Blues. It may have brought tears from the youngster at the time as he grudgingly obeyed his father's wishes, but if his emotions were tied up in fanciful dreams of playing for the Maroons, he could never have imagined the great depth of affection he would eventually harbour for Rangers.

It didn't take long for Greig to be assimilated into the Ibrox way. Leaving Edinburgh juvenile side Edina Hearts behind him, Greig, a useful inside-forward, found himself thrust into the glamour of a club that boasted some of the best players in the country. The young Edinburgh lad found that advice was always available from Jimmy Millar and Ralph Brand, two of the Ibrox legends who took him under their wing and taught him of 'the Rangers way'. He learned about the great traditions of the club and quite simply what it meant to be a 'Ranger' – how to dress, how to train and, importantly, how to look after himself.

Eager to progress, the enthusiastic youngster made rapid strides and seized his opportunity to break through to the Ibrox first team in the space of just two years when Jim Baxter's withdrawal from an impending tour of Russia left a vacancy in the squad. Greig impressed everyone with his maturity in a side that returned from the tour unbeaten. Few realised the significance of the events that saw the emergence of Greig. They had set off for Russia with their star man missing. They came back with a player who was to become the most important in their post-war history.

John Greig's football spanned eighteen seasons at Ibrox during which time he amassed five League championship medals, six Scottish Cup medals and four League Cup medals. He also reached the remarkable total of 857 first-class games including 496 League matches, a record 73 Scottish Cup ties, and another first of 121 League Cup games. In the international arena he earned 44 caps for Scotland. But it was in Europe that he achieved the pinnacle of his success. In 62 matches in European competition, he reached two finals and captained the side in the famous 1972 European Cup-Winners' Cup triumph in Barcelona. He was also voted Scottish Player of the Year in 1966 and then again in 1976, but one of his proudest moments came outside the football arena when he gained the recognition of the monarchy in his award of the MBE in 1977.

Greig served under four managers at Rangers, each of whom had his own style. He watched them carefully, because he always wanted to manage a football club. His interest in tactics extended back to the earliest days of his career and he would never miss the opportunity to discuss the ideas of great managers of the period when he came across them either on his numerous international trips or on their visits to Ibrox. A keen student of the game, he even visited the famous Sportschule in Cologne in the 1970s as he continued his quest for knowledge on modern coaching methods.

His enthusiasm for the technical side of football was clear. In his autobiography, *A Captain's Part*, published ten years before he moved into the Ibrox hot-seat, he provided some insight into the roots of his enthusiasm for management. He told of long discussions with Scot Symon about the game and how a football club should be managed. Greig told me that he never had any major disagreement with Symon, a man for whom he had great respect, but his early accounts suggest that he was at variance with his boss on managerial style. Symon was a traditionalist who believed that the manager of Rangers should follow Struth's tried and trusted ideas that had proved successful at Ibrox in the past. Greig considered this old hat. He believed in the new style of management where the boss pulled on his tracksuit and did his work on the training field. To him, the role of manager lay on the football side, leaving administration to others.

For all their disagreements on how the job should be done, Greig learned a lot from Symon and believed his manager had much more to offer the game. He felt that Symon knew modern tactics, but was reluctant to use them. Greig recounted an incident when he shuffled pieces around the tactics board as he showed Symon a move that had been worked successfully against Rangers on the previous Saturday, suggesting that the team give it a try. Symon listened, before counteracting the play in a move that Greig considered had been executed brilliantly.

The significance of the story is not so much in Symon's tactical ability, but Greig's fascination with that side of the game while his playing career was still very much in full flow. Just as Struth's captains Meiklejohn and then Young had been close to their manager, Greig worked closely with all four of the managers he played for. He listened and learned, often adding his own contribution to tactical discussions, with Wallace in particular. Jardine recalled, 'Jock [Wallace] used to call John and me into the wee boot-room on a Friday to talk about the game coming up and ask for our views on how things were working on the field. We used to have these meetings every week.'

Jardine and Greig were on the golf course shortly after they heard the news of Wallace's shock departure. 'We were stunned – couldn't believe it,' he said. Greig then received a call from Willie Waddell asking him to come to Ibrox as quickly as possible – to be offered the job as manager of Rangers. It was 24 May 1978.

Wallace's exit had left only one true candidate in the eyes of the fans and the media. As Jock Stein moved out of Parkhead, Celtic captain Billy McNeill was touted for the vacant hot-seat across the city. The two Old Firm captains, who had been head to head on the field for so many years, looked set to continue their challenge from a higher station. It seemed a natural transition for both. For Greig in particular it was the obvious move, although it came much earlier than he could have anticipated. He still had a couple of years at least left in him as a player and, with another treble in the bag, his third, he had an eye on further honours. McNeill did eventually move into the Celtic top job having served an apprenticeship at Clyde and then Aberdeen. Greig had no such opportunity for preparation. At 35 years of age, the Rangers captain would jump straight into the biggest job in the land. Quite simply, it was one he could not turn down.

When he faced the press after confirming his acceptance of the position, Greig said, 'I am delighted. It's a dream come true. Since my appointment, I've been in a daze.' Significantly, he added, 'I just can't believe that I will never play for Rangers again.' It was impractical for Greig to consider playing when he had the respon-sibility of management to deal with, but his decision to step back from the playing-field was one of the biggest problems he had to overcome in the early days of his management career. Finding a replacement for a player such as Greig was a task that would eventually face some manager at Rangers. Ironically, the difficulty fell squarely on the man himself.

Colin Jackson, who played alongside Greig for many years, said, 'He was a father figure to the team. He slowed up in his last season, but his sheer inspiration kept us going. He had been there through all of the other players' times at Ibrox. It seemed strange to imagine that he would not be beside us on the pitch.'

Greig had been the inspiration of the side for years, the marauding do-or-die captain who had seen his team-mates through thick and thin. With the wave of a fist he would often rally the side when their heads dropped. He was every manager's dream skipper. He was also an excellent defender who had latterly filled a vital role on the left flank to provide balance to the excellent Jardine at right-back.

In effect, Greig needed two players to replace himself – a left-back and a captain. With little money available from the board-room, Greig busied himself in the bargain basement, acquiring

Alex Forsyth for the left-back berth on a free transfer from Manchester United and Billy Urquhart from Inverness Caledonian for a modest fee. The captaincy was still a problem. Derek Johnstone was being publicly touted for the position, but Greig had some reservations about the striker – he wanted to leave Rangers.

Johnstone said: 'I roomed with Greigy so had no problems there when he took over, but I had been having problems with Rangers for a good few weeks before big Jock resigned. I had a feeling that I wasn't wanted at Rangers and had made up my mind to go. The papers said that I wanted the captaincy and that I wanted to play centre-half and was holding the club to ransom, but that wasn't the case. I just felt that the time had come to move on.'

Greig talked Johnstone around and offered him the captaincy because he felt that he could command the role long into the future at Rangers. The obvious choice, Sandy Jardine appeared to be nearing the end of his career. Derek Parlane would take the striking position vacated by Johnstone as he moved into defence.

These changes aside, Greig made no drastic alterations to the side that had been successful for Wallace, but he could not have imagined a more troubled start to the season. Losing to St Mirren at Ibrox on the opening game, Rangers did not record a victory in the championship until the end of September when six games had already come and gone. Despite this, the side was just off the pace in the League race.

But if the Light Blues fans had little to cheer in the League, Greig gave them something to smile about in the League Cup and, more significantly, the European Cup. Steady progress in the League Cup was matched by some remarkable progress in European competition. Greig had always been a keen student of the continental game and the new Ibrox boss relished pitting his wits against the top coaches in Europe.

Jackson recalled, 'He was great going into European games. His thoroughness was remarkable. We would all get pictures of players we would face and reports on how individuals played. He told us everything about the opposition. Greigy knew the game inside out, so we went into these matches fully prepared.'

The boss could not have picked a sterner challenge in putting his tactical ability to the test when Rangers were drawn against Juventus in the first round of the European Cup. They boasted nine players who were in the Italian World Cup squad, including such household names as Zoff, Scirea, Causio, Tardelli, Benetti, Cabrini, Gentile and Bettega.

In the first leg in Turin, Greig put out a defensive side who fought a rearguard action and emerged with a narrow single-goal defeat. When the Italians came to Ibrox two weeks later, Rangers could hardly have reason to be confident that they would get the two goals they required. After their dismal start in the championship, they had not won a single League game, their only victories of the season so far coming against lowly Albion Rovers and Forfar Athletic in other competitions. But the side had a confidence drawn from their performance against Juventus in the first leg and in fact the team responded magnificently, recording one of the club's finest European victories by the two-goal margin they needed. The Italians were out-thought and outplayed. Greig had given his men a new respectability. Wallace had been a hero, but the new boss provided some hope and optimism that a more successful era was dawning, an era when Rangers could compete with European sides playing refined, continental football.

As Rangers started to pick up their League form, they continued their progress in Europe, achieving another famous win, this time over Dutch champions PSV Eindhoven. After a disappointing goalless draw in the first leg at Ibrox, Greig's men overcame the loss of an early goal to sweep ahead in the tie, leaving Robert Russell to complete the scoring with one of the most memorable goals in the club's history, giving the Light Blues a 3–2 win.

Although Rangers' European journey was to falter in the next round with a narrow defeat at the hands of Cologne, the club continued to make strides in the League, recovering from the early-season lapse. By the end of February, Rangers were in second place, just one point behind surprise leaders St Mirren, with Celtic in touch, but with a backlog of fixtures. Rangers had gained the ascendancy on Billy McNeill's men with an extra-time 3–2 victory over their Old Firm rivals in the semi-final of the League Cup – a stormy tie that saw the dismissal of Celtic's Tommy Burns and Rangers' Alex Miller. They followed it up at the beginning of May with a 1–0 League win at Ibrox in the penultimate Old Firm fixture of the season. Greig was on course for a treble in his first season as manager.

The side went to Parkhead with three games remaining, knowing that victory would seal the title. Rangers got off to the perfect start with a goal in nine minutes, and when Celtic went down to ten men just five minutes into the second half, the championship looked to be firmly within their grasp. However, games are never over until the final whistle, especially an Old Firm fixture, and Greig's side slumped, sending the Celtic fans into raptures and the Rangers contingent plummeting to the depths of despair. With just five minutes left and the score locked at 2–2, Celtic took the lead when goalkeeper Peter McCloy palmed a cross out to the head of defender Colin Jackson who accidentally put the ball into his own net. A late goal from Murdo MacLeod gave Celtic an unexpected victory and the initiative in the title race.

Rangers played out a marathon Scottish Cup final with Hibs, which went to extra-time in the second replay. It gave Greig his second trophy as Rangers manager, but the championship was lost just a few days later. Rangers really should have won the title. They had it within their grasp, and even a draw at Parkhead, which seemed secure with five minutes left, would have cleared the way for the championship. They were in many ways victims of their own success. Having reached two finals and had a good run in Europe, they faced a Celtic side who hadn't qualified for Europe and who had played considerably fewer games. The situation was compounded by poor weather that caused a congestion of fixtures for the Ibrox side in the final weeks of the season. In the seven weeks leading up to the Celtic match, Rangers had played twelve competitive games. In the end there was no treble for John Greig and his men, but the Cup double was a fine consolation. For many, however, it was not enough. Rangers had lost the title to their rivals, and Greig would be challenged to win it back.

The manager's next season got off to the best possible start, providing little hint of the traumas that lay ahead. The team won the Drybrough Cup with a 3–1 win over Celtic including two of the best goals ever scored in a final, from Jardine and Cooper. The winger's effort in particular was special and was recently ranked as the best ever Rangers goal. He juggled the ball past a handful of Celtic defenders before stroking it into the net. The Drybrough Cup provided a joyous day in the sunshine for Rangers but it obscured the troubled skies that would soon appear above Rangers and Greig.

The side that had served Wallace well and almost gave Greig the
treble in his first season as manager were beginning to show signs
of deterioration through injury and form loss early in 1979–80.
Tom Forsyth, who had been the solid core of the Ibrox side's
defence for many years, found his contribution increasingly curtailed through injury. Greig juggled his resources to try to fill the
gap before eventually going into the transfer market for Gregor
Stevens, who cost around £150,000, from Leicester City.

Injuries also restricted Robert Russell's progress in the side,
while loss of form limited the appearances of Gordon Smith, Davie
Cooper and, eventually, Alex MacDonald. Greig's ability as a
manager was stretched along with his player pool as he struggled
to achieve some consistency in team selection. The boss was also
aware that the age profile of the side would need to be addressed
in time, but the youth squad did not appear to offer a great deal of
potential in the short term.

At the end of October and with the first quarter in the cham-
pionship completed, Rangers were four points off pace-setters
Celtic and out of the League Cup. Defeat at Parkhead in the
second Old Firm game of the season left the side even further
adrift in the title race as Greig struggled to find the right blend.
The Ibrox men also crashed out of the European Cup-Winners'
Cup to Valencia, inspired by their Argentinian World Cup hero
Mario Kempes, who scored a wonder goal at Ibrox to give the
Spaniards victory.

The Rangers boss was conscious he would need to go back into
the transfer market. The appointment of Lawrence Marlborough as
vice-chairman in September signalled the growing business strength
of the board, which Greig hoped would sanction the spending he
needed. The manager needed players for several positions. It was
clear that the team had no strength in depth, and although Stevens
provided some versatility in the centre of the defence, Greig's
options in the middle of the park and up front were limited.

With the title drifting away, Greig signed forward Ian Redford
from Dundee for a record fee of around £210,000. Redford slipped
into MacDonald's role as the little midfielder began to drift out of
the scene, but he was hardly a straight replacement. MacDonald
was a tenacious, hard-working player who used to cover an enormous amount of ground. Redford was less physical, although he

came from Dundee with a good goalscoring record. In truth, he was short of the quality needed to replace MacDonald.

Redford was asked to link on the left flank with Davie Cooper, but the talented winger was very inconsistent under Greig – occasionally brilliant, but often ineffective. Jardine recalled: 'Cooper was ultimately a magnificent player for Rangers, but in the first five years or so that he played with us he was substituted a lot. When he turned it on, there wasn't a finer player in the world and I've never played with anyone with a left foot like his – so accurate. But sometimes when we were getting beaten 1–0, we just didn't see him. To be fair, he was young, learning and improving. That was just the kind of player he was. But his true brilliance didn't show through until later, long after Greigy had gone.'

Although Greig had smashed the Scottish transfer record with the signing of Redford, the club recouped much of the fee when Derek Parlane was sold to Leeds United two weeks later. Redford took some time to settle, and any faint title aspirations Rangers still had dwindled and virtually died when Celtic won the last fixture of the League season between the two sides at the beginning of April. Rangers had hardly got out of fifth place since the turn of the year, let alone got themselves into position to win the title.

Celtic went on to take the championship as Rangers remained in fifth place, eleven points behind the winners, to the great disappointment of the fans who were growing frustrated by their team's inability to string a series of victories together. Rangers' best run of victories in the League was just three games – hardly the form of champions. They ended with just 37 points from their 36 games, the worst points total in the club's history. Greig did have the chance to salvage something from the season in the final of the Scottish Cup, where Celtic would once again be the opponents. The Cup provided no solace as the Parkhead side won with the only goal in extra-time.

Greig could be forgiven for believing that the gods were conspiring against him. His squad's limitations were cruelly exposed by injury and loss of form, but his signings failed to provide any real spark of inspiration to give the Ibrox support confidence that things would be better next year. Greig knew that he could not take the same pool into the new season and that further signings were needed. The board would have to relax the purse strings if

Rangers were to make any serious impact on the championship race.

Greig had a fundamental problem. He had inherited a good side from Wallace, but they were all of a similar age. With every year that passed, the ageing squad was becoming less and less effective. He would need to overhaul the squad completely, something he had not realised when he took over the reins. His success in the job would depend greatly on his ability to manage the transition.

'The nucleus of the team were all getting old together and Greigy knew that,' recalled Sandy Jardine. 'About eight of us in the side were in or close to the 30–32 age range. He knew that he would have to replace us, but the problem for him was that we were all international players. It is not easy to replace players of that kind of quality and he didn't get the budget he needed. The club were very tight about money at that time and I believe John needed an awful lot more than was available.'

In the light of the revelations of the departure of Wallace, it is easy to appreciate the difficulties Greig faced in getting the funds he required to bring the right quality of player to Ibrox to wrest the title from Celtic. He could have had his pick of almost any player in Scotland, but the best Scots were in the English First Division. Persuading them to come back to Scotland was almost always a non-starter – the wages in England still outranked those north of the border and traditionally the only players who came back were those who were looking to resurrect a fading career. The market in Scotland may have been wide, but the depth of quality was limited – as was evidenced by the Anglo-dominated Scotland national side at the time.

Greig persisted with his squad, adding youngsters such as Ally Dawson and John MacDonald into the side. In a flurry of transfer activity just as the season ended, Gordon Smith left to join Brighton for £400,000, providing valuable funds for the acquisition of Colin McAdam for £160,000 from Partick Thistle and Jim Bett from Lokeren for £180,000. Just as the campaign kicked off, he also added Willie Johnston for a fee of around £40,000 from Vancouver Whitecaps and Alex MacDonald exited to Hearts for £30,000. A major rationalisation was under way. The side that Greig took into season 1980–81 showed five changes from the one he inherited from Wallace. He may have had to juggle his finances with transfer income largely funding his acquisitions, but he did radically shake up the squad.

Greig was rewarded with a good start in the League race, opening up with a 15-game unbeaten run that included a Premier League record 8–1 win over Kilmarnock and two victories over Celtic. The second of these, a comprehensive 3–0 win, was a satisfying consolation in a bad week that saw the Light Blues humiliated in the Anglo-Scottish Cup with defeat by lowly Chesterfield by the same scoreline. The tournament seemed a reasonable compensation for Rangers' failure to qualify for Europe, but it turned out to be something of a disaster and never captured the imagination of the Ibrox crowd.

Rangers' disappointment with the Anglo-Scottish Cup was mirrored in an early exit in the League Cup as the momentum they had gained in the early part of the season stuttered. By March, a succession of poor results saw the Ibrox side slip to third in the table behind Celtic and Aberdeen. Defeat by a Charlie Nicholas-inspired Celtic in the last Old Firm game of the season just about sealed the title for the Parkhead side as Rangers headed for another blank season. Their only remaining chance of success was in the Scottish Cup final where Dundee United would provide the opposition.

Greig left Davie Copper and John MacDonald on the bench, with an out-of-favour Derek Johnstone excluded from the squad. In a dismal final, Rangers got the chance to break the deadlock with a penalty in the final minute. Ian Redford stepped up and missed, sending the game to a replay. It was not an outcome the club particularly wished, but destiny beckoned the recalled Davie Cooper in the replay. The winger was joined by Derek Johnstone and John MacDonald, who were also reintroduced to the side.

In what was later to be called 'the Cooper final', the winger produced a magical display to demoralise Dundee United, scoring the first goal and setting up two others as the Light Blues romped home 4–1 winners, giving Greig his third trophy as manager.

The Scottish Cup was a welcome addition to the Ibrox trophy-room, particularly in the light of the barren season that the club had endured a year earlier, but the fans demanded more. With the growing threat of the New Firm clubs of Aberdeen and Dundee United to add to the perennial challenge offered by Celtic, Rangers faced competition for the championship on three fronts at least.

Greig prepared for the new season with Irish international John McLelland added at a cost of £90,000 and new keeper Jim Stewart a £115,000 acquisition from Middlesbrough. Greig also tried to sign a young striker named Ally McCoist from St Johnstone, offering the Perth side £300,000 for him, but Sunderland stepped in with a bid of around £400,000. McCoist's time would come later.

The Rangers boss searched for inspiration, but injury and suspension foiled his plans. Things were not right in the dressing-room either, as Colin Jackson recalled: 'The older players in the squad knew how to look after themselves, eating properly and getting to bed at the right time, but many of the younger lads were unprofessional. As youngsters we would listen to the old players and heed their advice, but the new breed that Greigy inherited were different. They didn't have the same kind of respect for the manager or Rangers and that is probably why none of them went on to make a real name for themselves in the game, despite their ability.'

Davie Provan, who was head of scouting at the time, disagreed. 'I believe the youngsters were good enough, but many of the older players let Greigy down,' he said. 'Their respect was questionable, but we did turn out a lot of good players, although many such as Durrant, Ferguson and McPherson didn't really emerge until after he had gone.'

Greig's side started the new League season with a victory, but his first-choice back four of Jardine, Stevens, Forsyth and Miller played the opening game and then were never seen as a unit again. Within a few months, surgeons advised Tom Forsyth that he would have to hang up his boots. Greig's other central defender, Gregor Stevens, also found his season curtailed for quite different reasons. Off the field a quiet man, Stevens was lethal on it, known more for his rough-house tactics than his silky skills. When he was sent off for the fifth time in his career midway through the season, the SFA imposed the severest of sentences – a six-month ban. Stevens' appearances had already been considerably restricted up until then as the impact of his repeated dismissals and nineteen yellow cards mounted.

Greig reverted to a central defensive partnership of Jackson and McLelland, two very similar players. Without a settled back four,

Rangers haemorrhaged goals; but, if they had deficiencies in the back line, the front men were hardly inspiring. The title was lost to Celtic again as Rangers slumped to third place, scoring 22 goals fewer than the champions and fourteen fewer than second-placed Aberdeen.

Europe offered little respite as Rangers slipped out of the Cup-Winners' Cup in the first round to Sparta Prague, but the League Cup provided some joy for the fans. A late Ian Redford goal gave the Ibrox side a 2–1 win over Dundee United as Greig took his fourth trophy in as many seasons. His quest for a fifth in the Scottish Cup final was thwarted as Aberdeen ran out comprehensive 4–1 winners after extra-time. That match was something of a watershed for Rangers. The manner of their defeat suggested that a number of players were not of the class expected and some were well past their best. Indeed, Greig had suffered criticism that he had been too loyal to certain players. Cruel jibes of 'Dad's Army' were trawled out as the press had a field day at Rangers' and Greig's expense.

The manager was delivering some silverware to the trophy-room, but it could not appease the fans who demanded the championship and superiority over Celtic. Desperate to make a decent challenge in the title race, Greig knew that he had to stiffen the Rangers defence, but he was further thwarted by the loss of some of the old stalwarts who had played loyally beside him and served him well during his management career. In the close season, Sandy Jardine, Colin Jackson and Tommy McLean were all given free transfers. Now only McCloy, Cooper, Russell and Derek Johnstone remained from the Wallace era.

Greig plunged into the transfer scene again, bringing central defender Craig Paterson in from Hibernian for around £225,000. The season started reasonably well for the Light Blues as they showed some silky soccer on the way to carving out a twenty-game unbeaten run. A string of draws kept them firmly in the chasing pack as Celtic moved clear in the League race, but the turning point in Rangers' season arguably came in four fateful days at the end of October. The side, playing a smooth passing game, had made steady progress in the UEFA Cup, defeating Borussia Dortmund and then Cologne at Ibrox, before heading for the return in the German city on 3 November 1982. A few days earlier, however, they faced Celtic at Parkhead in the first Old Firm clash of the season. With Craig Paterson ruled out with a serious knee injury, Greig reshuffled his defence, drafting in Gregor Stevens for only his fourth appearance of the season. With a 2–1 lead at half-time, Rangers looked secure, but a late Celtic fightback, including a goal three minutes from time, ended the Ibrox side's unbeaten run.

After the game, Rangers travelled to Cologne, needing a draw to progress. It was to be a nightmare of a tie. Four goals down after nineteen minutes, they lost one more goal in the second period to go down 5–0. It was a devastating defeat. The character that had epitomised their stunning performances against the likes of Juventus and PSV was missing. The Cologne result sparked a miserable November for Rangers as they suffered a further two League defeats, although they also fought through to the League Cup final. But December offered little improvement. Celtic took the League Cup and Rangers continued to stutter in the championship.

Defeat in the Ne'erday Old Firm fixture left them thirteen points off the pace with any hope of the championship all but gone. Showing some of the resilience that characterised his performances on the field, Greig continued to battle against the growing discontent. In March he signed Sandy Clark from West Ham for £170,000 and signalled his determination to get things right by clearing out those he felt could offer Rangers no more. Stevens, whose indiscipline had been so costly, was put up for sale, along with McAdam, Johnstone, Stewart and youngsters Derek MacKay and Gordon Dalziel. The clearout at Ibrox indicated Greig's frustration with his position. He had persevered with some players and signed others who quite simply were not good enough to replace those who formed the nucleus of the successful side he inherited.

Rangers' form showed little improvement as the season drew to a close. On the final day they lost 2–4 to Celtic at Ibrox, but the honours had already been decided. While the Rangers fans could take some comfort from the fact that Celtic had not won the title, as Dundee United sneaked through to snatch the League on the final day, it was scant consolation for a dismal season. The Light Blues failed at their final hurdle in their attempt to salvage something from the season when they went down 1–0 to Aberdeen in extra-time in the Scottish Cup final.

The Ibrox board met to discuss the future of their manager. They were becoming increasingly impatient with a situation that showed little improvement in the team's performance or prospects, but they decided to remain behind Greig. Led by chairman Rae Simpson and with the support of Willie Waddell, the board voted 3–1 to back Greig. The board would await the fortunes of the new season, but there would be little money available to the Rangers boss to buy new players.

Greig was clearly entering a critical phase of his management. With Ally McCoist finally procured at a cost of £185,000, he entered the season with a settled squad, but one that was made up almost entirely of players who had failed him in the previous season. He tried to lower the average age of the squad by introducing some of the promising youngsters who were beginning to emerge from the reserves. But the manager needed more than the enthusiasm of his young bucks. He needed good, experienced players – but that would demand a lot more than the money that was available to him. He lost Jim Bett, who returned to Lokeren for personal reasons, swelling the Ibrox coffers by £240,000. He particularly needed to strengthen the full-back areas and midfield, which now looked distinctly out of its depth. If he had any confidence going into the new term, it was based on misguided optimism rather than any real substance.

Reflecting on the disappointment of the previous year, he said, 'Injuries crippled us last season, but I'm not making that an excuse. I'm happy with the way things have gone so far, but the fact that we lost Bett, a player I admire tremendously, does leave us a bit short in midfield. Players of quality are hard to get, but if one becomes available I will try to buy him.'

Interestingly, Greig added that he did have money to spend 'after his summer dealings', suggesting that he had been told to generate at least some of his own cash for transfers.

As the team shaped up for the new campaign by heading off to Belgium for a series of friendlies, he confessed, 'We haven't found the team to challenge for the Premier League title yet. We have the system, but we need these pre-season games to sort everything out.' Greig cited his uncertainties on how best to use the four central defenders available to him and talked of how he was encouraging his midfield players to get forward into scoring positions. The midfield had certainly been a problem area in the season past. The five players who regularly contested the midfield positions contributed a total of just fifteen League goals. Up front, he hoped that McCoist would boost the side and also the fans, because he desperately needed their support.

Rangers' pre-season went reasonably well, with victory over West Bromwich Albion at Ibrox, followed by a win in Belgium and victory over Celtic in the Glasgow Cup final, but the position was fragile, and in fact the opening weeks of the season proved disastrous. A draw in the opening fixture against St Mirren was followed by defeat by Celtic, despite McCoist opening the scoring on his Old Firm début in just 33 seconds. Further losses to Hearts and Aberdeen plunged Rangers and Greig into crisis. After the match against the Dons around three hundred fans gathered outside the main entrance of Ibrox calling for Greig's head. Many remained for an hour after the final whistle.

The manager was not ready to concede defeat, despite the side sliding to third bottom of the table with just one point. After the game a defiant Greig said, 'I've never ducked a press conference after any game in my life and I haven't ducked this one.' Regretting the loss of a bad goal that he felt changed the match, he admitted to being 'disappointed', adding that 'there is not much more I can say'. The press had much more to say, rounding on the Ibrox board, who seemed content to sit the situation out without offering any comment on either the manager's position or their plans for the future.

The hacks had more sympathy than condemnation for Greig. They called him the 'loneliest man in football'. It seemed everyone wanted to know Rangers' position on the crisis. They were offered no more than a few short words from Chairman Simpson: 'I am making no comment on this situation. There is nothing to say.' After the regular board meeting a few days later the message from the Ibrox hierarchy remained the same: 'No comment.'

Greig continued to put a brave face on the situation, stating unequivocally that he would 'bite, scratch and fight to ensure that Rangers are the team the supporters want'. He also confessed to being a 'prisoner' in his own home, but insisted he would go on. Showing remarkable resilience, he sent out a defiant message to everyone, saying, 'The players will be told exactly what is expected and they will be told in a fashion they can't misunderstand. I assure you that nobody will fight harder than me and the players to put Rangers where they should be.' In a message for the fans he said that he knew what was in their hearts because he was 'the biggest Ibrox fan of all'.

Ally McCoist, whose form had been disappointing in these early months at Rangers, said, 'Take it from me, the whole team is behind John Greig.'

The boss battled on gamely, but by mid-October Rangers had accrued just seven points from eight games when Motherwell, ironically now managed by Jock Wallace, visited the stadium. Two goals in the last fifteen minutes gave the Lanarkshire side a shock 2–1 win.

At the end of the match, a crowd of over a thousand gathered outside the ground calling for Greig to be sacked. Players and directors faced a wall of hate and derision as they made their way from the ground. Inside the stadium, a doleful Greig said: 'Some 15,000 fans paid good money to see the game – they have a right to shout at someone. If that happens to be me, I'll take the brunt of the shouting.'

The manager was at his lowest ebb and he was showing signs of the strain. A few days later, on 28 October 1984, he resigned. His decision, which was made without the prompting of the board, ended his 23-year association with Rangers.

Campbell Ogilvie, the club secretary, read John Greig's prepared statement to the press. It simply said: 'As you are no doubt aware, this has been a trying time for me and my family. I trust that you will now respect our privacy.'

Greig later added, 'This is obviously a very sad day for me as Rangers Football Club has been my whole life,' before offering his best wishes to the club and supporters for the future. Rae Simpson, equally saddened by Greig's departure, said that the manager 'put the interests of the club first and foremost', venturing this as the reason for his departure. He added his own personal tribute to John Greig, saying that 'he has been a great servant to this club as player, captain and manager. He is a man of total loyalty and commitment to this club.'

Simpson insisted that Greig had been under no pressure from the board but the Rangers boss had been subject to immense stress from the media and the fans who were calling for his resignation throughout the season.

The players were stunned. 'It's a complete shock,' McCoist said, 'I know that we haven't been doing well, but this is honestly a surprise.'

As John Greig reflected in the aftermath of these events, he tried to look to a future beyond Ibrox. 'I don't see me staying in the game. After spending so long with one club – and at the top in football – it would be very difficult to go anywhere else. The worst thing of all is the thought of not going into Ibrox in the morning any more.'

John Greig was unlucky. He was unfortunate that the job he so dearly wished for came at a time when he was scarcely prepared for it, but to reject the offer would be to turn down an opportunity that was unlikely to come again. He had little choice but to accept the position. But his misfortune did not end there. He inherited a squad that had been built by Willie Waddell eight years earlier and had enjoyed great success under Jock Wallace, winning two famous trebles. In the changing cycle of football life, few sides can maintain their momentum in the face of Father Time. Even the best sides, such as the Rangers of the 1960s, Celtic in the early 1970s and Liverpool in the 1980s, failed to maintain the dominance that they once thought would last forever.

Greig inherited a successful side but he did not have the ingredients that would allow him to successfully ford the river of transition to a new era of glory on the other side. It is true that a number of his signings failed him, but he had successes too. Where would have later Rangers managers have been without the likes of McCoist, McPherson, Ferguson and even Durrant, all groomed by Greig for future glory?

Did Greig fail as Rangers manager? Well, if failure is judged by an inability to turn the tide and bring the championship back to Ibrox then John Greig was a failure. But he did have his moments of glory, winning four domestic trophies and enjoying some good European campaigns.

What was he like as a manager? Probably the best placed to answer this are those who served under him. Colin Jackson was impressed by his tactical ability but felt that the inspirational qualities he brought to the field as a player were not so easily apparent when he was boss: 'The job definitely came too early for him and he would have been better prepared with some kind of apprenticeship. He also had the imposing figure of Willie Waddell behind him, and that could not have made it easy for him to be his own man.'

Sandy Jardine said, 'John Greig was the best manager I ever had. Tactically, there was no one to touch him, but I come back to the same point: he was unlucky in that he inherited an ageing team.'

John Greig left Ibrox, his dreams of management in tatters, but his pride and respect intact. After a few years on the sidelines where he was a frequent television and radio pundit, he was given the opportunity to return to Ibrox to head the club's PR department. His rehabilitation was complete when Dick Advocaat was appointed manager and called on Greig to assist him in the interface between the management and the press. As their working relationship progressed, Greig moved into the Advocaat backroom team where he once again found himself on the touchline at training sessions, assisting in any way he could.

As Rangers celebrated the championship win at Ibrox in May 2000 and the SPL trophy was passed around the side for display to the crowd, the loudest cheer was reserved for the manager. Then, as Greig was beckoned forward, there was huge emotion as the trophy was passed to him. Proudly, he raised it above his head to the deafening cheers of the Rangers crowd. Forgotten were the unhappy days at the end of his managerial career. The old Greig was back, the disappointments of the early 1980s behind him. The cheers rang out for the man they called 'the greatest Ranger'.

GRAEME SOUNESS

In September 1985, inside the Sampdoria ground that was to see so many of his virtuoso displays, Graeme Souness talked of his future. 'I have moved for money – I can't deny that. For that reason I can't see me ever returning to Scotland as a player. I'd love to be manager of Rangers, perhaps player-manager. Look out, Jock Wallace!' he said with a smile.

A year later, with his future financially secure, he didn't so much breeze into Scottish football as arrive with all the intensity and power of a hurricane. Not only was he Rangers' first player-manager, but no one else had ever taken the helm without at least some past involvement with the club. Struth, Symon, Waddell, Wallace and Greig were all reared in the old Ibrox traditions established by Wilton and his contemporaries, but Souness found himself propelled into an institution he knew little about despite his Scottish roots. He was not only expected to assimilate himself into this new role with the vigour and determination that marked his playing career, but hopes were high that he would secure the championship flag which had not flown over the stadium in nine years.

Many would have been overawed with the enormity of the task and the grandeur of a club that had all the trappings of a stately home but without the silverware, but Souness was not. Here was a man who had such confidence in his ability that he truly believed that nothing was beyond him. It was a self-belief that was often misconstrued as arrogance as he strolled around the playing-fields of Europe, tantalising and tormenting opponents. In fact, he was never contemptuous of his opponents. As a boy he had idolised Jim Baxter, but it was never his style to tease players the way the legendary Ibrox left-half had done at Wembley in 1963 and 1967, revered in the abiding memories of the Scotland fans.

It was that same self-belief which thrust Souness on to the front pages of the newspapers in 1970 when he walked out on Tottenham Hotspur at just seventeen years of age. He had arrived at White Hart Lane as a raw 15-year-old schoolboy signed by manager

Bill Nicholson on apprentice forms. He showed enough to earn youth international caps, but Souness believed he was good enough for the Spurs first team. With no sign that there was a place available for him, allied to a touch of homesickness, he returned to Edinburgh while still under contract.

The club threatened to suspend him until June 1972, and MP Tam Dalyell took up his case in the House of Commons. It was an early indication of Souness's strong will that he should endure such pressure as a youngster yet maintain his stance. Only after some cajoling and helpful words of advice from seasoned pros like Martin Peters and Martin Chivers did he relent and return to London.

Despite a brief appearance as a substitute in a UEFA Cup tie, Souness's fears that there would be no regular place for him at White Hart Lane in the near future were confirmed. Eventually, he was released and Middlesbrough acquired his services for £30,000 in 1973.

It was at Ayresome Park that Souness matured as a player and received guidance from the Middlesbrough boss Jack Charlton which would help mould his own management style in years to come. Souness recalled the Geordie's 'blunt, abrasive attitude', which hit home hard and helped him at a period when his career could easily have turned up a dead-end. 'Work hard and become a great player or continue as you are and you'll be finished in 12 months,' warned Charlton.

Souness felt it was a turning point for him and wondered whether such guidance at Spurs would have relieved the torment of these early years.

After five years with the Teesside club, Bob Paisley stepped in with a bid of around £350,000 to secure his transfer to the English champions, Liverpool. He joined an Anfield squad built on the foundations that Bob Shankly had put in place, winning three European Cups. Great players such as Dalglish, Kennedy, McDermott and Hansen provided the platform for his talents. When Phil Thompson relinquished the captaincy, Paisley threw the armband to Souness.

Anfield was now the Scot's stage and he relished the opportunity to lift the European Cup as skipper. That chance came in 1984 in the Olympic Stadium in Rome when Liverpool faced AS

Roma in front of their partisan home crowd. A dramatic penalty shoot-out brought victory for the Merseysiders and Souness achieved every footballer's dream of holding that tall trophy aloft.

Souness learned a lot at Liverpool that he would carry with him into his new career. He once spoke of the targets the backroom staff instilled in every new side at Anfield: 'Always strive harder . . . the team before you was better than you,' the likes of Ronnie Moran and Roy Evans would say. It was a philosophy that Souness took into management. At Rangers, he often highlighted the fact that the side had a long way to go to reach the heights of the great Liverpool team that he had once graced. Such comparisons were a constant source of agitation to the fans and to many inside Ibrox, who believed that there was no club like Rangers.

After three European cups, five championships and four League Cups with Liverpool, Souness decided that the world or – more accurately, the Italian Seria A – was his oyster. He joined Sampdoria and helped them to the Italian Cup. The style and panache of the Italian game was perfectly suited to Souness as he played out the closing years of his career – or so it seemed.

Back in Glasgow, meanwhile, Rangers were toiling with little success in a disappointing 1985–86 season. Jock Wallace had returned but had failed to recapture the glory days that the club had enjoyed during his first stint as manager, and there an air of disenchantment enveloped the club and its supporters. By April, Rangers were out of all competitions and watched meekly by the sidelines as Hearts and old rivals, Celtic, battled it out for the coveted League championship flag.

On 6 April 1986 they met Tottenham Hotspur at Ibrox in a friendly fixture that was of little consequence and, ordinarily, would have been lost in the record books. In fact, such was the apathy that surrounded Ibrox that a crowd of just 12,000 watched the Londoners win 2–0. The few who turned up that day had little inkling that the club was on the threshold of a major change of direction but just two days later Rangers called a dramatic press conference. They announced that Jock Wallace would leave the club to be replaced by new player-manager Graeme Souness.

The appointment of Souness was not precipitated by the result of the Tottenham match. In fact, he had first been approached a couple of months earlier, in February. Walter Smith recalled that

Scotland played Yugoslavia at Hampden the day he first heard of
Rangers' plans to lure Souness to Ibrox. 'Graeme asked me if I
would join him if he became manager of Rangers. I never heard
any more about it until we met up again at Turnberry before an
international and he told me he had been offered the job. I confirmed I would join him. Later, I discreetly went to Ibrox to watch
the Spurs game, joining the fans in the stand. The next day the
news broke.'

The appointment of Souness was in fact the last piece in the
jigsaw as Rangers underwent a massive overhaul from top to
bottom. Lawrence Marlborough, the director who had a 66 per
cent shareholding in Rangers, had responded to the sad decline in
the affairs of the club by enforcing greater control. He installed
David Holmes, a leading light in his construction firm, to manage
the change as three directors were ousted and the operations at
Ibrox were streamlined. Rangers could go forward again, but only
with a change in management. Jock Wallace sat quietly in his office
as the turmoil raged around him. In Italy, meanwhile, Souness was
preparing himself for the move that would astonish Scottish
football. The decision to appoint him was inspired.

The Ibrox club had become frustrated by years of decline in
which they had seen the power shift not just to Celtic but to the
New Firm of Aberdeen and Dundee United. These, in addition to
a resurgent Hearts, under former Rangers Alex MacDonald and
Sandy Jardine, had pushed the Light Blues to a mediocre position
in a Premier League of just ten clubs.

The appointment of Souness appeared to many to be a gamble
because despite his undoubted ability on the field of play, he had
no management experience. In fact, it was less of a gamble than it
looked. The acquisition of Souness the player was in itself great
value at the £300,000 required to buy out his contract from
Sampdoria. His nominated assistant manager, Walter Smith,
secured from a similar role with Dundee United, would join him.

Smith was a highly respected coach within the game, and was
Alex Ferguson's first-choice right-hand man when he was in charge
of the Scotland side in the 1986 Mexico World Cup. Both Souness
and Smith would fulfil their international duties before they could
take up the reins at Ibrox. Smith provided an invaluable prop to
the new manager, supplementing Souness's lack of both coaching

experience and intimate knowledge of the Scottish game. As he accepted the role, Smith confessed, 'I wouldn't take a number-two job anywhere else, but I'm a big Rangers fan.'

It seemed a marriage made in heaven and the Light Blue legions excitedly anticipated a bright new future. Smith echoed their thoughts when he spoke of Souness's arrival as 'marvellous news for Scottish football'. He also pointed out the new manager's 'leadership qualities . . . both on and off the field'.

Souness was under no illusions about the importance of what he was taking on. 'I know this is the biggest job in British management,' he said, 'and I realise just how vital success is to the Rangers supporters – and believe me, I intend to bring that success to this club.' It was what the fans wanted to hear – but just how was he going to do it?

With the financial backing of a board led by Lawrence Marlborough, Souness declared his intentions early in his tenure. He launched a massive £500,000 bid for Dundee United's young defender Richard Gough, following it up with an increased offer of £650,000 when that was turned down. The approach was rejected, but little-known striker Colin West was signed from Watford for a fee of around £175,000 and some of Wallace's squad made an early departure. Other signings followed, most notably that of England goalkeeper Chris Woods for a fee of £600,000, a record for a goalkeeper. Souness, meanwhile, was working on a deal that would send shockwaves throughout British football: the acquisition of England captain Terry Butcher!

Souness recognised that every successful side was built from a solid defensive base and he saw the formidable Butcher as the key to his plans. But it would not be easy luring a man who had only played for one senior club, at cosy Ipswich in East Anglia. What's more, the England skipper was also a target for some of the biggest clubs in the south.

Souness knew that he had to get Butcher to Ibrox so that the Englishman could see just how big a club Rangers was. As speculation mounted about Rangers' interest, Butcher played in a Rest of the World v Argentina charity match in Los Angeles at the end of the World Cup. Souness arranged for the player to fly directly to London where the two men met at a hotel near Heathrow Airport. A misunderstanding by Butcher saw him turn up at the wrong venue as Souness waited anxiously a mile away. The slip-up almost dashed the meeting, but the resourceful Souness managed to track down his bewildered target. The England captain, wearied by his transatlantic flight, heard what the Rangers boss had to offer and asked for some time to think things over. Souness knew that he had to maintain the pressure of his bid. He demanded that Butcher fly to Glasgow with him to have a look around Ibrox.

The new boss leaked the imminent arrival of his prospective signing to the press, 'to provide a touch of showbiz' and ensure an interested crowd at the front entrance. When Butcher saw the enthusiastic fans and the impressive stadium, he was 'simply bowled over'. He signed.

There is no doubt that it was not only the ebullience of the fans and the majesty of Ibrox that impressed Butcher. The financial package was undoubtedly the greatest lure to Scotland. As Arsenal boss George Graham, himself a Scot, later observed as a stream of players flowed northwards, 'They hadn't all gone to admire the scenery!'

Butcher and others who had reversed the traditional trend of transfers from Scotland to England were disparagingly called 'football mercenaries', and there is no doubt that money was the major factor in many of the transfers. It is also certain, however, that most would never have considered a move to Scotland but for Souness. Butcher, for one, was attracted by the prospect of playing under and alongside a player of the Scot's stature. The fact that the Rangers boss had made the journey back to Scotland suggested that a move to the Scottish League was not the retrograde step that many in the south believed it to be. If Rangers was good enough for Souness, most of the 'football mercenaries' believed that the club could more than match their ambitions.

Souness's big spending brought resentment from most other clubs who were unable to compete now the stakes were raised. 'People saw us as a group of bigheads, but they failed to recognise that we could be good for the Scottish game,' Souness recalled. 'They didn't see that other players would benefit from what we were doing. The interest we were creating in Scottish football alone was a benefit.' In spite of this, he was aware of the resentment towards him and the club. That resentment was manifested as a fierce determination to beat Rangers, an attitude that became very evident to the Rangers boss from as early as his first competitive game. On a balmy August day, the opening of season 1986–87, at Hibernian's Easter Road ground, Souness paraded his £1.5 million of new talent in front of a capacity crowd.

Hibs fought feverishly, winning every 50–50 ball, and hustling the new-look Ibrox side. They were rewarded with an early goal as the game ran anything but according to Rangers' plan. Suckered by players determined to unsettle him, Souness lashed out amid scenes of turmoil in the middle of the field. The centre circle became crowded with almost every player involved in a brawl that led to a flurry of yellow cards – and one red, for Souness.

Rangers lost the game 2–0, but it was an important lesson for Souness. He realised that Rangers would have to match other teams' efforts if his own side's undoubted superior quality was to have a chance to shine through. He also learned that referees would have little respect for his standing in the game. It was, in fact, only the beginning of a long struggle against officialdom in Scotland.

One positive aspect of the game was the confirmation that the new boss had real 'togetherness' in the squad. It may not have had flowing football, but when the side rallied as a unit in the face of their troubles at Easter Road, the manager knew he had men who would fight for each other. 'They were a spirited lot,' he recalled. 'Each morning as we assembled for training it would be a case of the Jocks versus the English. Durrant would give them pelters. The abuse they would give each other was frightening. Sometimes I would just walk out, sensing there were some things I didn't want to hear, but come the Saturday they were all pulling together.'

Using the camaraderie that Souness had engendered, Rangers recovered from their shock start and more than made up for that opening-day upset with victory over Celtic in the first Old Firm clash of the season. It put them top.

As Souness settled into his new role he continued to build the squad. By October, just three months into his first season, he delivered a trophy, the Skol League Cup, to the jubilant Rangers support. The signings continued and Spurs star Graeme Roberts arrived in December to bolster the defence.

By May, Rangers were on the threshold of their first championship since 1978. They had maintained their lead with an impressive run of 23 League games without defeat, coinciding with Souness's return to the side after injury and suspension. The solidity of the defence was highlighted in the record established by keeper Chris Woods, who kept a clean sheet in twelve consecutive matches, the run ending with ignominious defeat to lowly Hamilton in the Scottish Cup in January.

But everyone wanted the League title and no one more so than the Rangers boss. He took his side to Aberdeen for the penultimate game of the League knowing that a point would secure the title. Just as the red mist ruined his party on the opening day, an angry Souness was again despatched for an early bath at a time when his men needed him most. He had assembled a resilient bunch, however, and it was fitting that the man whom he had seen as the vital cog in the machine, Terry Butcher, rose to head the goal that delivered the precious point that secured the championship.

The pent-up emotions of nine long years without a title victory were released as the blue-and-white army swarmed onto the Pittodrie pitch at the final whistle. The jubilant fans carried Terry Butcher shoulder-high while other players, many without socks, boots and even shirts, cavorted amidst the masses before heading for the tunnel. They didn't care that the fans had snatched a little souvenir of the day, because they would return to Glasgow as champions.

Midfield star Ian Durrant recalled the events in his autobiography as a day when a great cloud was lifted from him. The game provided a welcome distraction from the media attention he had received after an appearance in court with Ally McCoist on charges of breach of the peace and assault. Durrant's case was eventually thrown out, but McCoist received a small fine for minor assault.

The case was the furthest thing from their minds as they enjoyed the celebrations on the journey back to Glasgow. With the party in full swing, Souness called the pair to the front of the bus. Durrant expected some thanks from the boss for their efforts. 'That business in the chip shop,' Souness said sternly, 'it's not on. You're both fined £1,500. Behave yourselves for the next six months and I'll give you it back.' True to his word, Souness did eventually return the money to the players. It shocked Durrant that the manager should act in such a manner immediately after winning the title, but, despite it all, he confessed that he respected

Souness immensely. The fact that the money was returned is evidence that Souness's sharp disciplinary measure was effective.

Discipline and professionalism were the watchwords during Souness's reign. As he settled into the historic manager's office at the top of the marble staircase he made it quite clear that he would be his own man, unfettered by many of the traditions upon which the club was built. Where players were once regarded as almost subservient to the great Institution that was Rangers Football Club, and were even forbidden to climb the staircase without authority, Souness ensured his players had a standing second only to his own. They were cosseted and guarded in a throwback to the manager's experiences in Italy. He was well aware of the distractions available to his young stars in a bright city like Glasgow. He had been just like them only a few years earlier, but he knew that they would have to show some professionalism. In fact, even though Souness was something of a party-animal as a youngster, he knew where to draw the line.

Jack Charlton related one incident during his time at Middlesbrough that indicated the young Souness's awareness of his responsibilities. Hearing that Souness had been out on the town, Charlton called the young Scot into his office. 'I've heard you like your nights out and you like the girls,' said the manager.

'I do like going out,' replied Souness, 'but I don't know who you have been talking to. I go out midweek and would never go out on a Thursday and Friday before a game!'

Charlton was impressed.

That set the philosophy of the Rangers boss, and to ensure that he could keep track of his players he insisted that the team stay together overnight at a hotel before every match. It was not a routine that was widely accepted by the players in the early days and on one well-publicised occasion at least one of them breached the security. Ted McMinn slipped out of the team's Glasgow hotel before one match and returned in the early hours – to find an angry Souness waiting. The discipline was swift and sharp. The winger was to find his days at Ibrox cut short.

While Souness's strict disciplinary measures were a reflection of his demands that the players should adhere to his rules, there is little doubt that he was influenced by the person he called the greatest man-manager he had seen. Souness had immense admiration for the former Celtic boss Jock Stein, who later took over as manager of the Scotland international side. Stein had made Souness captain in the World Cup qualification trail and the player had been at the older man's side in Cardiff when Stein succumbed to a fatal heart attack as the nation celebrated the dramatic success that guaranteed Scotland's place in the Mexico finals.

One occasion he felt the wrath of Stein was when he returned late from a shopping trip with Kenny Dalglish while the remainder of the squad gathered for a team meeting. The pair had got their schedule wrong, but it cut no ice with Stein, who gave Souness, as captain, a humiliating dressing-down in the public lobby of their Brussels hotel. The captain was berated all the way along the corridor and for half an hour into the meeting. As Souness recalled, 'He didn't miss you if you stepped out of line! You only did it once.'

It was an attitude to discipline that he himself was to display several times while he was in charge of Rangers. Ally McCoist was often on the receiving end of disciplinary action as the boss singled him out for being what he considered unprofessional. On one occasion, an errant McCoist was found to have gone to Cheltenham without authorisation to pursue his interest in racing. Souness rebuked the striker, then arranged a press conference for him to offer a very public apology. The striker was a hero to the supporters, with a popularity that often seemed to irritate the manager. The incident gave him an opportunity to highlight some of McCoist's deficiencies to his adoring fans. If there was ever any doubt, it also gave Souness a chance to demonstrate that things would be done his way. He was the boss, and the players were well aware that they had to play by his rules – or, quite simply, they wouldn't play at all.

Souness was hard on McCoist throughout his managership, but the former Rangers boss nowadays goes to great pains to explain that there was never a feud between them. 'The way I treated Ally may have seemed hard but I believe it has helped him stay at the top for so long,' he said recently. 'The truth is that I felt that Ally was too comfortable with life. He was in a comfort zone and it was no good for him.'

He went on to admit that during his spell at Rangers his attitude was 'confrontational'. 'Everything was black and white,' he confessed. In fact, the decisions to leave McCoist out of the team were not solely down to Souness's judgement. Walter Smith was an intense analyst of the game and showed a keen interest in some statistics I was compiling on a match-to-match basis. These illustrated the performance of players in key areas. He enquired if their decision to leave McCoist on the bench was justified by the statistics. The figures had highlighted a slip in form by the popular striker. In typical style, McCoist came bouncing back in the following weeks.

Apart from the matters of discipline, Souness was a fitness fanatic and did his utmost to ensure that his players were in tip-top condition. Nothing was too good for them. No treatment was beyond them if they needed it. He even insisted that they wear sandals around the dressing-room to ensure that they didn't pick up any foot infections. He took a particular interest in diet, something he had learned about during his career in Italy.

Golf was barred as a pastime as the manager sought to ensure that the players neither over-exerted themselves outwith Ibrox nor subjected themselves to sports that might aggravate injuries. The ruling was unfortunate for a young reserve player, Angus McPherson, who later joined Kilmarnock. The youngster withdrew from the final of his local golf club's Junior championship final for fear of incurring the wrath of Souness.

On the training-field, the players worked mostly with Walter Smith, although Souness did contribute various stretching exercises he had learned during his time in Italy. Unlike the Wallace era, Souness's philosophy of training lay firmly in ballwork. 'If you do your work well with the ball in training, there is no need to do training without the ball, except in pre-season,' he argued. He was an ideal example for his players to follow. Although one of the older members of the international squad for the Mexican World Cup, he was undoubtedly the fittest, as indicated by medical tests. When he arrived at Ibrox just after the tournament, the training at altitude had left him in peak condition. It is little wonder that the players were impressed.

The interest that Souness had stimulated in Rangers was reflected by a dramatic increase in attendances. The average crowd for League matches in Scotland rose from 21,000 to over 30,000 that first season, with the average at Ibrox rising by around 12,000 to

36,000. As the crowds flocked back to the stadium, Rangers finally moved to capitalise on their commercial value with a number of initiatives designed to fuel the on-field investments with corporate money.

The first executive area, the Thornton Suite, provided corporate hospitality packages as Rangers tried to match Souness's ambitions with the cash he would need to lift the club to a position of sustainable strength. Rangers had to generate funds; although they looked like a club with unlimited funds, Souness did not have an open chequebook.

Enhanced shirt sponsorship deals and other initiatives designed to capitalise on the incredible interest in the club finally dispelled the myth that football was 'only a game'. Souness had recognised that the high transfer fees seen in Italy and France would set the standards for top-quality players and, if Rangers wished to compete on a continental level, they would have to be able to contend with the financial demands of the top clubs in Europe.

The fans revelled in the glamour of the big transfers as Rangers were linked with major names around the country and even beyond the insular shores of British football. As the club forged ahead with seemingly no end to their resources, Celtic showed a hesitancy to match the spending power of the Ibrox side. In fact, they appeared almost bewildered for a spell as the Light Blue legions taunted rival fans over their comparable poverty.

Into the new season and Souness continued to add to his squad; again, most of the new players came from England. He was very familiar with the scene south of the border and that undoubtedly influenced his bias towards England, but the Rangers boss was quick to dismiss criticism that he had turned his back on Scottish players. In fact, he found that many Scottish clubs operated a double standard in their valuation of players. Rangers, because of their needs and apparent unlimited financial resources, were often quoted excessively high transfer fees. One club in particular, Dundee United, indicated a reluctance to sell any player to the Glasgow club, not surprisingly unwilling to contribute to the strengthening of the champions.

Souness therefore had good reason to look south of the border and to Europe, where he invariably found better players at good value. Into his second season, an impressive list of new recruits was added including former England stars Trevor Francis and Ray Wilkins. The latter, a classy midfielder, was great value at £150,000 from Paris St-Germain. He went on to play arguably his best football at Ibrox.

Having pursued him for around 18 months, the Rangers manager also finally secured Richard Gough for a fee of £1.1 million, making the defender the first player to break the seven-figure mark in Scotland. Souness greatly admired Gough, having seen him at first hand in the international scene. 'He was a very special player,' he enthused many years later. 'I was impressed with how he looked after himself. Even at the age of 37 he was Walter Smith's best player at Everton in that first season he played at Goodison.'

Mark Falco (Watford), Mark Walters (Aston Villa) and John Brown (Dundee) were other notable additions as Souness took his spending to over £5 million.

The side was now better equipped to meet the challenges of Europe and the manager took his troops into the European Cup competition that had brought him so much glory in his Liverpool days. The draw threw Rangers into a first-round tie with Dynamo Kiev and an opening away leg in front of an intimidating crowd of 100,000. In a disciplined performance carefully marshalled by Souness, the Light Blues returned with a narrow 1–0 defeat.

He had a surprise in store for the Soviets on the return leg at Ibrox. Conscious that an away goal for Dynamo would all but end Rangers' hopes of progressing, the manager realised that the greatest threat would come from their pace as they counter-attacked on the flanks. The Kiev coaches knew Souness would try to negate that threat but what they most certainly didn't expect was for the Rangers boss to physically remove the flanks altogether from the field.

Consulting UEFA regulations to find out just how wide or narrow a football field could be, Souness found that he could slim the Ibrox pitch by around five metres. Early arrivals at the stadium that night were astonished to see the lines had been moved inward by the requisite amount. The Kiev officials protested but there was nothing the UEFA observers could do. They simply hadn't come across such a situation before. Director/Secretary Campbell Ogilvie recalled the anger of Rangers' opponents that evening. 'At the end of the match, after the stadium had been cleared, they went out to the field with a tape. They would not even allow any of our people to hold the other end of the tape for them. It was a bit tense, but thankfully the tape showed that the pitch had been adjusted to acceptable dimensions.'

The game was played in front of an excited capacity crowd of 44,500. Goals from Falco and McCoist were enough to see Rangers into the next round.

As Souness continued to mould his side he was dealt a savage blow in November when the linchpin of his defence, Terry Butcher, broke his leg in a midweek League match at Ibrox against Aberdeen. The manager had lost not only the heart of his defence but also his inspirational captain.

Celtic, spurred on by their centenary celebrations, went on to take the title, but many of the Light Blue fans reckoned that Rangers' championship hopes went off on the stretcher that carried Terry Butcher from the field that cold November night at Ibrox. 'We missed him so much and I'm convinced it cost us that title,' Souness later reflected.

The following season, with more additions to his squad including Gary Stevens, Kevin Drinkell and Ian Ferguson, Souness recaptured the championship and sent the fans into raptures with two comprehensive victories over Celtic. The first, early in the campaign, saw the side slam five goals past a stunned Ian Andrews, with almost 25 minutes remaining. The fans and some of the Rangers die-hards within the team bayed for at least another two goals to level the tribal rivalry that had seen them suffer in silence for over thirty years as Celtic fans baited them over a 7–1 Cup final defeat. Souness, though, was content to play out time and savour the victory. In the cold light of football management he was right, but it was certainly an occasion when he wasn't entirely at one with the Ibrox support. 'Victory over Celtic was only worth two points,' he would tell them, but to the fans it meant so much more than that. He would later admit that he had failed to realise the importance of the match.

If he failed to come to terms with the significance of an Old Firm victory, he could not hide his contempt for Celtic boss Billy McNeill who, he felt, was often enveloped in his own self-importance. 'When we won anything at Liverpool, we never gloated, never had the big heads on,' he told me. 'It was the way I was brought up there. At Ibrox, when we won an Old Firm game our attitude was that we had had a good day today, a good day at the office. We realised that another day it might be their turn.

'When he [McNeill] won an Old Firm game, it was about how "Tactically I did this today – tactically we were superb. All week in training I have been working on this because I knew a weakness was there." He always made out that it was all down to him and his clever football brain.'

If his failure to appreciate how much winning the Old Firm contests meant was hard for the traditionalists to accept, he was about to cause even greater furore over the old vexed question of the club's signing policy with regard to Catholics. Like countless prominent Rangers figures in the past, Souness was continually asked if he would break with the club's apparent policy of signing only non-Catholics. It was a constant source of agitation that the media should be preoccupied by the issue, with one notable journalist raising the hackles of the board on the very day that Rangers secured that long-awaited championship at Pittodrie in 1987.

But Souness could not hide his distaste for sectarianism. 'I hate every aspect of it,' he said, pointing out that his wife was a Roman Catholic and that his children were also raised in the faith. 'How could I refuse to sign Catholics, then go home to a wife of those same religious beliefs?' he would ask. He also would reflect on the words of Jock Stein, himself a Protestant, who told Souness that Celtic's scouts were always more anxious to tie up good young Protestant talent quickly – they knew that they could generally deliberate longer over Catholic youngsters, because there was no way they would end up at Ibrox!

Souness, supported by new chairman David Murray, wanted to break with the past and sign a Catholic, but the move had to be considered from every angle. The two men had a fair idea that there would be a hostile reaction from a section of the Rangers support, and whichever player was to come to Ibrox would arrive in a whirlwind of media attention. It would take a strong personality to withstand the inevitable severe pressures.

Souness found support from his assistant Walter Smith and the pair deliberated over possible candidates. They were determined to make it happen, but it had to be a player who fitted into their overall plans. An approach was made to Glasgow-born Ray

Houghton, a Republic of Ireland international, who 'fancied it' but backed out and went instead to Liverpool. Ian Rush was also considered but Souness claimed Rush 'wasn't keen at all from a religious point of view'. Hibernian's John Collins was another who was lured to Ibrox. He was on the verge of completing the move before deciding against it at the last moment.

Souness had another candidate in mind: the former Celtic star Maurice Johnston who was at that time plying his trade with French side Nantes. In Johnston's case the transfer was not so much carefully conceived as born out of chance and opportunity.

On 13 May 1989, as Rangers welcomed Aberdeen to Ibrox for the final League match of the season, Souness left his office and bounded down the marble staircase just before kick-off to watch the unfurling of the championship flag. He spotted Johnston's agent, Bill McMurdo, an unashamed Rangers fan, standing by the radiator in the hallway at the bottom. Souness had just seen a photo of Johnston on the back pages of the newspapers wearing a Celtic jersey as the Parkhead side announced that he was returning to Parkhead.

Souness went over to McMurdo. 'I thought you were a Rangers supporter,' he said.

McMurdo replied, 'What do you mean?'

'Letting them sign Johnston,' said Souness.

'The deal isn't done yet,' replied McMurdo, as he discussed the complications that belied the suggestions in the press that the transfer was concluded. In fact, it was far from completed.

'Would he come here?' asked the Rangers boss.

McMurdo replied, 'I think he would – I'll ask him.'

Maurice Johnston confirmed his interest in a move to Ibrox, meeting Souness and the club's chief executive Alan Montgomery in the most discreet place they could find – a little café in France. Another meeting was arranged in Scotland and the parties agreed to rendezvous at the carpark of the Royal Hotel in Edinburgh. Campbell Ogilvie, the secretary, and Alan Montgomery sat in a car with the player and his agent discussing the mechanics of the transfer. By chance, just at that very moment a minibus full of Orangemen appeared. As they walked into the hotel, they had no idea of what was going on in a car a short distance from them as Johnston cowered out of sight. The deal was done amidst a flurry of telephone calls and on 10 July 1989, Mo Johnston was presented to the excited press pack in the Blue Room at Ibrox.

It was a huge move for Souness and an even bigger one for Johnston, and the financial package he received reflected the importance of the transfer in terms of its impact on Rangers. As dissenting fans gathered outside the stadium and shockwaves reverberated around the world of football, the player stood nervously inside the doorway of the Blue Room as the press pack left to spread the word. It was a moment of calm in a day of frantic activity as Alan Montgomery and Souness joined him, alone but for Willie Waddell who sat quietly in the corner.

Johnston turned and caught Waddell's eye, almost seeking approval for his arrival. The legendary Rangers figure peered over his glasses and said caringly, 'Keep your head down, son. Keep your head down.' Johnston smiled and nodded with respect. In a moment he knew that he could play at the club.

The signing of Mo Johnston was one of the most pivotal events in the long history of Rangers FC. Long the 'Presbyterian club' of Scottish football, it stubbornly resisted the criticism from all quarters that it was practising a sectarian signing policy. In truth, the club was not exclusively Protestant. Players of other religions were welcomed, but Catholics were never knowingly signed. Despite the claims of Rangers managers through the years that they would and could sign whoever they wished, the club *did* exercise a sectarian policy on the field of play. No Catholic player would ever have been bought by Rangers from at least the latter stages of Struth's era until Souness broke the tradition with the signing of Johnston.

Some players, most notably the great Ibrox favourite Don Kitchenbrand, did slip though the net but, as he once remarked, no one asked him his religion so he never felt any reason to tell them.

The assumption that Rangers would continue that policy under Souness was anathema to the new boss. Coming from the east of Scotland, where religious divisions were less intense than they were in the west, he had no time for sectarianism. The club's signing policy was not on the agenda when David Holmes wooed him to Ibrox. Quite simply, the new boss would tolerate no restrictions on whom he could sign. He told me, 'I would never have taken the job if there had been any restrictions.'

The signing of Maurice Johnson provided Rangers and Souness with some respite from the press fascination with the club's policy, a fascination that often seemed to go too far. When Mark Falco was signed a year into Souness's reign, the media's focus on the player's religion became almost farcical. Fired by the suggestion that 'Mark' was a Catholic name and 'Falco' suggested distinctly foreign origins, one of the tabloids telephoned the player's mother to enquire of his creed. When told that Rangers had never before signed a Catholic, she replied, 'Well, you don't have one now!'

In breaking Rangers' sectarian policy, Souness had demonstrated that he would not be deflected from his desire to run the club the way he saw fit. It was a self-will and determination that the club thrived on – although his stubbornness led to frequent conflicts with the press and the footballing authorities.

He could not stomach criticism if he felt it was unjustified. His time at Ibrox was littered with accounts of confrontations with reporters who had dared to question his ethics in dealing with favoured newspapers or, more particularly, his management of the team. Invariably, Souness was indiscreet in rounding on any hack he felt had misrepresented him.

On one journey back from a disappointing European defeat in Belgrade, he stormed up the aisle of the plane for a face-to-face exchange with controversial sportswriter Gerry McNee. Only the intervention of Rangers officials prevented the two from coming to blows. On another occasion, during a post-match press conference, he spotted another writer, James Traynor, who had written a disparaging piece a couple of days earlier. Souness cut through the assembled pack to launch a tirade at the bemused Traynor.

Souness admits nowadays that he was too inexperienced to manage the press aggravation. 'At Liverpool, we were positively discouraged from talking to the press. If you had a bad game then you maybe had two interviews, but other than that they kept us away from the media. When I joined Rangers, I had no training in how to deal with the press. There is no doubt that I would handle things much differently now. I didn't have the experience back then.'

As for the Scottish Football Association, Souness appeared contemptuous of the old-style attitudes that he felt hindered the game in Scotland, and he was never slow to reveal his thoughts. With almost a siege mentality, he insisted he never got a fair crack of the whip from the SFA and routinely faced the beaks for a series of on- and off-the-field indiscretions.

It was not only outside Ibrox that his stubbornness and confrontational character led to difficulties. He had trouble coming to terms with the position of chief executive Alan Montgomery whom he claimed interfered in team matters, an allegation that was strenuously denied. In a test of strength, Souness effectively ruled that there was no room in the set-up for the two of them. The decision was placed firmly in the domain of David Murray, and Souness instinctively felt that his position was secure. Montgomery left the club.

By this time Souness was well aware that his popularity didn't extend far beyond the Rangers support, but that didn't worry him. He would still continue to plough his own furrow, even if it did not meet the general acceptance of others.

But this was the public face of Souness. Behind the hard-nosed, determined individual who had dragged Rangers to the top of Scottish football was a compassionate man who rarely displayed his softer side to the public. Walter Smith said that the public face of Souness was not a true representation of the man.

One incident which revealed the compassionate side of Souness received no public coverage, because the Rangers manager never sought to improve his image, but the story is important to gain a better understanding of the man. A young Rangers groundsman, David Roxburgh, was back at work just after suffering the tragic loss of his wife when he was called to the manager's office. He feared that Souness was unhappy at the state of the pitch, because he was a perfectionist who had a compulsive interest in the quality of the playing surface. The nervous groundsman knocked then entered the room where Graeme Souness sat behind the desk. The Rangers boss pushed an envelope across the table and instructed Roxburgh to take himself and his young family away for a holiday. Inside the envelope were tickets and spending money for a dream trip to Walt Disney World in Florida. It was typical of the generosity of Souness, but not an image that he publicly fostered.

On 16 April 1991 Souness rocked Rangers with his resignation. It came only a few months after he had publicly pledged his long-term future to the club. He announced that he had been offered the vacant manager position at Liverpool, a club he had always loved. In a hastily convened press conference at Ibrox, he announced: 'I feel I've gone as far as I'm allowed to go in trying to achieve success at this football club,' a clear reference to the growing frustrations he faced on and off the field.

David Murray told the gathered press corps that Souness would leave immediately. The manager had wanted to end the season at Rangers and told Liverpool that he would not join them until the League was over in Scotland, but Murray felt that this was not appropriate. 'It's not Graeme's wish, but he's free to go. We have a championship to win,' he announced defiantly. Eager to ensure that the show would go on at Ibrox, and with echoes of Struth, Murray told the stunned pressmen that Rangers would not be deflected from their goals. 'No one is bigger than the club. Not Graeme and not me. The championship is the biggest thing right now.'

Admitting his own dismay at the events, he went on to say that he felt 'personally let down' by his friend's decision. 'I think he's made the biggest mistake of his life, and time will tell.' Souness, who claimed he felt too emotional to deal with questions, left to speed south immediately. The Anfield that held so many happy memories of past glories would now be his future. No one knew what lay in store.

While there was much speculation about Souness's reasons for leaving, he revealed to me that there were a number of factors that led him to accept the Liverpool post, a position that had in fact been offered to him a number of times. He said that every day at Ibrox brought a big problem, although he insisted he loved the place. Despite his defiant nature, his resilience was becoming eroded by certain things. On the footballing side he felt targeted by players and officials alike. 'I felt that if people tackled me in a certain way, it was okay, but I got cards,' he recalled. 'I suppose it is in the Scottish mentality – "I'll show you" kind of thing. I used to say to Phil Boersma as I took to the field, "Is the target straight on my back today?"' Off the field, the media attention wore him down: 'Everywhere I went, I was being scrutinised in a negative way.'

There were other problems, too – his marriage had gone wrong and his children were living in England. But his 'biggest problem' was 'all the aggravation I had living in Scotland'. This exacerbated the heart trouble that would afflict him a few years later, but which was already developing during the latter stages of his Ibrox career. 'I had permanent headaches through the high blood pressure,' he said, although at that time he had little notion that the headaches were not stress related, but a symptom of a potentially fatal illness.

His departure left some financial business to be squared. He was a club director and a shareholder in Murray's holding company that controlled Rangers. Souness had a 10 per cent shareholding in the company which held a 76.29 per cent share in Rangers. The matter was resolved without fuss by Murray and Souness, as the chairman turned his attention to gaining compensation from Liverpool.

It was a sombre-looking Souness who left for his hero's welcome at Anfield. At Ibrox the fans were bitter. They felt betrayed by a man who seemed to have pledged his future to the club they loved. Many found it difficult to accept that he had chosen to go elsewhere when they believed there was only one place to be.

The fans may have been disappointed but there is little doubt that Graeme Souness will go down as the most influential character in the club's modern history. He inspired a revolution in Rangers that saw a new era of big-money players come to the club, and not just from within Scotland. Walter Smith spoke of the excitement of that period as the crowds more than doubled and continued improvements to the stadium kept pace with the growing commercial interest that enveloped Rangers. He recalled that everyone wanted to know about the club. They were not just local news, but often made national headlines as the press flocked to Ibrox from far and wide.

Souness generated a renewed interest in Rangers and Scottish football that many in his homeland failed to appreciate. In truth, they did not deserve him. Today, he says that he would have done many things differently, offering his increased experience for the mellowing of his character. Perhaps the traumas of his illness have provided a sense of perspective to something that is, after all, only a game, but which seemed much more than that at times. Souness's strength was his single-minded determination to succeed. Without that, it is doubtful if he would have had the resilience to withstand the immense pressure that his revolution brought to bear on him and Rangers.

While Phil Boersma, his long-time friend, chose to follow the manager south, Walter Smith decided to remain. As the door closed on Souness, Smith turned the latch to push through his own claims for the position. Souness's tenure at Ibrox was perhaps the most dramatic and controversial in the club's history, but with his departure came the opportunity for Rangers to enter a new era. Smith's time had come.

As the new manager carved his own little piece of history, Souness exorcised the ghosts that lured him to Liverpool, then began a journey that would take him to Turkey and Portugal before returning to England. A long time has passed since those heady days of the late 1980s.

'Can you ever see yourself back at Ibrox?' I asked him.

'You can never say "never",' he replied.

WALTER SMITH

Having served as a capable and loyal assistant to some of the greats in the game, it had always been Walter Smith's desire to manage his own side. When the opportunity finally arose, he could not have wished for better. Always a Rangers fan, he had dreamed of playing for the club, but although he did show some ability in the game, his destiny as a player was never to lie at Ibrox.

Born in Lanark on 24 February 1948, he was brought up in Carmyle in the east end of Glasgow. He may have remained there, working at the nearby Dalmarnock Power Station where he was serving his apprenticeship as an electrician, but a career in football beckoned. As a young aspiring star, he first attracted the interest of Ashfield, a Junior side, who took him on to their books, but he quickly moved up a grade to full professional level, joining Dundee United in November 1966. His father, aware of the uncertainties of football, made him finish his apprenticeship as an electrician while he was on Tayside. In football, however, the young Walter carved out a useful career at Dundee United, initially under manager Jerry Kerr and then under his successor, Jim McLean. An uncompromising wing-half, Smith served United well although success was limited.

Along with his brother, he was among the crowd of 80,000 who watched the Old Firm match at Ibrox on 2 January 1971, the game that will forever be remembered for its aftermath rather than the events on the field. As the final whistle sounded, turmoil on the fateful Stairway 13 at the Copland Road end of the ground left 66 fans dead in what will forever be known simply as the Ibrox Disaster.

Smith left by the same exit and was almost caught up in the mayhem. He recalled, 'I wasn't playing for Dundee United over the holiday period, so my brother and I went to the game. As we left the terracing to make our way down the infamous Stairway 13, we were caught in the top half of the stair when everything just came to a standstill. There was terrible crushing and when the barriers on the stairway went, everyone went over to the side and my impression was that the wooden fences at the side of the stairway collapsed, but I saw a photograph a few years ago and it showed the fence intact. We must have climbed over the top of them, because I can remember scrambling down the grass verge and out of the other gateway at Edmiston Drive. Because we left from the other exit, we weren't aware of how serious the situation was. Some of the boys thought there had been a wee bit of trouble at the bottom of the stairs, but nothing more.

'We got back on to the supporters' bus and all of the boys in the supporters' club who were on the terracing around Stairway 13 had returned. The bus set off back home to Carmyle and by the time we got to the drop-off point, there were a lot of people waiting. There was no radio on the bus at that time, so we were completely oblivious to what had happened until we met all the families waiting for us. Then we heard the news.'

Two weeks later Smith returned to Ibrox to make his Dundee United début against Rangers. It was the first game the Light Blues played after the trauma of the disaster and Smith took his place in the sombre, almost surreal atmosphere as the match was played out to a 1–1 draw. It was a sad return to the stadium for many, including Walter Smith.

Although United were a fine and emerging side that were rarely out of the top half of the table, the opportunities for honours were limited. Smith's one realistic opportunity of a medal came in 1974 when he was part of the United side that lost out to Celtic in the Scottish Cup final. But his interests in the coaching side of the game were already brewing in the early years of his career.

'I was always interested in the coaching side of the game and thought that it would be good to follow that through,' he said. 'I started doing my SFA certificates when I was 24 and got through them in a couple of years. Jim McLean then asked me if I wanted to take the schoolboy training, which was once a week. I enjoyed that, and then when I was 27 I got a pelvic injury that kept me out of the game for eight months. Jim suggested I help him with the training through that period.

'When I was fit again, he asked if I wanted to go into the coaching side for the team saying I was better at that than I was at playing anyway!' laughed Smith.

Smith found his appearances in the Tannadice side becoming less frequent. Dumbarton were interested in signing him and he served for 18 months under Alex Wright. He continued to live in Dundee, though, where he had a part-time job in the technical college and was also still coaching at Tannadice. 'I stayed there during the week and came down for the games, but United got a lot of injuries that year and Jim bought me back to Tannadice in 1979,' said Smith.

Rangers featured again in Smith's career, when they were the first side he faced on his return to Dundee United. Despite playing a makeshift side, United left Ibrox with a 3–2 win after being 2–0 down.

As well as making progress in his coaching apprenticeship at Dundee United, Smith was assisting in coaching responsibilities to the SFA. He eventually helped Andy Roxburgh as coach to the Scotland youth team where he assisted for nine seasons. It was a successful partnership, with the pair going on to win the European Youth Championships.

By 1982 McLean, well aware of Walter Smith's potential as a good tactician, appointed him assistant manager. His return to Tannadice coincided with the emergence of Dundee United as one half of the New Firm challenge to Rangers and Celtic for the country's top honours. In tandem with Aberdeen they not only turned Scottish football upside down, but they also made an incredible impact in Europe that belied their meagre resources. A UEFA Cup final and European Cup final were the rewards for stirring campaigns that saw the likes of Barcelona vanquished in their own Nou Camp Stadium.

Jim McLean, who by now had assumed virtual control at Tannadice, recognised his assistant's contribution to Dundee United's achievements by appointing him to the board. It was a short-lived stay: Smith's credibility in the game had not gone unnoticed by the national administrators – or by Rangers. He had worked with a number of the senior SFA coaches, including Jock Stein, with the national side. Apart from his service to the youth team, he also took the Scotland Under-21 side for four games. After Stein's untimely death in 1986, Alex Ferguson was asked to take Scotland to the Mexico World Cup. Ferguson asked Walter Smith to assist him.

Smith worked alongside some of the most renowned coaches in

Scottish football, but who had greatest influence on his career?

'Probably Jim McLean,' he replied. 'He was a tracksuit manager who was heavily into the tactics and formation of sides, and having worked with him for about eight years as coach then assistant manager, I picked up a lot. I was lucky at the start with Jim because he had already laid the foundation for the success that United later earned. I don't think he gets the credit he deserves for winning the League championship and then taking United to the semi-final of the European Cup and the final of the UEFA Cup. He did it – I just helped,' he said modestly.

'I picked up a lot working with Alex Ferguson over that short period of about six or seven months, because he was a different personality from Jim. I began to see that there wasn't just one way to be successful. Alex had a different view on things from Jim in tactics, training and man-management, but it showed that different people had different ways of working and could still be successful. That opened my eyes. Andy Roxburgh was different again. He was very good – meticulous in everything he did – and he had a great spell with the Scotland team. So, I picked up ideas from lots of different people, but you develop your own ways. It was all good experience.'

As we spoke my mind drifted to William Struth's account of his early days as manager of Rangers. He spoke of keeping his ears open and his mouth shut. Smith, clearly, was of a similar opinion in the formative years of his coaching career as he gleaned the secrets of management from some of the best in the game.

IBROX BECKONS

When Graeme Souness sent shockwaves throughout Scottish football by taking on the Rangers job, it was generally acknowledged that he needed an assistant who was familiar with the game in this country. Souness knew Walter Smith from the international scene and when his name was put forward as a suitable assistant, a natural partnership evolved: Souness with his flamboyance and awareness of the wider European scene; and Smith with his coaching background and intimate knowledge of what it took to be successful in Scotland.

'Graeme came in with a player's perspective of management, which is different from the guys who came in from the coaching side with a more formal background. He brought experience of being a player at the top level, and that was interesting. It was a new outlook,' said Smith.

Smith was the perfect assistant to Souness. Always a calming influence, he was easier to deal with than his uncompromising boss. But if Smith rarely became embroiled in the very public controversies that surrounded Souness, he never failed to support him. Indeed, he was the perfect foil: Souness with the grit and single-minded determination; Smith with the studious approach providing calm reasoning to his boss's decisions.

Smith recalls it as a 'fantastic' period. 'We had a great five years there, being part of the resurgence. Looking back, everything was great: the changes to the ground, the excitement, even the bad things – they were all part of the package. I really enjoyed that spell. It was a valuable period, because it gave me a good insight into management with a top club. Graeme had seen it as a player, but working alongside him through these early years provided me with a sense of it as his assistant.'

It was to be a great partnership. Souness was the motivator and taskmaster who instilled his own fiery determination to succeed in the squad, and Smith was the tactician.

Souness's decision to quit Ibrox did not come as a great shock to Smith. He was aware of the manager's increasing frustration with life in Scotland, and when the opportunity came to manage Liverpool there was little surprise that he took it. Souness asked Smith to join him at Liverpool. He could undoubtedly have carved out a new and more lucrative career for himself in a new, refreshing environment, but Smith declined. 'I felt that it would be difficult for me to fit in at Anfield. They had been a successful team and they already had Ronnie Moran and Roy Evans in the backroom. I didn't see a role there for me. I told Graeme I was grateful, but that I couldn't see how it would work out. But he left the position open for me should I change my mind. I really thought that the natural outcome would be that I would have to leave if the club [Rangers] brought in a new manager, but I just couldn't see a position for me at Liverpool.'

Souness, who was later chastened by his experience at Liverpool, said, 'I think he read the script better than I did and foresaw the problems I was walking into there.'

Smith recalled the moment he got his first inkling that he might be in line for the vacant manager's position. 'When the news broke, David Murray phoned me up and I went to see him the next day. He said that Graeme's departure had caught him unawares and that it would take him a few days to make up his mind. That took me by surprise, because I realised that he was considering me for the job. A few days later we met inside Ibrox and walked down the tunnel and he told me the job was mine if I wanted it. He didn't need to ask.'

Smith remains full of admiration for Murray's courage in appointing him. 'It was an unbelievable decision, because there aren't many assistants who go on to become managers at the same club and continue to be successful. It is more difficult than simply moving to a management position with another club. He must have been tempted to go out to recruit someone else with a track-record of success who could continue things at the club. It was a remarkably brave decision by the chairman and I will be eternally grateful for the opportunity he gave me.'

WALTER SMITH: THE NEW MANAGER OF RANGERS

Smith was presented to the Scottish media on 19 April 1991 as the ninth manager of Rangers. 'I supported Rangers for a great number of years and I'm delighted to take this job,' he announced. His appointment was given a ringing endorsement by Souness, David Murray and the players. 'Walter was the only choice,' Murray said.

Richard Gough, the captain, confirmed that the news was welcomed by the players and dismissed any suggestion that Smith would be weak in comparison to Souness. 'Walter is no soft touch,' he said, 'but he's a bit different and that will go a long way to helping our difficulties with the SFA and the press.' Smith did indeed provide a contrst to the often confrontational management style of Souness and there is no doubt that many in the media and the football authorities were glad to see a change in leadership at Rangers.

Even Manchester United boss Alex Ferguson weighed in with some support for the man who had been his assistant in Mexico five years earlier: 'Smith is an absolutely first-class choice. He has a magnificent knowledge of the game.'

For Walter Smith, the appointment was a natural progression in his footballing education. 'I've worked under two of the best managers in Scotland, Jim McLean and Graeme Souness,' he explained. 'I've been with Stein and Ferguson in Scotland squads and I've handled international players on a daily basis.' But, for all his experience, he admitted candidly that 'at the end of the day, it's results that count'.

Despite the endorsement of those closest to the Ibrox scene, the fans did not universally welcome Smith's appointment. Having seen the power that Souness had in attracting the top names to Ibrox, the supporters worried that Smith would be unable to entice the same quality to Rangers. Some players, like goalkeeper Chris Woods, were quite open in their acknowledgement that they came to Ibrox because of Souness. Former Rangers star Andy Gray was another who questioned Smith's ability to attract the top talent from England.

There were other reservations. Some were anxious that Smith, an apparently quieter personality than Souness, would not be able to impose himself on a side of seasoned internationals. These concerns were ill-founded. While Smith was quieter than Souness to the public eye, he was as firm behind the scenes as his predecessor.

Smith ignored the doubters, completely confident in his own ability. As Gough said, Smith had been very much hands-on during the Souness era in any case. There would be no drastic change because the team were playing largely as he would have them in any case. 'I like a passing game and that's how we play. We will never adopt tactics of kicking the ball up the park in my time here,' he said.

He was determined that it would be business as usual at Ibrox, for all the turmoil caused by the departure of Souness: 'Things will be done exactly as before. I was responsible for the day-to-day running of the team anyway.'

It may have been a seamless transition, but Smith could not have inherited the side at a more perilous time – despite their place at the top of the table. For weeks they had haemorrhaged points as they suffered an unprecedented run of injuries and suspensions that decimated the squad. Two matches against Celtic in the closing weeks saw the dismissal and suspension of three players. Oleg Kuznetsov, the £1.4 million signing from Dynamo Kiev was lost to Rangers with a bad knee injury just weeks into his Ibrox career. Trevor Steven and Ian Durrant were also long-term injury worries. Terry Butcher had left the club early in the season and poor form pushed Mo Johnson to the sidelines. Smith's worries were compounded by a suspension for Richard Gough. And there were others who were unavailable.

At one stage in the season, Rangers had an apparently unassailable lead. When Smith took over with just four games left, Rangers had the slenderest of leads over Alex Smith's Aberdeen who were on a charge with seventeen points taken out of a possible eighteen.

The new manager's first game in charge was against St Mirren at Love Street. He fielded the best players available to him in a makeshift side which included some youngsters and players newly returned from a long spell out of the side. With the game drifting towards a goalless draw, young Sandy Robertson popped up with only seven minutes to spare to give Smith the perfect start to his management career.

Although the Love Street victory preserved their lead, the team lost out to Motherwell two weeks later in the penultimate game of the season. It left Aberdeen ahead in the race with one game to go. The two sides were locked together on 53 points with the same goal difference, but Aberdeen had scored two goals more to give them the edge in the championship. The final game, ironically, would be Rangers v Aberdeen in one of the most thrilling finales the League race had ever seen. The Dons needed only a point to secure the title. Rangers needed the victory.

Smith recalled that his men went into the match in the worst possible shape. 'We just didn't have a team. We couldn't name the team until the Friday morning because we just didn't know who would make it. Boys like John Brown showed enormous courage. He was desperate to play and risked a bad injury by playing, and did eventually go down, tearing his calf completely. We were in a shambolic condition. By the end we had Terry Hurlock, a midfielder, at left-back, and striker Mark Hateley wide on the left, but we still managed to give a team their first defeat in twenty-odd games. That day taught me the power that supporters can generate. I had never felt an atmosphere like that. You could have cut it with a knife. If a team could get carried along then that team were carried along by the crowd that day.'

Mark Hateley, who had joined the club at the beginning of the season but failed to excite the fans, was the hero, scoring both goals in the Ibrox side's 2–0 victory as Rangers put aside a shaky start to send the Light Blues fans into raptures. Smith sighed with relief. The title had not been his to win, but it was certainly his to lose in the eyes of his doubters. Had he not succeeded, his credibility would have been severely dented. He may even have been irreparably damaged.

Smith survived, however, and proved much to the fans and to himself. Rarely would a manager be subjected to such pressure. 'The match gave me a chance to show the fans that I could handle that situation,' he admitted. 'The championship was important, but in a selfish kind of a way, the match had that other perspective for me.'

He prevailed with a side that was so makeshift that the eleven who performed that day had never before played together and who, despite their success, would never appear together again. Smith praised the character and determination in the side that suffered more injuries on the day and celebrated at the end like walking wounded on VE Day.

THE THREE-FOREIGNER RULE

Fresh from his championship success, Smith began his preparations for the new season in Scotland and Europe. In the latter he was hindered by a UEFA rule change that restricted the number of 'foreign' players who could appear in the side to a maximum of four initially and then eventually three. This presented major difficulties to the new boss – he had inherited 12 foreign players from Souness. Souness himself had failed to guide Rangers to any real success in European competition, their best showing being a European Cup quarter-final appearance. But for a club that had been for so long in the domestic doldrums, the Scottish championship more than compensated for the disappointments in Europe. Walter Smith's tenure was quite different. To a club that was becoming acquainted with championship glory, the demands for some tangible return on the transfer investment were growing. Smith found his hands tied, however, by the UEFA rule change. It was a major issue for the manager to address. If Rangers were to make any impact in Europe, they would have to change the squad and signing policy completely. Where Souness had quite happily scoured the English League and abroad for players, Smith needed to assemble a team for Europe that contained a minimum of eight Scots. It was a major problem. Smith had to find the right quality of players while releasing others from the Ibrox books.

Even though just three foreigners would be able to play in European ties, Smith could not afford to dispense with the bulk of his foreign stars – for all the desire to make some headway in Europe, he still had to nurture a side capable of maintaining the momentum in Scotland. He and Souness had been aware of the impending change for some time, and moves for some players were already under way by the time Smith took over. It was the new manager who would have to play the cards he had been dealt, though.

One of the first casualties of the ruling was Chris Woods, who lost his place when Scotland international goalkeeper Andy Goram arrived from Hibernian with a £1 million price-tag. Smith's reasoning was simple: foreign players in outfield positions had more versatility. A foreign goalkeeper, for all his ability, took up one of three valuable places. Woods would have to go. Trevor Steven was also on his way out, transferred to Marseille for around £5 million. Smith wanted to keep the former Everton star – he was one of his best, if not *the* best player at Ibrox at that time – but the money offered by the French side was too attractive to turn down.

Maurice Johnston also left in October 1991 in a £1.75 million move that took him to Everton. The striker had failed to recapture the form he showed in his first season at Ibrox and his departure represented good business for Rangers. Mark Walters rejoined Souness at Liverpool in a deal worth around £1.25 million.

Completely disproving the theories of those who suggested he could not attract the top names, Smith signed Alexei Mikhailitchenko from Sampdoria for £2.2 million. It was a major coup for the manager, who had shown that Rangers were the attraction and not Souness, even though money was undoubtedly the lure. David Robertson also came in at a cost of around £970,000 from Aberdeen, followed by Stuart McCall for £1.2 million from Everton and Dale Gordon from Norwich for a similar fee.

In the first few months of season 1991–92, Smith had been very active in the transfer market, bringing in six new players to his first-team squad and shedding eight. Despite the UEFA restrictions on foreigners, his changes did not markedly increase his room options in the side. He had a fundamental problem: he wanted to increase the number of Scots in the pool but he could not afford to compromise the quality of the squad. When he took over at Ibrox he had 12 foreigners on his books. By the end of the season, he had reduced that number to nine, but key players like Stevens, Hateley, Spackman, Huistra and Mikhailitchenko remained at the core of his side.

Smith's first European match in charge was a first-round Champions' Cup tie away to Sparta Prague. Shedding Mikhailitchenko from the side, Rangers were comfortable if not entirely impressive until a bad misjudgement by the new keeper gave the Czechs the only goal. Goram made a vain attempt to reach a swinging cross that swirled over his head and into the top corner of the net. Rangers were disappointed but felt that in the return leg they could easily overcome a side that one of the players reckoned was 'no better than a pub team'. But they didn't: when the Czechs scored early on to gain a vital away goal, Rangers were left scrambling. A 2–1 victory was not enough to overcome Sparta, who went through on away goals.

Smith recalled the criticism from one Scottish commentator, who reckoned that Sparta Prague 'looked like a village amateur team'. Smith said, 'He criticised us for not being able to beat them, but they went on to knock out Barcelona in the next round and do well in the competition. I was disappointed at the time, but looking back I should have expected the problems we had in the early stages. It was a bedding-in period for the side which had a lot of new players.'

Disappointed but not disheartened, Smith continued to pursue the prize that he considered would always be Rangers' goal – the championship. The Premier League was increased to twelve teams, meaning that there would be 44 games in the title race. It was to be a long hard season for a Rangers side that remained plagued by injuries, but it proved a successful one. The prolific striking partnership of McCoist and Hateley plagued defences up and down the country as they notched 55 League goals between them, McCoist hitting his best total of 34. His season's tally of 41 earned him Player of the Year awards from the Scottish Sportswriters and also from the Scottish Professional Footballers' Association. The player who had been used inconsistently by Souness was unbridled. He rewarded Smith with a lethal touch that proved vital to the side.

The Scottish Cup was also secured in a 2–1 victory over Airdrie in a final that proved something of an anticlimax after one of the most dramatic cup-ties in years against Celtic. Minutes into the semi-final at Hampden Rangers had found themselves reduced to just ten men when Davie Robertson was dismissed for a challenge on Celtic winger Joe Miller. Robertson later said that he had been told by Smith to put in a hefty challenge on Miller early in the game, but he completely mistimed his tackle and body-checked his opponent.

In torrential rain, a reorganised ten-man Rangers swept into the lead with a first-half goal from arch-predator McCoist. Through-out the remainder of the match, they fought off a Celtic onslaught. Celtic threw everything at Rangers but created few clear-cut chances. It was a vital game for Smith and his men. He said, 'After that night we had the inclination that we were not involved with an ordinary team. There might have been a lot of other teams in Europe with far better players, but this team stuck together, worked together and didn't like getting beaten. That night at Hampden was a tremendous performance.' He knew that the team had incredible spirit and resilience. The match confirmed that they had the will and determination to succeed. It was a spirit he carefully nurtured.

1992–93: A SEASON TO SAVOUR

Smith had won the double in his first full season as manager. It was a great achievement given the introduction of so many new players and the troubles of an unrelenting injury list. On the transfer front he had spent just over £7 million, but his income from transfers, boosted by the Stevens deal, brought him over £10 million. Smith had shown prudence in the transfer market and had continued the momentum at home that had been begun by Souness. Rangers were now celebrating their fourth successive championship. The thoughts of some drifted towards Celtic's record of nine titles in a row, but that seemed too far in the future to contemplate. Walter

Smith was, however, moulding a side, his own side, that could continue for many years to come. What's more, he felt that they were on the verge of something bigger.

While the new boss enjoyed his championship success, life for Souness at Liverpool had not turned out as he expected. Indeed, his problems were far away from the football field. While Rangers celebrated their title win, Souness lay in intensive care a week after undergoing a triple heart bypass operation.

Smith entered the new 1992–93 season with further additions to his squad. Dave McPherson returned to Rangers from Hearts for £1.3 million as the manager made strenuous attempts to change the side's foreigner-to-Scots ratio. Trevor Steven also returned to Ibrox as Marseille failed to fulfil the terms of the transfer that had taken him to France a year earlier. Smith recouped some of his expenditure with the sale of Spencer, Rideout and Spackman for a combined fee of over £1.5 million.

It was to be a remarkable season for the Rangers boss. The team lost 3–4 at Dens Park in August in a thrilling League match against Dundee. From there, they put together a 44-game unbeaten run that saw them take the League Cup with a 2–1 win over Aberdeen in the final and sweep to the top of the League. But it was in Europe that Rangers really made their mark and proved that Smith had assembled a squad that was something special. Having disposed of Danish side Lyngby in the first qualifying round of the Champions' Cup, Rangers were paired with Leeds United for a place in the newly formed Champions' League set-up (incidentally, a format first promoted by Ibrox secretary Campbell Ogilvie).

In what was billed 'The Battle of Britain', Rangers defeated the English champions home and away in one of the most dramatic contests in years. With away fans barred from attending either of the two matches, it was an eerily silent Ibrox Stadium that saw Gary McAllister put Leeds ahead in the first minute of the first-leg tie. The Light Blues rallied with goals from McCoist and an own-goal by Leeds keeper Lukic, but the 2–1 lead seemed perilously slender to take to Elland Road.

There was so much at stake in the second leg for both sides, but particularly for Rangers and Smith. Forever taunted by the English press about the supposed lack of any real quality in the Scottish game, Rangers knew that failure would diminish their achievement of successive League titles. They also knew that if they were to achieve any recognition in the game they would have to qualify for the lucrative Champions' League to boost their international credibility and generate the funds that would allow the club to compete regularly and successfully at that level.

As Rangers headed south, the English media were already dismissing their chances. Even Leeds manager Howard Wilkinson appeared cocky and condescending. The players did not need any extra motivation from Smith – they were well fired up long before a ball was kicked.

Inside Elland Road an hour before kick-off, I met one of the Rangers officials who had just arrived with the team by coach. He told me that the mood among the players was 'electric, frightening even'. With the music they always played on the coach booming out, the players were vociferous and firmly focused. They were ready. It remained to be seen if Leeds could match them.

In a reflection of the Ibrox leg, Rangers stunned the Leeds fans with an opening goal from Mark Hateley, a man on his own mission to show that he was still a great striker despite being rejected by England boss Graham Taylor. The goal shocked Leeds and, despite heavy pressure, they could not breach the resilient Rangers defence. The Ibrox side sealed victory with a sweeping move on the counter-attack when McCoist reached to head a Hateley cross beyond Lukic. A late consolation goal from Leeds salvaged nothing. Rangers were through. They had beaten the English champions home and away.

If Rangers' victory over Leeds was impressive, it was only a taster for a Champions' League run that took them almost all the way to the final. Drawn in the same section as Marseille, CSKA Moscow and Bruges, Rangers continued their undefeated run to the penultimate game of the League phase needing a win to go through to the final. 'I used that as the basis of my team-talk to motivate the players. I told them that this was their chance. They almost took it,' Smith said.

Marseille had the same incentive. Despite going down in the second half, Rangers fought back to score an equaliser through Durrant. In the closing stages, Gary McSwegan had a chance to take the match for Rangers but the ball flew a foot wide of the post. The game ended 1–1 and Rangers went into the last game against CSKA knowing that their fate was no longer in their own hands. Marseille got the victory they needed to seal their place in the final, a game in which they triumphed over AC Milan.

Rangers went through their entire European campaign of ten matches undefeated. They failed at the final hurdle, although Marseille were to be later discredited and have the Cup stripped from them following a series of malpractice allegations with club president Bernard Tapie at the centre of most. There were rumours of match-fixing and even the CSKA coach told of attempts to bribe him. These were later withdrawn after threats of legal action from Marseille, but the rumours persisted. There was no recourse for Rangers, however, who sportingly acknowledged the French to be the better side. 'They were a good team,' Smith said. 'They gave us a lesson for an hour at Ibrox. They were terrific – could have been four goals up, but we came back. If there was anything going on behind the scenes with Marseille, so be it.'

With Europe gone, Smith turned his attention towards the championship, which could be secured a few days later with five matches remaining. The title was duly won at Airdrie's Broomfield Stadium, but Richard Gough's words in the aftermath sent out a chilling warning to their rivals that this fifth successive championship would not be their last. 'It's up to others to catch us because we will never get bored winning the title,' he said. 'We seem to get stronger each year, while others have got weaker. I would expect us to strengthen. I don't expect us to stand still and that means others will have to take up the challenge.'

Rangers went on to win the Scottish Cup and seal the treble with a 2–1 win over Aberdeen at Celtic Park. It had been a magical season for Smith, a season he called 'one of this club's best ever'. McCoist and Hateley remained the potent strikeforce that had devastated defences in the preceding season. Once again they scored a remarkable total of 88 goals between them, 55 of them coming in the League. McCoist was awarded his second Golden Boot as Europe's top goalscorer, but he suffered a broken leg in Portugal in April while on international duty.

Smith could look back on that season with a justifiable glow of satisfaction. He felt that the side had a special ingredient that was the essence of their success. 'It was chemistry. I can't put my finger on it, but it doesn't happen that often.' The side did gel, but although he could not precisely identify the magic of that side of 1992–93, it is important to recognise that the Rangers boss himself was the main motivating force in the success. Coping with a catalogue of injuries and the difficulties presented by a 44-game Premier League and lengthy Champions League competition, he still prevailed, sweeping almost all before him.

Rangers played a total of 64 competitive games that season, each one with something at stake. Most of the team played over 50 games and some missed only a handful throughout the season. It was a rewarding season, but it took its toll.

Smith at last enjoyed virtually unanimous approval from the masses and was hailed by some as the best manager the club had had. He was rewarded with a place on the board in a ringing endorsement from his peers. Souness was gone and forgotten. With five successive championships in the bag, Rangers dared to dream the dream – nine in a row.

THE MARCH TOWARDS NINE CONSECUTIVE TITLES

The success that Rangers enjoyed in 1992–93 was almost their undoing the following season, although they still managed to keep up the title run, winning their sixth successive championship and almost repeating the treble success of the previous term. Smith boosted his challenge with the acquisition of Gordon Durie for £1.2 million. Durie weighed in with 12 League goals at a crucial stage.

The ravages of the preceding term's long campaign created major injury worries for Smith. Robertson, McCoist, McPherson, Stevens, Brown and new signing Duncan Ferguson (a £3.75 million acquisition from Dundee United) all found themselves in the treatment-room for extended periods. If the success of 1992–93 was down to Smith's indefinable ingredient which he saw in the squad, the next season was a tribute to his own resourcefulness in managing a squad that was stretched to its limits.

Despite their injuries Rangers took the League Cup, but Europe was an immense disappointment following the success of the previous season. Needing to progress through a qualifying round to reach the final-phase group matches, they were paired with Bulgarian champions Levski Sofia. Smith's men should have progressed and were, at various stages, well set to win the tie, but they did not. A Levski goal in the dying minutes of the away leg put paid to Rangers' European ambitions for the season. It was a cruel blow to Smith who had watched his side surrender a 3–1 lead at Ibrox then come so close to the final phase of league matches with a disciplined display in Sofia only to have it snatched from them with a wonderful 30-yard goal from Todorov at the end.

The manager lamented the fatigue that afflicted the squad that year. 'We suffered a bit from the previous year when a lot of the players went through the season not missing many of our matches and then having internationals to contend with too. If you look at our team list you can see that we were short of regular players.' (The team read Maxwell, Stevens, Wishart, Gough, McPherson, McCall, Steven, Ferguson, Durrant, Hateley and Hagen.) But if Smith felt that Rangers were weakened, he was also keen to highlight that Levski were no Euro minnows. 'They had six players who had helped Bulgaria get to the World Cup semi-final, so it was no disgrace to be shaded out by them.'

Putting aside their European disappointment, Rangers met Dundee United at Hampden looking to secure a historic second successive treble. Their hopes were thwarted in the first half when a mix-up between goalkeeper Ally Maxwell and Dave McPherson gave United the easiest of chances to open the scoring. There were no more goals as a tired and jaded Rangers subsided.

Although they had not prevailed in the Scottish Cup, the League championship gave Rangers their seventh successive domestic trophy, a record of which Smith could be proud.

Smith's attention was now focused on two fronts – progression towards a possible nine in a row and a return to the success the club had enjoyed in Europe in 1992–93. Desperate to make some impact on Europe, he acquired Brian Laudrup for £2.7 million from Fiorentina and Basile Boli for £1.8 million from Marseille. The manager was investing heavily to try to further his European ambitions, but he wasn't spending more than he was earning. In his three years in control, he had spent in excess of £20 million on new players. That was balanced by selling others to the tune of around £20 million, a figure swelled by the departure of Dave McPherson to Hearts for £400,000 and Duncan Ferguson to Everton for £4.26 million. The latter was sold following a troubled spell that saw the striker end up in jail on an assault charge after an off-the-ball incident in a game against Raith Rovers.

The signing of Laudrup was a master stroke by Smith. The Danish winger had become disillusioned with football after a torrid spell with Fiorentina when he suffered a backlash from the Italian fans who had lost patience with their troubled side. A loan spell to AC Milan failed to placate him. A star of Denmark's successful European Championship-winning side of 1992, Laudrup was internationally renowned, having served Brondby, Bayer Uerdingen and then Bayern Munich. He had won great success in Germany, being nominated 'best foreign player' shortly after he arrived there at the age of 21. When Fiorentina failed to make any impact in Seria A, Laudrup was one of a few foreign players who were singled out for abuse by the baying fans. Fearful for the very safety of his family, he moved them out of the region while he made the best of a situation he could do little to alter. He wanted out but when Walter Smith made approaches to sign him, the Dane was reluctant. He took counsel from his father and brother Michael who was then with Barcelona. They advised him against the Scottish League, but Laudrup was encouraged to visit Ibrox by Smith and Murray. What he saw and what he heard were enough to convince him that Rangers were the type of friendly club he needed as he tried to get his football career back on the tracks.

While Smith had turned up an ace in Laudrup, the Boli signing hardly proved to be a trump card. From the moment he arrived, he looked nothing like the formidable player Rangers had faced a season earlier in Marseille. A misfit, he seemed off the fast pace of Scottish football and prone to making errors. Laudrup was every-thing that Boli was not.

It has often been said that Rangers are always just a match or so away from crisis. If Walter Smith enjoyed the plaudits of the past seasons and his run of seven successive trophies, he had little time to revel in his achievements before the hawks began to gather again. In perhaps one of the worst weeks in the club's history, the team tumbled out of Europe in the qualifying round, lost to Falkirk in the League Cup and were then beaten by Celtic in the first Old Firm clash of the season. The disappointment was compounded by the fact that all three games were played at Ibrox.

The defeat against AEK Athens in the Champions' League was hard for most to stomach. It was the second year in succession that Rangers had failed to qualify for the league stages, losing out on revenue estimated at around £5 million. Each season the Light Blues fans entered the fray with great optimism as the club paraded big-money signings, fulfilling David Murray's philosophy of always changing the menu. For a club that had now come to expect to win the championship, defeat in Europe at an early stage was unacceptable.

Smith came in for pointed criticism for his tactical approach to the first-leg match which ended in a 2–0 defeat. Having played the opening games of the season in his routine back-four formation, Smith shifted to five at the back. There were claims that none of the players was familiar with their changed role and it was folly to experiment in such an important tie. 'I adjusted the formation to accommodate the players we acquired,' Smith explained. It did not work, but he suffered more criticism from one of his own players after the return leg, where Rangers could not overturn the deficit, losing 0–1. Smith had deployed Basile Boli on the right flank and the Frenchman later claimed in his country's press that he had been played out of position. Boli suggested that Laudrup had also been critical, a statement that incensed Laudrup who denied making any criticism of the manager.

Smith was angered by the situation. 'We were short of cover on the right and Boli actually volunteered to play there, telling us that he had done so many times for Marseille and had scored a few goals from that position. It was a bit rich to hear him criticise me later after it was he who suggested the move in the first place. As usual with many foreign players, he later claimed to have been misquoted,' explained Smith.

The supporters were not appeased. But the week had more woes in store. The defeats by Falkirk and Celtic left the fans and Smith troubled. The massive expenditure to lure Laudrup and Boli to Ibrox was intended to give the club a decent run in Europe. With only two weeks gone, they were out of two of the four competitions they contested.

With no Cup football (they exited the Scottish Cup in February), Rangers put aside their early-season disappointments and customary injury woes to concentrate on the one thing the fans did care for: another championship to add to their run in the quest for nine. Led by the magical Laudrup who was playing like something of a free spirit, he danced around defenders and contributed his fair share of goals in a series of performances that had the likes of former wing hero Davie Cooper singing his praises. No one could touch him, or a Rangers side inspired by him. The club won the title by fifteen points from second-placed Motherwell.

Smith paid tribute to the players who had carried the side through a troubled season. Of Laudrup, he said, 'Brian has settled in very quickly and has had outstanding performances throughout the season. His form has without doubt been the highlight.' Of the others, he added, 'In the early part of the season Andy Goram, Richard Gough, David Robertson, Stuart McCall, Mark Hateley and Brian Laudrup were called on to produce their best form to help the team. It is to their credit that they did just that.'

Winning the title vindicated Laudrup's move to Scotland. He said, 'For the first time I have found a manager and team that give me all the back-up and support I need.' Laudrup was an international star without question, but Rangers needed more players of his quality. Midway through the close-season they dramatically signed Paul Gascoigne from Lazio for a fee of around £4.3 million.

It was a risk for the club, but a calculated one. The player's career had been plagued by injury and controversy, but these flaws reduced his price-tag. If he could reach top form, the club would have a player worth considerably more than what they had paid for him.

Smith was convinced that Gascoigne could do a job for Rangers. He had met the player two years earlier while on holiday in Florida. The two had built up a friendship which became crucial in Gascoigne's decision to come to Rangers when other clubs, including Arsenal, were interested in buying him from the Italians. 'I obviously thought about other clubs, but that was before I knew Rangers were in for me,' Gascoigne said. 'When I met Walter Smith it only took me minutes to decide. And there was no messing about with the chairman either.'

Exuberant after their championship success, the fans were refreshed by the arrival of the larger-than-life Gascoigne. Who could stop them now, they thought. 'Gazza's here for nine in a row,' they sang.

If the fans eagerly anticipated the new season, the meticulous Smith reviewed the campaign past, looking to make a greater impact on Europe than in the past couple of years. His team would have to play an early-season qualifying round before they could even think about progressing in the tournament. He could not afford to fail.

Smith put the poor early form of the previous season down to the club's close-season preparations. He reckoned that they had travelled too much in the pre-season, playing matches in Denmark and Germany after their initial sessions in Italy. They would concentrate on local matches in the future. On the injury front, Smith was faced with the disruption of his striking partnership of McCoist and Hateley which had brought so many goals in the previous years. Throughout the season the pair did not play an entire ninety minutes together. Hateley's time had come and gone. In the summer he moved south to Queens Park Rangers.

Persistent injuries to key players plagued Smith throughout his tenure, bringing criticism that the Ibrox training methods were flawed and that the backroom staff were incapable of serving the players' needs. The manager bitterly refuted these suggestions, pointing instead to the heavy match schedule that the players had to endure. 'Most of the injuries have been wear and tear,' he said. 'When players are getting into their late twenties and early thirties they're bound to suffer with the demands of modern football.'

While most players had no particular complaints about the training, some later expressed dissatisfaction with the diagnoses they received for serious injuries and the treatment they subsequently received at Ibrox. These alleged misdiagnoses only came to light when they moved on to other clubs.

Regardless of any individual problems, there is little doubt that Smith and his backroom staff were subjected to criticism that was patently unfair given the heavy schedule of matches they had to endure, particularly with the shift to a 44-game Premier League. They were also extremely unlucky with a number of injuries to key players – injuries that could be put down to more bad luck and circumstance than anything related to the Ibrox backroom.

Despite this, the team did maintain their magnificent championship run and, with season 1994–95 heralding title number seven, there was a growing awareness that Celtic's remarkable record of nine could be reached and perhaps even surpassed. The club's objectives became increasingly divided. The purists saw progress and success in Europe as the *raison d'être*. For the loyal footsoldier, whose attention never strayed from what was happening on the other side of the city, the number nine was the prize, the stuff of dreams. Walter Smith had to satisfy both camps, but he became increasingly aware that while Europe was a season-to-season challenge, the quest for the nine was a once-in-a-lifetime opportunity. To win would remove one of the monkeys that had sat on the club's back since the day Jock Stein's team completed the sequence for Celtic. To fail would diminish Rangers' succession of championships secured to date.

Smith knew his side had a real chance of matching Celtic's achievement. So did Murray. But while winning nine titles in a row would appease the fans and provide an opportunity for some commercial spin-offs, the real money lay in Europe. 'Two years without the Champions' League has meant no money for the club,' Murray said. 'We need to play in Europe from both a football and a financial point of view. If we make it next season it'll be worth £5 million to the club and that's why our accounts showed a healthy profit three years ago.'

Murray knew that he had to make some money available to the manager to enable the club to progress in Europe. Concerns had been raised by some doubters that Rangers were not capable of competing at the highest level. 'We'll spend £8 million net on players during the next few months,' announced the chairman. Eager to drive the club forward to achieve its aims on every front, he launched an initiative named 'My Blue Heaven' which was designed to raise the capital for investment in the squad and finance some additional redevelopment of the stadium.

The new additions included Oleg Salenko, Steven Wright, Gordan Petric and Derek McInnes. While it was hoped that the injection of finance would help to stimulate Rangers, the recent acquisitions, excepting Gascoigne, did little to improve Smith's squad. Steven Wright was lost to injury a few months into the season, Salenko looked a shadow of the player his reputation had suggested, and both Petric and McInnes, while solid players, were hardly the quality needed to help the side make any impact on Europe. From being a side of good players with excellent teamwork and spirit, Rangers were becoming a club dominated by the class of key individuals. At the heart of it all were Gascoigne and Laudrup, ably supported by the resilient Gough and dependable Andy Goram. As Smith later conceded, his key players helped to 'paper over the cracks which were appearing in the side'.

They helped Rangers to qualify for the Champions' League after narrowly defeating Anorthosis of Cyprus in the qualifying round, but the League stages of the competition proved somewhat disappointing. A poor start to the campaign with an away defeat from Steau Bucharest was followed by a draw against Borussia Dortmund at Ibrox then a double whammy from Juventus. Clearly outclassed, they succumbed to the Italian champions in a tortuous first half when they lost four goals. Although Gough pulled one back, Rangers never looked at ease. Despite a more spirited performance at Ibrox, the Light Blues again lost four, and went down without reply.

There was little point in stating that Rangers were not in the class of Juventus but Smith did venture that his men were in the middle group of teams with the likes of Dortmund, who had failed to beat the Ibrox side over the two legs. Regardless of where they were ranked either by opinion or the complicated UEFA co-efficients that decided their seeding each year, Rangers had not made any significant impact on Europe, despite their expenditure.

The team continued to dominate on the home front, however. Inspired by the genius of Laudrup and the inimitable but often wayward Gascoigne, Rangers swept to the championship, sealing it in dramatic fashion against Aberdeen in the penultimate game of the season. Needing all three points to secure the title but level at 1–1 with nine minutes remaining, Gascoigne picked the ball up deep in his own half then launched forward in a run that took him past several despairing Dons defenders before he carefully placed the ball in the net. A penalty near the end completed his hat-trick and gave Rangers an eighth championship.

For the first time in several years, Celtic offered the main challenge to the Ibrox team as they put boardroom problems behind them to try to thwart Rangers' hopes of achieving the nine. The Parkhead side, bossed by old Celtic favourite Tommy Burns, had a remarkable season, losing just one League match (to Rangers), but still they could not overcome Smith's men.

The title won, Rangers went on to complete the double with victory over Hearts by five goals to one, with Gordon Durie snatching a hat-trick in a final that was orchestrated by Laudrup. The season was a personal triumph for Smith. He had seen some of his old faithfuls depart the scene but had juggled his resources to maintain the winning formula. He had even changed his defensive formation, switching to three at the back instead of the four that had brought him so much success in the early years.

NINE IN A ROW

Of the 31 players Smith used in his first season in charge just five years earlier, only five now remained: Richard Gough, John Brown, Ally McCoist, Ian Ferguson and Ian Durrant. He had built and rebuilt his team over and over again. Now, with his ageing stars nearing the end of their careers, he prepared for the most important season in the club's history – the year in which they hoped to seal the long-desired ninth title in succession.

Walter Smith added Joachim Bjorklund (£3 million) and Jorg Albertz (£4 million) to his squad in the close-season. Over at Parkhead, meanwhile, Tommy Burns, determined to preserve Celtic's record of nine titles, bought Alan Stubbs for £3.5 million and Paolo di Canio for £1 million. The battle lines were drawn. Titles were not always won on the results of Old Firm clashes, but the resurgence of Celtic in the previous year showed that the destiny of the championship would rest heavily on the outcome of the great Glasgow derbies.

Before Rangers could even consider the outcome of the title race, however, they had Champions' League business to attend to. Again it was dismal for Rangers as they tumbled out following a series of unimpressive performances against Grasshopper Zurich, Auxerre and Ajax. The match against the Dutch champions was particularly disappointing for Smith. He watched any hopes of a result in the Amsterdam Arena disappear down the tunnel with Gascoigne as the midfielder headed off with a red card high in the air behind him after an off-the-ball kick at Ajax defender Winston Bogarde. Gascoigne found no support from his team-mates. McCoist called it 'inexcusable'; Gough bemoaned the difficulty the side had playing against the Dutch with eleven men let alone ten.

Smith suffered further criticism of his tactics and his failure to make an impact on Europe. Clearly irked, he recently pointed out that it was often overlooked that on most occasions teams win quite simply because they are better: 'Every time Ajax win a match, is it because the other team gets the tactics wrong?'

On the quality of Rangers compared to other European sides, he added, 'It was interesting to hear Dick Advocaat suggest that Rangers cannot win the European Cup considering the value of players that the club can realistically afford compared to the top sides in Europe. If Dick feels that, having some money at his disposal and with no restriction on the number of foreign players, you can imagine that expectations were perhaps too high during my period with less to spend and a three-foreigner rule to contend with.'

Smith faced an altogether different situation on his return to Glasgow when he was confronted with press coverage of an altercation Gascoigne had had with his wife Sheryl at Gleneagles Hotel. It was the final straw for many fans who had become increasingly concerned at the well-publicised antics of the player. Smith had always publicly stood by the player's side, out of sympathy with him for the unrelenting media fascination with his life. In a world where there was rarely any privacy, Gazza was an easy target for hacks seeking controversy.

And Gascoigne was not Smith's only problem. Rumours of players nightclubbing and drinking caused concern that discipline inside Ibrox was waning. When some members of the team were caught drink-driving, this feeling was confirmed. The issue was raised at AGMs but Smith continued to defend his players and the way he treated them. To those on the outside, it seemed that he was weak on discipline. In fact the opposite was true. The players knew when they had let him down and he enforced a series of sanctions on players who stepped out of line, but everything was done behind closed doors. It was Smith's way, and a code of silence among the players ensured that little left the dressing-room to fuel stories of misbehaviour behind the scenes. Indeed, while Celtic were crippled by a series of controversies leaked from within, their rivals remained tight-lipped on most issues.

In the goldfish bowl that is Glasgow, any players out for the evening inevitably came under the spotlight and when they did gather for some celebration or other, stories exaggerating their behaviour would occasionally appear. While a few did sometimes go overboard, the players were generally responsible and there was a deep-seated belief within the dressing-room that they were more often than not misrepresented by the media. In truth, Rangers were no different from most clubs in this respect and the players did mix socially. Although this was worrying, it was also an important part of Smith's management style. He bonded with the players, especially those who had known him from the earliest days of his managerial career. Richard Gough once famously said: 'The team that drinks together wins together.' It may not have made much sense in terms of physical conditioning, but what Gough meant was the incredible team spirit that grew within the squad. Smith had engendered this spirit. It was the essence of his team and their success. So long as they remained with clearly defined bounds, the sessions were accepted and to an extent encouraged.

Smith feels that the whole issue of the players' behaviour was exaggerated. 'The players were too open at times for their own good. When they talked about bonding and drinking together it was easy for people to misconstrue that, but there was a culture about the Scottish player that doesn't really exist since the influx of foreigners. There were never any complaints about behaviour when the side were winning, but in the last couple of seasons when the pressures started to mount, the stories came out. But it was certainly exaggerated.

'It was true that they had built up a tight bond in the dressing-room, and that worked in our favour. Interestingly, when Celtic won the championship, they spoke about how their boys got together for a drink and that it had helped them to bond. It was always okay when you were winning.

'When they did actually cross the line on what was acceptable, we dealt with it, but never publicly.'

Smith was walking a tightrope with his *laissez-faire* attitude. While the team were on top, criticism of the discipline inside Ibrox was muted. When the side lost, particularly in Europe, the questions about how prepared the Ibrox stars were started again like an old gramophone record. The dissent was infectious and grew, especially among the older fans who recalled the days of Symon and Struth. Concerns were also raised in the boardroom.

In the case of Gascoigne, who was at the heart of most of the controversy that affected the club during the 1996–97 season and the previous year, there were real practical considerations for Smith and Murray. Had the player been less influential, he may well have found himself on the first train out of Ibrox, but Gascoigne was important to Rangers. They had a championship to win. Like it or not, that would dictate the priorities of the Rangers boss. For all his flaws, the player would not be sacrificed to safeguard the club's reputation. Smith stood by him because he had a genuine liking and sympathy for the player. In addition, he quite simply needed him.

With Europe behind them and Gascoigne's endless troubles set aside, Smith focused on a championship that placed unprecedented levels of stress on him and Celtic boss Tommy Burns. Rangers took first blood in the championship clashes with Celtic, then added another win over their rivals with victory at Parkhead. Ahead in the title race, Smith bought Sebastian Rozental for £2.2 million from Chilean side Universidad Cattolica; haggling over the terms delayed the player's move until January, however. Rozental had been sourced by the club's new senior scout, former Celt and Liverpool boss Kenny Dalglish. The presence of Dalglish seemed to represent a threat to Smith and the manager bristled at interviews when the announcement of the appointment was made.

At the end of November, Rangers met Hearts in the final of the Coca-Cola League Cup at Parkhead, a match that was of some significance to Smith, not just for the explosive second-half performance of Gascoigne who scored two goals to help the Light Blues to a 4–3 win. As the Rangers players took their customary bows in front of the fans there was a sense of apathy in the air. The supporters were happy, but the outpouring of joy that they showed in the early years of Smith's tenure was not evident. Rangers had become victims of their own success. Although the importance of the League Cup had certainly diminished over the years, it was still a trophy and one of the major domestic honours. The fans had simply come to expect success. Even Smith felt that there was something missing. He was to reflect on that day later.

By the New Year, Rangers had chalked up another victory over Celtic as they marched into an apparently unassailable fourteen-point lead in the championship. Meanwhile Tommy Burns made some pointed remarks regarding refereeing decisions that he regarded had been crucial in the outcome of two of the Old Firm matches. Smith remained dignified and detached from the controversy, but the pressure was building on both managers.

As the teams neared their final clash of the season, scheduled for Celtic Park, injury troubles for Rangers disrupted the side and Tommy Burns' men had closed the gap to just five points. Celtic gained a psychological edge by putting the Light Blues out of the Scottish Cup just nine days before the match that the press were calling 'the biggest Old Firm game of the century'. Smith, troubled by injuries and loss of form to front players, recalled Mark Hateley from Queens Park Rangers just two days before the game. The big striker was well past his best but he had a physical presence and experience that would be vital at Parkhead and in the tense closing stages of the championship. With goalkeeper Andy Goram ruled out through injury, Rangers relied on Andy Dibble, on loan from Manchester City.

In one of the most dramatic games in years, Rangers snatched the lead when Ian Durrant broke past the opposing defence and lobbed Celtic keeper Stewart Kerr. As the ball bounced over the line Brian Laudrup raced in to ensure that it remained on course for the net and Rangers on course for the championship. Despite the dismissal of Hateley in the second half, Rangers held on to record their fourth win out of four against Celtic – a Premier League record, in the most vital of seasons.

At the end of the match the exuberance of the players led them into a huddle down at the corner of the Parkhead pitch, mocking the pre-match ritual that Celtic had adopted a few years earlier. Although only a few Celtic fans were still in the ground when this happened, Tommy Burns felt moved to criticise the behaviour of Smith's men.

'At the Cup game, Celtic did the huddle, for the first time to my knowledge, at the end of the match,' a raging Walter Smith retorted. 'That was to produce more embarrassment to Rangers' players, management and supporters. Our players didn't show any disrespect. It was to show that we can be together as well. If Celtic can do it and no one complains, why not Rangers?'

He went on, 'After we lost the Cup game, Celtic had the pleasure of reading the next day's papers with Rangers saying they deserved their victory. Yet, when we turn to Sunday's game, we're to blame for bad sportsmanship.'

It was a rare show of emotion from a manager who normally kept a dignified silence in front of the media that often belied the deep discontent that football inevitably brings. However, an Old Firm match is no ordinary match, and the final clash of season 1996–97 was quite extraordinary. Smith later admitted his regret over the war of words with Burns: 'I regret that two people in high office within the Old Firm became involved in a public debate of that nature, but it was not of my doing, although I still regret what happened.'

The victory over Celtic was not in itself enough to give Rangers the title, but the championship was sealed a few weeks later when a rare Brian Laudrup header gave the Light Blues a 1–0 victory over Dundee United at Tannadice and the points they needed. The dream that few had dared to dream just a few years earlier had been realised. The words that had been banned from even being mentioned within the Ibrox dressing-room were now shouted throughout the land – 'nine in a row'.

In his moment of glory, Smith paid tribute to the Celtic side which won nine successive championships in the 1960s and 1970s: 'During the period I've been Rangers manager, Celtic's achievement has become even greater in my eyes because I know what Mr Stein had to go through to do it. He suffered the same thing that by winning [the Championship] so often it becomes devalued, because it becomes accepted by everyone. But you cannot devalue your championship.'

A SEASON TOO FAR

His goal achieved, Smith set his sights on a tenth championship. But if the pressures of the quest for nine in a row were relieved, there would be no respite in the demands for success in Europe, particularly since the manager had a massive cash injection at his disposal. David Murray had converted the revenue from a share transfer, delivering £40 million to be spent buying players and on various commercial ventures including the servicing and elimination of some of the club's mounting debt.

Smith set about a complete revamping of the squad and finding a replacement for his captain, Richard Gough, who bowed out to continue his career in the United States. David Robertson also left to join Leeds United. Brian Laudrup looked to be heading for Ajax before Murray and Smith convinced the star that he should remain at Ibrox for the final year of his contract. It was a huge gamble by Murray, who realised that he would forgo the fee of around £4 million that the Dutch side had offered, leaving Laudrup the opportunity to depart for no transfer fee at the end of the season. Laudrup was moved that he was valued so highly by the club and decided to put his departure on hold, to the dismay of Ajax.

With bulging pockets from Murray's smart financial manoeuvring, Smith zealously entered the transfer market, acquiring Marco Negri, Lorenzo Amoruso, Sergio Porrini, Jonas Thern, Tony Vidmar and Staale Stensaas for a total of £14 million. It was a massive injection of new talent, but there were concerns that the manager might have difficulties attaining a balance and a blend with so many new players.

Smith's problem with the new recruits was not in assimilating them into the side, but something more fundamental. Amoruso hardly kicked a ball for Rangers before a lingering ankle injury necessitated surgery. Thern was another who suffered a catalogue of injuries, but principally some ligament damage that ultimately ended his Ibrox career. Negri burst on to the scene, scoring a remarkable total of 30 League goals by Christmas before disappearing from the scene amidst rumours of a rift with Amoruso.

The boost that the fans had received with the announcement of Smith's new signings evaporated amid the despair of failure in the early stages of the side's quest for European success. It had become clear that nothing less than qualifying for the later stages of the Champions' League would be enough for a club that had invested heavily with no tangible return beyond Scotland's shores. Rangers' hopes of progressing in the tournament were lost in a miserable performance in Gothenburg where they conceded three goals without reply and failed to overturn the deficit in the return leg.

With automatic qualification to the UEFA Cup, there was at least the thought that a good run in this tournament could bring greater revenues through television rights than may have been on offer from the Champions League. It seemed scant consolation, but it also assumed progress and, with French side Strasbourg in their way, Rangers' European form hardly gave any comfort that there would be a future in the competition.

Their first-leg performance was a continuation of the anticlimax and disappointment that had punctuated the Ibrox side's Euro ambitions in the previous five years of Smith's management. Going down 2–0, the team had a mountain to climb if they were going to progress. I spoke to a dejected Smith in the airport outside the French city as the sombre party assembled for the journey back to Glasgow. He talked of the early-season injury to Amoruso that had wrecked his plans for the Rangers defence. 'He was to be the cornerstone, but we have no one with that kind of influence available,' he rued.

In truth, Smith never got the benefit of the players he signed. Shortly after the Strasbourg match he sat down to talk about the future with David Murray. 'We chatted around the subject, but generally agreed that it would be better if I finished. I had had my day and it was time to move on. I considered that I would leave there and then, but the chairman asked me to stay until the end of the season to try to get the "ten in a row". He suggested that I announce my intention to leave at the AGM. I agreed that it may be best, because many of the players were out of contract at the end of the season and would leave. I felt it would be better for them to realise that we were all going together. I thought that we might get that extra bit of togetherness that could drive us to the title. Archie [Knox] disagreed. He wanted to leave it until the end of the season.'

Smith delivered his historic speech to the hushed shareholders inside Glasgow's Royal Concert Hall. 'When I started, I could not have been prouder and we had a very successful first three years including the great run in Europe,' he told them. 'That pleased me, but the expectations of the club became greater every year on us to win the championship.

'Last season could have been better than it was, and when it wasn't to be, the players and the manager had to bear the brunt of that. Bad performances led to a lot of criticism, especially when we lost to Strasbourg this season, and there were calls for the manager to leave. I accept that me being the manager may lead to problems with the playing staff.'

Talking about his disappointment that the Coca-Cola Cup win over Hearts was seemingly taken for granted, he went on, 'There is no divine right for this club to continue to be successful. I have decided I would like to leave at the end of the season, regardless of what happens.'

David Murray paid tribute to Smith: 'This is the end of an exhilarating era and all the success of the last decade would certainly not have happened without Walter. He will go down as one of the greatest managers in the history of Rangers. In the shareholders' meeting I genuinely had a tear in my eye when Walter walked on to the stage to a standing ovation. When he told me of his intentions, it was one of the saddest days in my chairmanship of Rangers.'

Walter Smith believed that his players would bond with him in the knowledge that many of them would leave at the end of the season. Most did, but the spirit of the dressing-room sagged as the new players arrived and failed to deliver and Rangers' title challenge stuttered. With Richard Gough called back from Kansas as Smith desperately tried to consolidate his defence in the absence of Amoruso, Rangers were troubled. Injuries and suspensions interrupted Gascoigne's influence. Laudrup, too, was a shadow of the player he'd been in previous years as he succumbed to illness and injury. The players that Smith had used to paper over the cracks in the side in the last few years were debilitated. The new arrivals were largely ineffectual.

Ahead of Celtic in the title race at Christmas, Rangers slipped into second place by February. The championship challenge virtually ground to a halt in March when three successive draws and then defeat at Motherwell left the Ibrox side trailing. Celtic were themselves unconvincing, but held out for victory on the last day of the season. They won the title but there is little doubt that it was parcelled up in blue ribbons by Rangers. Smith recalled, 'We were about twelve points short of the total that gave us the nine in a row, but Celtic won by just two points in that final season. We effectively gave them it.'

One controversial moment in the closing stages of the season was the sale of Paul Gascoigne to Middlesbrough for a fee of around £2.5 million. The fans were torn about the wisdom of the move. On the face of it, the deal looked good: Murray, chastened by the loss of revenue on the Laudrup deal, had an opportunity to get some money for a player whose value would be significantly diminished by the end of the season. The Teesside club made it clear that they could not wait until then. It was a dilemma for Rangers: the midfielder was inspirational, but his form leading up to his departure was disappointing. The club decided to cash in.

Whether the move was wise at such a critical stage is still the subject of much debate. Critics would point to the fact that the side failed to land the title, but it should also be recognised that Gazza played in two of the three games in late February–early March when Rangers surrendered six points. Opinion will forever be divided on the wisdom of the move.

The championship lost and dreams of ten titles in a row washed away in sadness, Smith and Rangers turned towards the Scottish Cup final at Celtic Park. They went into the match against Hearts without Jorg Albertz who was suspended after lashing out in frustration at a Dundee United player in the final League game. The disappointment of the season was carried into the Cup final with Rangers going down 1–2 to a spirited Hearts side.

Television evidence confirmed the match to be a tale of two penalties, one given, one not. Rangers were incredibly unlucky. They conceded a dubious penalty in the opening minute and then had a valid claim of their own turned down in the latter stages as they pushed for an equaliser. At the final whistle, many of the team slumped to the ground in tears. 'It remains my biggest disappointment in football,' said Smith. 'I felt for them. This was their last game and I wanted them to go out on a high.'

There was no happy ending for him or the men who had shared so much glory in the past. As he left Parkhead that evening, the curtains had come down on an era, one that was arguably the most successful in the history of Rangers. Smith had 12 great years at Ibrox. In seven of these he carried the challenge to win the nine in a row and fulfilled his dream. It was a glorious spell in the club, one in which the trophies came so thick and fast that the achievement of winning became diminished – almost expected – such was Rangers' dominance of the game.

If Europe was often disappointing, it also brought some memorable moments, none more so than in the great run of season 1992–93. That Smith failed to make the impact that everyone, including himself, had hoped, is as much down to circumstance as to any failing on the part of the manager. Crippled by rules that limited the number of foreign players available to him, he balanced the desires of European success with the demands for the championship. Ultimately, domestic triumph was the most important. It was not always seen that way by others.

Smith closed the chapter on one of the most exciting periods in the club's history – a chapter that opened with the flamboyant Graeme Souness. The two men arrived when Rangers were at their lowest. Smith left disappointed but unbowed. With nine flags flying over Ibrox, he lived the dream, a dream that he shared with thousands of Rangers fans, because he was one of them.

Walter Smith left with his head held high, a domestic goal fulfilled. Europe remained to be conquered. It was a quest that was to be laid before a new man. Rangers cried out for a 'European coach'. Before Smith departed, the new man was already in place. Dick Advocaat prepared to take Rangers forward into an exciting new era.

DICK ADVOCAAT

David Murray travelled to four different countries, interviewing several candidates for the hottest job in football. On Monday, 15 February 1998, five months after Walter Smith announced his decision to vacate the manager's chair, Murray proclaimed in the club newspaper *Rangers News* that: 'I am delighted that Dick Advocaat, one of the game's most respected coaches, has accepted the position of manager of Rangers. He is 100 per cent the right man for us. When I first met him, I had no doubts that he was the right man for the job.'

Murray was understandably pleased. He had snatched Advocaat from PSV Eindhoven and thwarted a number of other European clubs who coveted the Dutchman's signature. Indeed, one Spanish side had reputedly offered him a salary in excess of £10,000 per week more than was on offer at Ibrox. However, the Dutchman had given his word to Murray and would not renegue on the deal. The chairman could not hide his delight: 'In Dick we have one of the biggest figures in world football. This shows that Rangers can attract the best in the world in terms of coaches and players.'

He explained that he had announced the new boss four months before he was due to take office to put a stop to the unrelenting speculation that surrounded the post. Murray felt that the move would allow Walter Smith and his players to concentrate on their title challenge free from the persistent press coverage of the club's attempts to find a new manager. The move suited Advocaat too as he prepared to exit from PSV. He had a job to finish in Eindhoven, but he relished the thought of the new challenge. As the news of his impending arrival at Ibrox reverberated around Europe, Dick Advocaat explained: 'I have a very clear vision of the direction in which I wish to take the club and I look forward to working with everyone at Rangers to ensure that direction brings even more success to this great club.'

Murray had every reason to feel satisfied. He had worked feverishly to find the right man for the job before he approached

Advocaat, one of the most respected coaches in the game. The Dutchman first knew Rangers were interested 'around December or January', but Murray did not have to tell him about the club. He was already well aware of Rangers, having carried out his own intensive research before the two men met. He recalled the preparations he made before that first fateful meeting with the chairman: 'Before I went to see Mr Murray, I informed myself about the club through the Internet, but I already knew a lot about Rangers from visits to Ibrox while with the Dutch Football Association.'

Indeed, he visited Ibrox regularly during his time as assistant manager of Holland under Rinus Michels, when he turned up to watch Rangers winger Pieter Huistra. Advocaat was impressed by Ibrox from the very first moment he walked through the front doors. 'It was around 1992 when I first came to see Huistra. What I will always remember is that when I came here, there was a man in a uniform at the front entrance and when I collected my tickets he took me to my place and offered me some tea or coffee. It was all very polite the way they [Rangers] treated people when they came to the ground – totally different from other clubs. They showed a real interest in you and that is why I was always very pleased when I visited Ibrox.'

He also found the stadium an attractive venue, modern and fresh on the outside and very traditional on the inside: 'I was impressed with the stadium, but not so with the corners which were still open at both sides at that time. When I came in 1997–98 and saw that the corners had been filled in I was very pleased. It made the stadium look much nicer that it was. On the inside, there is a sense of tradition and everyone who comes to visit me talks of it – the wood, the pictures, the paintings. I like all of that.'

As the news emerged of Rangers' prospective new manager, the press set to work to find out who exactly this man Advocaat was. He was well known in football circles, of course, but to the ordinary Rangers fan he was just a name. They had heard of his association with the Dutch national side but little else. It did not matter, however. They had what they had longed for: a European coach. He was the first non-Scot to be appointed manager of Rangers Football Club.

Dick Advocaat was every bit the kind of man they desired to

lead the club into a new era. Born on 27 September 1947, his professional football career commenced at the comparatively late age of 23, and he became something of a free spirit, drifting through the Dutch and Belgian Leagues and even serving for three summer seasons in the US National Soccer League. A solid midfielder, his clubs included ADO, FC Den Haag, Roda JC, FC VVV, Chicago Sting, Sparta, Berchem Sport and FC Utrecht. He played 513 first-class games and scored 35 goals. His career coincided with the emergence of Dutch football in the 1970s, initially through Ajax and Feyenoord who between them kept the European Cup in Holland from 1971 to 1974, and then the superb Dutch national side which took the World Cup by storm in 1974 and 1978 despite returning as beaten finalists.

The hallmark of the Dutch was their controlled passing game from defence all the way through to the front line in what was dubbed 'total football'. It was an exciting period to play in Holland and Advocaat loved the game. But his enthusiasm was not confined simply to playing. From an early stage he developed an interest in coaching although there was no single coach who influenced him. Indeed, much of his inspiration came from within himself. He recalled, 'I really developed this interest from my youth and my own playing career. At almost every club I played for, I was captain and then I began to consider that I may follow that responsibility through to coach or manager.' His ambition drove him to acquire the necessary certificates that would allow him to coach and he grasped his first opportunity with open arms.

It came in 1981 at amateur side DSVP 7 Pijnacker where he was appointed coach at the age of 34. He handled the job impressively and quickly attracted the attention of the coaching hierarchy at the Dutch FA. After four years with Pijnacker, and to the astonishment of many, he was propelled to the highest levels of coaching in the Dutch game with his appointment as assistant to Rinus Michels, the manager of the national side. He remained there for three years before leaving to take up the position of coach at Holland's oldest club, FC Haarlem, in 1987. By now Dick Advocaat was revered as one of the best coaches in the country, his status enhanced by the credibility he had gained in his senior role in Dutch football. He remained at Haarlem for two years before joining Second Division SVV, where he combined the role of coach with that of assistant to Michels once again in the Dutch national side. Working in tandem with technical director and former Celtic boss Wim Jansen, Advocaat took SVV into the Dutch First Division in his first season. His tenure there was short-lived, however, as the national team called for him.

When Michels left Holland in 1992, Advocaat was the natural choice to replace him. It was an exciting time for the Dutchman as he took his country into the quarter-final of the 1994 World Cup where Brazil shaded them out in a thrilling tie. When he returned from the World Cup, he relinquished control of the Dutch side to return to club football with PSV Eindhoven. In four great seasons, he brought success to PSV. They won the Dutch League Cup in his first season, but in the next he took them to a League and Cup double, ending Ajax's domination of domestic football in the country.

By 1998 he was ready for a new challenge. He could have gone to any of number of clubs but he chose Rangers. 'I was leaving one of the biggest clubs in Europe at PSV, but it was the challenge that brought me here,' he said. 'I had many offers from many countries, but I was interested in the challenge that the club presented in the years after Walter Smith.'

DICK ADVOCAAT: THE NEW MANAGER OF RANGERS

When David Murray came to call, it took several meetings before an agreement was thrashed out between the pair, but Advocaat was excited by the prospect of managing Rangers. When they concluded the deal that would take him to Ibrox, with a promise of a healthy budget for players, Advocaat started work immediately, even though he would not officially take up his duties until 1 July 1998. He met Murray several times before he took office, in Jersey, Monte Carlo and Edinburgh, as the two men mapped out the future of Rangers.

Videos of every match the team had played in that fateful final season for Smith were despatched to Holland for the prospective Ibrox boss to assess and analyse. He even made an undercover trip to the ground to watch one game, taking in the match from the stadium's Club Deck, away from the eagle eyes of the press pack. Advocaat knew that many of the players he saw that day would not be available to him. Richard Gough, Brian Laudrup, Ally McCoist,

Stuart McCall, Andy Goram, Ian Durrant and Alex Cleland were all scheduled to leave as they drifted out of contract. Paul Gascoigne also went as the season drew to a close. There were still a number of players left in the pool, but Advocaat knew that he had a massive rebuilding programme on his hands.

'Walter did an excellent job here, but there were and still are some players here who in my opinion were not good enough. It has been difficult to move some on to other clubs, because they are on good salaries, but we had to build a new team. When I came there were only two players left who had played regularly for the first team, so although Walter did a great, great job, I hope that when I leave there is a better team than when I arrived.'

If some of the players were not of the quality he believed to be adequate, there was one he was particularly keen to retain: Barry Ferguson. 'I saw Ferguson on tape and live at Ibrox and I saw his qualities. He was a similar type of player to Ian Durrant, another player I admired, but Durrant was older and played in the same position as Ferguson. It was better to have the younger player.'

Barry Ferguson was, however, disenchanted with Ibrox, feeling that his precocious talents were not given a chance under Walter Smith. He saw no future at Rangers. The pleadings of reserve-team coaches John Brown and John McGregor encouraged him to bide his time, at least until the new manager arrived. When he did, even Ferguson could not have expected the ringing endorsement he received from his new boss.

The youngster was asked to David Murray's Edinburgh office to discuss his prospects. Murray called Advocaat on the telephone, then passed the receiver to the startled Ferguson. Advocaat made it very clear that he wanted to have the player in his squad. Ferguson felt wanted. He decided to commit his future to Rangers, and to Advocaat. The impact the new manager has had on his career has been immeasurable. Growing in stature both physically and as a player, the youngster made a quite meteoric rise in the first two years of Advocaat's stewardship. A regular fixture in the side, playing a midfield holding role, he quickly gained international recognition for a series of sterling performances, and sealed it all by capturing the Scottish Sportswriters Player of the Year award for season 1999–2000.

Advocaat had great hopes for Ferguson, but the dearth of

quality in other key positions left him with a major headache. Such was the influence of both Brian Laudrup and Paul Gascoigne in Walter Smith's teams in the last couple of years that when they left the deficiencies in the side became even more obvious. Advocaat would have liked Laudrup to remain but the Dane had already decided to move on to Chelsea. He had postponed his move once. He would not do it again.

Although there would have been a place for Laudrup, there was no room for Paul Gascoigne at Ibrox under Advocaat. When he left for Middlesbrough in March 1998 there were suggestions that Advocaat had had the final say in his departure. 'I would have liked to have had the Gascoigne of ten years ago or so, but not the player of the latter period. I knew about his problems, so it was better for Rangers and Gascoigne if he found another club. Then again, he was one of the best players in Europe in the good days. When I started it was better for him to leave. At his peak, there is no question that I would have liked him in my team. When I was team manager of Holland we knew all about him as an England star. We watched him and saw what a high-quality player he was.'

But Gazza was not at his peak when he left Rangers and Advocaat knew that he would rebuild without a player who once was the fulcrum of one of the great Smith sides.

The new boss realised that he would need to integrate some of those who were less capable in the squad as he stretched his budget as far as it would go. He could bring in a number of quality players, but he could not replace a full team, at least not in the short term. He set about the transfer market with some vigour, spending just under £18 million in his first few weeks. Defender Arthur Numan, who had spent most of his career under Advocaat, came to Rangers from PSV, and fellow Dutchman Giovanni van Bronckhorst joined him. Andrei Kanchelskis, Lionel Charbonnier, Gabriel Amato and Rod Wallace were the other early starters. While most came with sizeable price tags, Advocaat's prudence and network of scouts secured Wallace on a free transfer under the Bosman ruling. The Englishman was to go on to become one of the stars in the formative season under the new manager.

Advocaat also added to his backroom team, bringing in long-time friend and Dutch FA coach Bert van Lingen. Both had gone through their coaching education together and while Advocaat progressed to senior coaching roles at club and national level, Van Lingen continued to forge a career in the academic side of the game with the Dutch FA, educating young coaches in modern methods. Pieter Huistra, himself keen to pursue a career in coaching, recently told me that most of the Dutch coaching manuals had been written by Van Lingen.

The influx of the many new foreign stars and the exit of some of the old characters created a rather uncertain atmosphere in the Ibrox dressing-room in the early stages. The players had heard that the new boss was a strict disciplinarian and some of the Scots players cautiously probed to get a feel for his sense of humour. They knew how far they could go with Smith. In Advocaat's case, they were dealing with a completely different character. Regardless, the remaining Scots players, led by Ian Ferguson and Derek McInnes, took up the cudgel left by the likes of Durrant and McCoist to keep up the dressing-room banter that many believed would be lost. They found that the multinational dressing-room entered into the spirit of the joviality, even if the humour was lost amidst translation difficulties at times. Little by little, they came to terms with a man who was indeed humorous, although much of his banter was played out over the airwaves as he toyed with countless radio and television commentators. One pundit in interview said, 'You have lost one central defender through injury and another through suspension – you are going to have to reorganise your back four.' Straight-faced, Advocaat replied, 'You tell me this?'

Humorous he may have been, but in the early stages the Rangers players got a taste of the discipline that they had heard so much about. They were required to gather together for lunch at the same time each day. Any latecomers were instantly fined. Players were also fined for failing to adhere to instructions for parking at the ground. Advocaat enforced strict guidelines in dress in keeping with the long-standing traditions of the club. He had been informed of this attention to smartness before he joined, and embraced the guidelines with vigour. Indeed, even today he is at the heart of all decisions taken on the subject of club uniform. 'I am involved with the outfits on the pitch and the Rangers suits,' he said. 'I believe it is important on and off the pitch for the players to look good. I was told about Rangers' traditions for smart dress, but I already believed in these things in any case for a football club.'

But when the team travelled to pre-season training in Norway, it was in his fastidious attention to time-keeping that he emphasised his expectations of everyone who worked for Rangers. At the airport, a flippant comment to customs officers from the *Rangers News* photographer led to a further search of the embarrassed snapper's bag. Advocaat was not prepared to allow the flight to be delayed. It took off, leaving the stunned cameraman behind, facing a sixteen-hour air and ferry journey to catch up with the squad.

Speaking in the Rangers monthly magazine, Advocaat said, 'Sometimes you need to set that kind of example and for me it was the right moment not to do it to a player, but to someone else. It showed the players how I am. They knew it already, but that let them see I wasn't kidding. He was late so I left him.'

Although Advocaat had a reputation for being a strict disciplinarian, the players found that Ibrox was not oppressive if they operated within the manager's framework for the organisation. Indeed, they found that the disciplines that they were adhering to were simply good professional attitudes. Advocaat was uncomfortable with the suggestion that he was strict. Indeed, he saw the rules that he established at Ibrox to be responsible, frequently drawing comparisons with the domestic family environment: 'I feel that discipline is the basis of success, but I would not want to overplay that point. It is like a family and children. You give your children some rules to work to and they adhere to that. It is quite simply the framework that we all have to work within.'

For those who had been troubled with the apparent indiscipline of some of the players during the later stages of the Smith era, Advocaat's attitude was refreshing. He had, however, to match his predecessor's achievements on the field.

EUROPE: THE PROGRESS CONTINUES

The new manager had got everything right off the field. A new sense of discipline and professionalism was instilled and the reconstructed first-team squad seemed to offer hope and optimism for the future. It was time for Advocaat to show what he could achieve on the field. From the earliest stages the continental influence was evident as Rangers adopted a distinctly European style of play, built upon a passing game where possession was all-important and the ball was king. To surrender it cheaply was a cardinal sin. It is a philosophy of football that the manager maintains to this day. The movement of the players is unmistakably Dutch but Advocaat denies that he adheres to a system that could be given the clichéd label of 'total football'. Indeed, he suggests that his ideas are a compendium of the best in the game from around the continent working within the limitations of the players at his disposal. He said, 'One of the qualities that I try to bring to the job is my involvement in every aspect of the game, although the basis is Dutch. I am very much involved with what is happening in other countries, looking at the way they play, the players, etc. I operate a system, but much depends on the players you have at your disposal. If you have the right players, you can play the system. If not, you have to work with what you have.'

For those not quite up to the required standard, the system relies on the cover and work of others in critical areas, but adjustment to the system can be difficult not only for weaker players. Even the great individuals who cannot fit easily into a team pattern have to be accommodated in the eyes of the Rangers boss, quite simply because of their brilliance. Walter Smith was criticised in his final years because of his dependence on Laudrup and Gascoigne. Would Advocaat have adjusted his team to accommodate their type? 'There is no question about that, because they are special players – they are the kind who can decide a game in a minute. But you have to give them some players who can work for them.'

A GLORIOUS FIRST SEASON

In the early stages of his management, Dick Advocaat did not have the luxury of knowing how his men would fit into the system. While he knew some of them well, there were others he knew little about, for all of his researches. In many ways he was asked to perform what may have seemed impossible to many. In his first competitive match in charge, before the team had even embarked on domestic football, his difficulties were compounded by the UEFA Cup draw that put Rangers in a preliminary round and facing a crucial tie against Irish side Shelbourne Rovers. The match was scheduled for Prenton Park, Tranmere, due to concerns of possible crowd trouble if the game took place in the Irish Republic.

The Rangers boss, reluctant to throw too many of his new players into the opening tie, started with a team that included Gio van Bronckhorst as the only newcomer. It was to be a roller-coaster ride for the manager. With the side 0–3 down at one stage, Rangers looked to be heading for an embarrassing exit against the little Irish side. Inspired by substitute Amato, the team came roaring back to win 5–3. The team safely negotiated the return leg to progress to the next round as Advocaat turned his attention towards his first Scottish Premier League match, against Hearts at Tynecastle.

The Light Blues slipped to a 2–1 defeat against the capital side, but Advocaat was unperturbed. He had seen enough in the second-half performance to be satisfied that the team could build towards a decent run. Settling into the system he had mapped out for them, the team did in fact embark on a seventeen-game undefeated sequence that carried them through successive UEFA Cup hurdles against PAOK Salonika, Beitar Jerusalem and Bayer Leverkusen. The win against the Germans in particular was greeted with delight. For fans who had been starved of any meaningful success in Europe for so long, that victory was a huge boost. The significance was not just in the side's progress to the next round, but in the manner of the win, which inflicted a rare defeat on the Germans at home. In one season, Rangers had gone a long way to restoring their pride in Europe.

The trail ended in Parma when ten-man Rangers slipped to the Seria A giants after going 2–1 ahead on aggregate in the first half. The dismissal of Sergio Porrini was the turning point in the game, but even when Rangers fell 3–2 behind on aggregate they were well in the tie until a late penalty sealed it for the Italians. The Rangers fans were unbowed as they remained for half an hour after the final whistle singing Advocaat's name as he gave post-match interviews on the touchline. It was an emotional moment for the 'Little General'. Humbled that so many fans should travel from all over to watch Rangers in Italy and then remain behind to sing his praises in the midst of defeat, he resolved to bring them some real success in Europe.

Rangers had the fans, the stadium and the manager to guide them to success. What they needed was a team, but Advocaat was meticulously assessing his squad. He knew that some players, such as Numan and Van Bronckhorst, were of the requisite quality. He also knew that others were not of the class he needed. For most, including some of his new signings, the jury would remain out.

If Advocaat was encouraged with the progress the side had made in Europe, his first Old Firm fixture at Parkhead provided a rude awakening to the tribalism that dominates Scottish football. Debilitated by the loss of defender Scott Wilson who was ordered off in the first half, Rangers lost five goals with Van Bronckhorst getting a single goal in reply. Celtic were so overjoyed with their win that they commissioned a video to be sold to the public. Advocaat studied the video, too, but from a quite different perspective. In truth, he probably learned more from the game than the victors. 'We were so desperate to score that we didn't play from our organisation and left too many open spaces,' he recalled. It was a bitter blow for the manager, who detested defeat at the best of times. That his side should fail in one of the most important games of the season while losing their shape and organisation was unforgivable. Advocaat was finding out about the capabilities and the deficiencies of the squad. The players would learn that any honeymoon period would be short. They would also learn that the manager would ruthlessly dispose of those he felt had little to offer Rangers. While there were many who did not perform that day and some defenders were left exposed, it was a disappointing afternoon, particularly for one of the managers' new signings, Colin Hendry.

The Scotland captain had been troubled by injury from the beginning of his Ibrox career, but he never made the impact that many expected. Gabriel Amato was another whose brilliance at times was more regularly overshadowed by mediocrity. He was not a bad player and indeed was quite superb at times, but he seemed unsuited to the Scottish game. Another who joined early in Advocaat's reign was French striker Stephane Guivarc'h, a £3.5 million acquisition from Newcastle United. Their cumulative value was £11.7 million. Despite the massive investment, Advocaat was not prepared to compromise the quality of the side by retaining players he ultimately felt were not suited to Rangers. All were shipped out at an overall loss of around £5 million, but, guided by David Murray, he felt that with the players failing to hold down a regular place in the side, they were a diminishing asset. The losses could be controlled with the rapid disposal of the players.

The Rangers boss continued to strengthen his squad, adding Neil McCann and Stefan Klos as Murray provided more funds, emphasising that the success of the club would be more important than the balance-sheet in that first season.

The heavy defeat at Parkhead behind them, Advocaat put the smile back on the faces of the supporters by winning the League Cup with a 2–1 win over St Johnstone. The New Year Old Firm fixture ended in a 2–2 draw, but it stimulated a run of nine successive victories for the Light Blues as they increased their claim on the championship. By May 1998 they were six points clear of Celtic and had the chance to seal the title with victory at Parkhead. It was an opportunity to erase the memories of their heavy defeat of just six months earlier. Even the staunchest of Rangers fans could not have dreamed of the contrasting fortunes of the two Glasgow teams.

With the title at stake, Rangers kept their head while all around were losing theirs in a quite remarkable match. It was a game that had everything, although little of the events will be remembered with relish by the Celtic contingent. Rangers won 3–0 with goals by McCann (2) and Jorg Albertz and secured the League championship, but the discipline that Advocaat had instilled in the squad was the key to the victory. In a match marred by mayhem both on and off the field, Rangers players and fans alike conducted themselves impeccably, while Celtic suffered the ignominy of seeing two players dismissed, some home fans enter the field, and referee Hugh Dallas felled by a coin propelled from an area of the Celtic fans.

Although delighted with the victory that sealed the championship for Rangers, Advocaat was disappointed that the disgraceful scenes at Celtic Park overshadowed the achievement of his side. Unbowed, he called it 'one of the greatest days of my career', a day when his newly constructed side showed that they had the spirit and determination to wipe the nightmare of their last visit to Celtic Park from their minds, to wrest the title back from their rivals. The team that won that historic match showed seven changes from the one that opened Advocaat's Rangers career against Shelbourne. The boss used 26 players in the League while searching for the blend and assessing the squad. It was a rapid evaluation of the resources, but the disruption had little effect on Rangers' surge for honours.

They continued the torment of Celtic in the Scottish Cup final when a goal by Rod Wallace proved enough to take the trophy, completing a remarkable treble. Dick Advocaat became the fifth Rangers manager to achieve the clean sweep of Scotland's domestic honours, but was the first to complete the set in his first season.

It was a huge achievement for Advocaat, freshly introduced to a new League with a new set of players and facing opponents that just a year earlier he had known little about. But, despite his massive rebuilding programme and his unfamiliarity with the set-up, Advocaat had remained focused on his targets. 'For me it was quite simple. We tried to win everything, but the main thing was the championship after Celtic had won it in the previous year. But, with all the changes we had to make, all the new players in and players out, it was a very difficult task and I don't know how we did it.'

Win it they did, and the additions of the Scottish Cup and League Cup completed a wonderful first season for the Rangers manager. Now, with the League flag fluttering over Ibrox, the boss took the side into his second season in charge, with the prospect of a tilt at the Champions' League. Europe's senior tournament had been a major attraction for Dick Advocaat and many of his players when they signed up at Ibrox. With the compliments of many observers ringing in his ears, he had to show that Rangers had matured in a short period under his stewardship and that the good European run they enjoyed in that first season was no fluke.

2000: A YEAR OF PROGRESSION

Continuing to mould his squad, Advocaat added Dutch striker Michael Mols, a £4 million signing from FC Utrecht. The move was inspired. Mols had failed to secure a place in the Holland national side, but Advocaat knew his capabilities. What is more, in an inflationary transfer market where even average strikers were hard to find under £6 million, the deal looked good. Rangers did not realise quite how good – Mols was a revelation, twisting and turning defenders inside out, providing pace and real class to the Ibrox front line.

In just over a year, Advocaat had shaped a side that looked

capable of giving Europe's best a run for their money in the continent's premier tournament – and they did. A place in the Champions League first phase of group matches was achieved by ousting one of the favourites for the competition, UEFA Cup-holders Parma. It was sweet revenge for the side's exit from the UEFA Cup to the Italian side a year earlier. Faced with a tough draw in the sectional matches, Rangers once again displayed the remarkable progress they had made under Advocaat. A disappointing defeat in Valencia in the opening match was followed by a draw against Bayern Munich at Ibrox, then victories home and away to PSV Eindhoven.

The Germans had been lucky to salvage that draw when they were awarded a dubious free-kick in the dying moments of the tie, then benefited from a deflection which landed in the Rangers net behind goalkeeper Lionel Charbonnier. If Rangers felt they were unfortunate at Ibrox, they were positively jinxed in the return in Munich at the end of the group phase when they needed just a draw to qualify for the second phase of matches. Once again, Bayern benefited from a dubious refereeing decision that gave them an early goal from the penalty spot. For the remainder of the match, the Light Blues bombarded the German goal, hitting the woodwork or the defiant hands of inspired German goalkeeper, Oliver Kahn. His Bayern team-mate Mehmet Scholl later said Kahn 'was a man of a thousand arms'. Dick Advocaat had nothing to comfort him other than pride: 'I am very disappointed. However, I am also very proud of my team. They showed that they are very strong and that we can compete very well with other European top teams. Unfortunately, we weren't able to score despite creating a lot more chances than Bayern.'

Advocaat's dismay was not confined to the scoreline. He also lost Michael Mols, who suffered knee-ligament damage in a freak challenge with Kahn near the touchline after just 25 minutes. Ironically, the Rangers striker sustained the injury as he tried to pull out of a tackle that may have led to some injury for the Bayern keeper. Mols was not seen in a Rangers jersey again for eight months.

Rangers went out of the tournament with their heads held high. Advocaat had learned a lot from the Champions' League matches. He discovered that Rangers had the quality to compete with the top sides in Europe but that he also needed to continue to strengthen the squad. The team had created many chances in Bayern, but they did not have the cutting edge to convert them. Rod Wallace had arrived for no transfer fee and did not owe the club anything. He had scored many vital goals for the club, including the winner in the Scottish Cup final, but Rangers needed a quality finisher to play alongside Mols. Unfortunately, the Dutchman would be missing for much of the season.

Advocaat knew that Rangers had made progress, but he still needed to improve the team in some key areas. Apart from the obvious deficiencies in attack, Advocaat also felt that the defence could do with strengthening, with the right-back and central positions in focus. The midfield was also an area that required bolstering. Rangers' shortfalls were cruelly exposed in the UEFA Cup when, as first-phase Champions' League fallers, the Ibrox side were entered into a competition that was regarded as something of a consolation-prize. They were drawn to face Borussia Dortmund. Despite beating the Germans 2–0 at Ibrox, a late goal from Bobic in the return levelled the scores on aggregate before the Ibrox side slumped out of the competition on penalties.

The speculation surrounding the midfield area and the sporadic use of Jorg Albertz in the early stage of the season proved unsettling for the German. A prolific goalscorer from the middle of the field, he was a hero to the fans, but his work-rate and positioning frequently left Advocaat troubled. Indeed, he was hauled off at half-time in the UEFA Cup tie in Dortmund with the Rangers boss concerned that 'players were running past him [Albertz]'.

The German was at a crossroads. He could buckle down and demonstrate his value, or he could leave. There was apparently no shortage of clubs interested in securing his services. He remained and his attitude and displays earned him a regular place in the side. Advocaat showed that he was not a man to hold any grudges. Albertz was embraced as a key player and offered a new contract, which he happily signed. There was only one way and that was the Advocaat way. Players would have to live with that, but he frequently emphasised that he would only keep players who wanted to remain at Ibrox. Any who were not happy to persevere on the touchline could leave, but the resolution of the Albertz position was crucial to the manager and Rangers. While the German midfielder maintained the right attitude, he was a great asset. Albertz knew that he had to keep up his standards and his overall play improved noticeably as he won himself a regular place in the side.

The disappointment of Dortmund followed an extra-time defeat from Aberdeen at Pittodrie in the League Cup. Rangers had lost one of their trophies, but they maintained a firm grip on the title race. With new striker Billy Dodds signed from Dundee United, Rangers effectively sealed the championship in a double-header against Celtic in March. A late goal from Wallace won the match at Parkhead. At Ibrox 18 days later, the rejuvenated Albertz scored two goals as his team surged to an emphatic win that put them fifteen points clear in the race. It was the one hundredth meeting of the Old Firm in the Premier League. As Celtic crumbled in the last lap, Rangers took the championship with a record 21-point margin.

Despite this, Advocaat was insistent that the race had been a lot tighter than the eventual margin suggested. 'Everybody abroad thinks that it is an easy competition but although not every game is hard, away games are all difficult. Every game is a final for our opponents, so nothing is easy. We finished 21 points clear but there was more to it than that gap suggested. We got the points at the right moment and Celtic lost them. Despite the margin of our victory, it was still a very difficult season for us. There were no easy games.'

The championship won, Dick turned his attention to the final trophy of the 1999–2000 season – the Scottish Cup. In a remarkable show of devotion and respect for their manager, the fans responded to calls for them to wear the orange of Holland. Advocaat was astounded when he walked through the Hampden tunnel and looked out upon a stadium awash with colour, but not the traditional red, white and blue of Rangers. The spectacle looked more akin to a Dutch international match than a Scottish Cup final.

Rangers turned on the style to trounce an Aberdeen side debilitated with the loss of their goalkeeper Jim Leighton who was replaced by outfield player Robbie Winters. The 4–0 victory was simply a procession as Rangers marched on to take the Cup, Advocaat's fifth domestic trophy out of six. Rangers looked to be unstoppable in Scottish football.

SEASON 2000–2001: A NEW CHALLENGE

Dismayed by their failure to match Rangers, Celtic sacked rookie boss John Barnes and appointed Leicester coach Martin O'Neill to take the challenge to the Ibrox side. As O'Neill unleashed a new wave of spending, the Parkhead squad was strengthened. Advocaat was conscious that there would be a sterner challenge from the east end of Glasgow and that domestic success could not be guaranteed, but he was looking beyond Scotland. The manager wanted to build on the relative success that Rangers had enjoyed in Europe in his first two seasons. As David Murray once again conjured up some additional finances for the manager, new players were secured. They included Bert Konterman, Fernando Ricksen, Kenny Miller, Peter Lovenkrands, Paul Reid, Allan Johnston and Paul Ritchie. Konterman and Ricksen, who were acquired from Dutch football, maintaining the manager's strong links with his homeland, cost £8.2 million between them. The others took Rangers' total spending to around £12 million in the close season.

As Dick Advocaat led Rangers into his third season as manager, the focus of the club's attention switched again to Europe. They safely negotiated a preliminary tie with Danish champions Herfolge to secure entry into the Champions' League first group phase. Before the signing deadline, Rangers plunged back into the transfer market to make what is potentially one of the most significant signings in the club's recent history. Ronald de Boer, a Dutch international with a host of honours behind him including five championships in Holland, a Spanish title and a Champions' Cup medal, was lured to Ibrox from Barcelona for a fee of around £4.5 million. He cited one of the reasons for his move as Dick Advocaat: 'He is a trainer I know very well and who has always had a lot of belief in me.'

The arrival of Ronald de Boer confirmed Rangers' credibility as a club that could enhance the careers of the continent's best players. Just as Terry Butcher had provided a gateway to Ibrox for many English players who had previously turned their noses up at a move to Ibrox, de Boer's acquisition was a sign that the Scottish League and the chance of regular European football was an attractive proposition to many foreign players. If it was good enough for him, it would be good enough for anyone. There was also speculation that Rangers would eventually enter a European league, which would increase their profile even further.

But there was more to the signing of Ronald de Boer than a simple PR coup for Rangers. He added immense quality as Advocaat continued to assemble a squad that could compete at the highest level.

The arrival of de Boer also took the minds of the Rangers fans off a devastating 6–2 defeat by Celtic in the first Old Firm fixture of the season. It was a rather surprising loss given that the club had suffered a similarly heavy defeat to their oldest rivals two years earlier, but Advocaat comforted the fans with the observation that the Light Blues had gone on to win the treble that season and, indeed, Celtic had not beaten them in the intervening years. Murray put the match into context and reminded the fans of Rangers' wider ambitions, saying he would prefer the club to qualify for the second phase of matches rather than top the League by the turn of the year.

While the arrival of de Boer was greeted with some delight by the Ibrox faithful, Advocaat was still frustrated as he scoured the continent looking for a striker: 'All we have bought is a right full-back and a central defender. I don't think that we have a much better side, but I know that we have much more experience and that can be a big advantage for us. I think we face a very difficult future – difficult in the sense that we don't know what is going to happen with transfer fees and players' salaries. If we want to compete, something has to change here. The players are not coming any more. They stay away. There is a lot of competition for players.'

Despite his concern for the future and the impact that legislation may have on football, and Rangers in particular, he reflected on the progress of the side with some satisfaction. 'We have to be very pleased with the way Rangers have improved in two and a half years, after so many players and so many changes abroad. We are an average club spending-wise, but we have an advantage in a great stadium and excellent fans. However, we can never compete with the likes of Barcelona and other similar clubs. But we can compete with Bayern Munich, Valencia, PSV, Rosenborg and these kinds of teams, and that is where our challenge lies.

'We cannot win the Champions' Cup. We have to be realistic. A player worth £40 million is better than a player worth £5 million.

The gap is getting wider and that will always be the case. Our most expensive player is Andrei Kanchelskis at £5.5 million – how can we compete with the bigger clubs? We can compete, but at the end you still lose.'

Although he realised that domestic success remains the key to the door of Europe, the manager poured cold water on the preoccupation of some with the desire to beat Celtic. Citing the targets that lie beyond Glasgow, he said, 'I don't build my team to beat Celtic. They are an important part of the competition, but if you ever want to improve it is not good to focus on beating Celtic. We have to look at the wider game. How is the competition in Europe? How is the game played there? But for the Rangers fans, there is only one thing that counts and that is to be champions.'

So with two seasons behind him, and the side edging closer to the quality he desires, what are Advocaat's reflections on Scottish football and the future for Rangers? On the overall standard, he believes that the game is misrepresented and that despite their apparent superiority, every match represents a challenge for Rangers. Of the style of play, he observed, 'Some people say that it is more physical in Scotland than elsewhere, but that is no problem. If you can play here, in Scotland and England, you can play anywhere. With the time and space available, you have to be very quick in seeing the game and passing. That improves your game.'

Comfortable with the pace of the game, he had no reservations about his ability to succeed and the suitability of his system to the Scottish game. 'I was never concerned that the system we played would work in Scotland. You could see in the last couple of years that our system worked here and in Europe. We have good players who can play football, but if during any games I see that the system isn't working, I change things to play another system, but we are not a team that would rely on long balls. We move the ball around and our players move off the ball. I would never want to change that system.'

Off the field, Advocaat has found the experience of managing Rangers fulfilling, but there have been frustrations. One area that did perplex him in the early days of his management at Ibrox was the apparent reluctance of the press to accept his word on some matters, particularly where new players were involved. Prior to some matches he was also accused of playing mind games. He pointedly refutes any suggestion that he would mislead the press. 'I am the same here as I was in Holland. I don't like to tell lies. I think truth is the best way to deal with them [the press]. If I don't want to tell them something, I won't say anything. Everything else I say to them is true.'

For all his candid dealings with the media, he is also aware that many eagerly seek out some negative publicity and he remains guarded against such eventualities. 'I feel that they are just waiting for something to go wrong, because bad news sells newspapers better, but I expect that. I knew what it was like before I started. It is part of the job.'

He has also become increasingly dismayed at what he sees as intransigence in the authorities as he urges change to enhance Scottish football. In a clear reference to the reformed Scottish Premier League set-up, which he was vigorously opposed to, he says, 'I feel very frustrated with the authorities. We have tried everything in the past two years to change things, not just for Rangers but for the whole of Scottish football. If we want to compete, we have to take the rules that are used in the best countries. Why do we have our own rules in Scotland? Are we something special? No, we are not something special. As for the influence of foreigners, foreign players and coaches come in because the talent and quality is not there in Scotland.'

On youth development, an area he feels that has been neglected in this country, he says, 'A lot more has to be done in youth development than is being done at the moment in Scotland. A lot of people are talking about youth academies, but we are the ones to have started. But why don't the SFA and SPL take the initiative on this? Why should we have to take this initiative? The coaches at the SFA should be pushing for this kind of initiative in youth development.

'When we started here we discussed it every day with David Murray and now we are the only club building a youth academy and training centre for the first team. You need it because that is the future, but it will take years before we see the benefit. We have to bring the best youth players of Scotland and abroad to Glasgow. If we get talented players in and show them the facilities, that is how we can keep them. That is the most important thing. We can do our own thing, but there is a responsibility on the people of the SFA to get things right.'

Despite the frustrations, however, Dick Advocaat has enjoyed his time at Ibrox although it has proven to be a more taxing role than he expected: 'I realised that this club takes up not just seven days a week but eight days a week. It is a very demanding job, more so than in Eindhoven, and more than I expected. That has a little bit to do with David Murray, but that is good. It is part of the relations between us. It is a hard-working job, but that is what I am paid for. The club has fulfilled my expectations totally. It is a great club to work with. There is one man who decides virtually every-thing, Mr Murray, and I can work with him. I also know that if I ever go to another club I won't get the same relations [with the chairman] that I have here.'

Of the team's prospects for the future, he is encouraged: 'After all the turmoil and changes of the first two years we are now moving into calmer waters. All the players know each other. Most of the players know their place. It makes everything a little easier. The structure is there. We know each other a little better. All of these things are important.'

And of his own future? 'My wife and I are wondering what we will do in the future, because time goes fast. It will be a judgement based on how I feel, but at this time I feel good. But, again, I can't go on. I have never given a statement on my intent because it could all change within a week. But, so far, everything is going the right way. The relationship with the club is good, the relations with the players are good, as are the results, but there are always two sides. Things could change. If I leave the club at least there will be a platform to build upon.'

The great success of Liverpool from the 1960s to the 1980s was based on promoting from within the club a succession of managers who were raised in the ways of the Anfield side. Advocaat con-siders that this would only be appropriate if the quality was there. In essence, he sees future managers being appointed for their capabilities rather than on the back of any emotional tie.

While he still has a lot to achieve at Rangers, he already has clear ideas of how he would he like to be judged when he finally leaves the club. 'I would like people to say that "he brought success to the club, not just with the first team but with the training ground." People can see that we were not only interested in the first team because the money we are spending could have bought us one of the best players around. But for the future of Rangers, it is more important to get the training ground. In the next ten years the talent will come. In the future if we cannot afford the salaries and transfers of players it will be a big advantage for us if we can bring our own players through.'

On the face of it, it could be some time before Dick Advocaat decides to close the book on his Rangers career. When he finally does leave the club, these formative years in his tenure at Ibrox will be recalled as a period when he completely rebuilt a side and guided it towards the success that the fans had come to expect in the domestic scene. He also re-established the club's fine reputation in Europe, turning them once again into a team that was feared and respected throughout the continent. But he offered so much more than this. Potentially his greatest achievement was in establishing the framework for the club's future success through the development of homegrown talent. Continuing to pursue his vision of a future when Rangers could see a conveyor-belt of young players feeding through to the first team, he presided over the plans for the state-of-the-art soccer academy – the hothouse of new talent that could secure Rangers' future in the modern era.

Having swept the board of Scottish honours and continuing to further his ambitions in Europe, Advocaat would have every reason to be pleased with his contribution to the club. How would he like to be remembered? When I asked him, he replied quite simply: 'I would like people to think of me as a good manager of Rangers.'

He need not fear: he has already achieved that. But who knows what the future holds? Greatness in the context of football management is measured in a number of ways, not least of which is service. But in his short period so far with the club, who would wager against Dick Advocaat going on to achieve unprecedented levels of success both on and off the field in a new exciting era for football. The greatest manager of Rangers? No, comparisons with managers from other periods are illogical, but there is little doubt that Dick Advocaat is well on the road to being remembered as one of the finest managers of Rangers.

THE GREAT LEGACY

'There's not a team like the Glasgow Rangers,' the fans sing, and who could deny that? What is it about this football club that sets it apart from many? Indeed, what is the Rangers Football Club? Tradition, success, wealth, good, endeavour, ambition, class? Yes, it is all of these things to the thousands of fans around the world. For the loyal supporter, the magic of Rangers is indefinable, but if the seeds of the club were sown on Glasgow Green in 1872, they were nurtured by ten men who are and who have been Rangers managers.

From the early days of Wilton and Struth who shaped the Ibrox traditions, to the modern cosmopolitan era of Souness, Smith and Advocaat, the managers have revelled in the glory and shared the bitterness of failure in the red, white and blue tapestry that is Rangers FC. Managers? No, more than that. When the champagne flows, they are deified. As the tears stream, they are cast aside like pariahs. Football followers are fickle. A great manager is only great while his side is winning. When success on the field of play can spin on a moment of genius, or luck even, their fortune can be beyond their control. It is arguably only in football that a great manager can become a bad manager in the space of a few games. But what makes a great manager, and how do they lose that adulation? If a manager wins a trophy one year then loses it the next, is he any less effective in failure than he was in his moment of triumph?

Success and failure for the manager of Rangers has been gauged by one factor only – his ability to stay ahead of great rivals Celtic. So how do we judge the managers of Rangers? By their performances against Celtic? Sadly, this has often been the case. Symon, White, Greig and, to some extent, Wallace all succumbed in the face of a superior Celtic side. But judgement of the respective managers is far more complex that can be ever ascertained by a comparison of honours.

So who was the greatest of them all? Some gave service that

could best be described as fleeting while others dedicated a life-time to Rangers. Some won a multitude of honours, while one failed to capture any silverware. It is impossible to make any reasoned assessment of the capabilities of the managers based on a simple tally of trophies.

Each manager presided over their own little microcosm in the history of Rangers. Their domain was an assembly of circumstances that was comparable with the others in some senses but widely variant in others. Their destiny was shaped by themselves, but there were other factors that determined their success or otherwise. Some had money available to them, others did not. Two toiled in the face of Celtic's greatest ever side. Those who 'failed' were invariably in the right place but at the wrong time – a failure borne of a cruel twist of fate rather than any reflection of their ability.

The factors that determine success are almost limitless, but the Ibrox hierarchy has been the single most powerful reason for the club's recent triumphs. In the boardroom, the support of David Murray has been a vital element in the achievements of the last three managers. Without his determination and financial acumen, it is doubtful whether Rangers could have maintained the dominance they regained with Souness in the late 1980s. No other manager has enjoyed such tangible support from the board. Campbell Ogilvie, the secretary, highlighted one of the reasons for Rangers' success as 'the manager–chairman relationship' where Advocaat and Murray discuss every decision with a common goal – to make Rangers better; the teamsheet before the balance-sheet.

If some of the earlier managers had good support at board level they did not have the same capital that was enjoyed by the more recent managers. Indeed, their cash resources were meagre.

Today, Advocaat has his own frustrations as he attempts to lure the best to Ibrox, but at least he can cast the net wider than most of his predecessors ever could. Ironically, for much of the club's history, blind allegiance to traditions that never were prevented the signing of players of the Roman Catholic faith. In truth, Rangers never started out as a Presbyterian club; indeed, for a number of years, their great rivals in Glasgow were Clyde, not Celtic, whom they regarded as 'great friends'.

It was a sectarian policy that was continually denied by Rangers but which was patently obvious for most of the last century. It was borne in the Irish immigration to the west of Scotland, mirroring a social divide that grew up within the community. William Struth did not sign many or any celebrated Catholic players, but he did once try to introduce Barney Battles, a Catholic youngster who had impressed him on one of the club's North American tours. Battles was denied the opportunity of signing for Rangers by his mother who feared the taunts her son may endure from the crowd. Struth resolved to find him another club, which he did, at Tynecastle. He went on to become a big star with Heart of Midlothian and was capped for Scotland.

No other manager of Rangers dared brave the sectarian cesspit until Souness. The signing of Maurice Johnston blasted away any notion of restrictions being placed on the players open to Rangers. It was a watershed. Without it, the club could never have hoped to attract future bosses of the calibre of Advocaat. The move paved the way for talent of all creeds to come to Rangers, and both Smith and Advocaat enjoyed the benefit. Walter Smith had other restrictions to contend with, of course. Limitations imposed by UEFA on the number of foreign players he could use radically affected the whole structure of his squad.

The Souness revolution of the 1980s will be remembered for the shattering of the sectarian policy, but the period was the threshold for many other radical changes. Campbell Ogilvie, who has served with five managers at Ibrox, recalls the impact of Souness: 'When Graeme came here it was a very exciting period with so much interest from England. We had so many calls from the English media and I recall Rangers even featuring on *News at Ten*. It was an exciting period that took us on to another level.'

The Souness era signalled the beginning of an explosion of media interest in football as television muscled in on the enormous viewing potential of the game. Souness often found it hard at times to come to terms with the tabloids' preoccupation with Rangers, but newspapers and television have evolved as an integral part of the fabric of the game, good and bad. The manager of Rangers nowadays finds that he is in the glare of an intense media spotlight that is never dimmed, in a country obsessed with the fortunes of the club and those who serve it. The media has been a double-edged sword: intrusive it certainly is at times, but without it the game would not have received the prominence it now has.

Souness's arrival stimulated more than the interest of the media. 'The wage structure at Ibrox used to be very rigid,' said Ogilvie. 'I recall us losing one player because we refused to alter the structure. The first thing Graeme did when he arrived was to smash the standard wage structure. When he arrived each player was on £350 per week top line. He lifted wages to compete with the higher salaries of the English clubs and that allowed us to attract the best English players. With English clubs out of Europe after Heysel, players were encouraged to come here for European football, and Graeme's change to the wage structure allowed that.'

Today, players come to Ibrox from around the world. Gone are the days when eleven Scots players took on the best of the continent and won that famous Barcelona triumph of 1972. For most of the fans, however, the success of the side transcends everything. But if the composition of the team and the style of play bears little resemblance to the great Rangers sides of the early years, the legacies of the past managers remain as the guiding hand in other ways for others to follow. Campbell Ogilvie recalls that every one of the last five managers showed an interest in the historical background to the club and remained loyal to many of the great traditions: 'We gave Dick Advocaat some books on Rangers and he has been keen to maintain some of our traditions. He has shown a particular interest in the dress of the players, for example, choosing all the club outfits both on and off the field, although the players no longer need to wear a tie to training. That is an example of the need to keep the good traditions, but dispense with those that are out-of-date.'

The fastidious Wilton and the great father figure Struth are generally credited with the tradition for smartness that Rangers players were known for, but the first two managers instilled more than simple dress-sense in the club. Their maxim that 'Only the best is good enough for Rangers' has been the guiding light. Reared in an era of Edwardian splendour, they provided respectability, honour and class to a club that emerged while many withered and died. Where now the Rentons, St Bernards and even Queen's Park who once ruled the Scottish game? For over fifty years, Wilton then Struth managed Rangers, mapping out the future of the club, but the role of manager they once held with esteem bears little relation to the office that Dick Advocaat holds today.

Wilton's responsibilities were so wide-ranging that his death spawned two jobs, that of manager and another of secretary. Struth was relieved of many of the administrative duties, but threw himself wholeheartedly into the development of the team and turned the Ibrox Sports into one of the most famous athletic events of the calendar. But if Wilton and Struth found themselves at times overworked, the role of the modern coach has become altogether more mentally and physically taxing. It is an 'eight days a week' job to Dick Advocaat. Many of the early managers would nevertheless have good cause to envy the role that the current boss now enjoys. Where once the manager's every decision, including team selection, was judged and ratified by the board, the organisation is now very different. Campbell Ogilvie said, 'When I first arrived here there was an item on the agenda for board meetings called 'football-related matters'. The board went through everything. Even prospective signings were referred to the chairman by the manager who would then table it at the board meeting for approval of the spend. Nowadays it is all streamlined. Rangers works well because of the chairman–manager relationship. Dick and the chairman sit down to discuss most things. On the general administrative issues, I will either make the decisions myself for routine matters and sit down with Dick to canvass his opinion on others before taking our views to the authorities. When we make up our mind, that then becomes the club view.'

While it is unquestionable that circumstances determined the fortunes of some managers, it is eminently arguable that none failed Rangers. All contributed to what the club is today. Even Davie White, who was unable to add any trophies to the honours list, was a catalyst for change in his own way. In the wake of the disgraceful dismissal of old loyal servant Scot Symon, White introduced a style of management that bore greater resemblance to the trends of the modern coaches of today. Radical is acceptable only when successful. The club wanted change and success, but principally the latter. Arguably, no one could have fulfilled the club's needs during his period as Celtic swept all before them.

But White's demise was the signal for Waddell to fulfil his destiny and guide Rangers back to the top. The European Cup-Winners' Cup would be enough for any man to rest his laurels upon, but Waddell's achievement transcended the glory on the field of play. His contribution to Rangers in its darkest hours after the 1971 Disaster and the later reconstruction of the stadium is immeasurable. 'Safety, comfort and a theatre-style atmosphere' were the design criteria for Ibrox. The magnificence of Ibrox is his legacy.

Then there was Wallace, best summed up in two words – 'character' and 'trebles'. No other manager fired the determination of a side more than he did. His two trebles remain unequalled by any other manager. John Greig followed and almost bagged one in his first season, but his period in office coincided with a team in transition. The decline in Rangers' fortunes needed an overhaul from top to bottom to put it right, and the scene was set for the radical change of the Souness years. It was a change that would provide the platform for Walter Smith to deliver a procession of titles in the most successful period in Rangers' history.

So where now for the club and Dick Advocaat? The new millennium signals the dawn of an age where television will undoubtedly dictate how the structure of the game develops, with new leagues and spiralling wages determining the natural selection process that will inevitably lead to the demise of many clubs. Rangers can embrace the future with confidence. They have always been a big club – one of the biggest, in fact. They are destined to become even bigger as they are carried along in the commercial tidal wave that has engulfed football. Sink or swim has been the philosophy that has guided the club in the deeper waters of continental football and no one knows where it will all end. Many clubs will surely be washed up on a beach in time, but Rangers will always survive because of the depth of their support.

For anyone who knows Rangers comes the realisation that this is no ordinary football club. It has evolved as an integral part of the Scottish community, led by a succession of managers whose instincts have been to embrace change while holding dear the great tradition that only the best is good enough. Every manager has played a part in raising the club to the standing it enjoys today, providing a higher platform for every successor. Dick Advocaat holds the keys of office and he too has enhanced the club and his role in a comparatively short period. In time, he will leave, but his legacy will remain alongside those of his nine predecessors; a unique group of men – the managers of Rangers.

STATISTICS

Summary of games played in major competition

	TENURE	LEAGUE CHAMP.	SCOT. CUP	OTHER DOM. CUPS**	EUROPE	TOTAL	WON	LOST	DREW	PERCENTAGE POINTS#
W. Wilton+	1899–1920	661	64	173	–	898	564	184	150	73
W. Struth*	1920–54	975	150	215	–	1340	896	189	255	74
S. Symon	1954–67	446	59	163	54	712	465	133	124	75
D. White	1967–69	74	10	17	18	119	77	22	20	74
W. Waddell	1969–72	88	17	20	11	136	67	33	25	61
J. Wallace	1972–78 & 1983–86	304	33	97	21	455	279	91	95	71
J. Greig	1978–83	189	34	58	21	302	158	72	72	64
G. Souness	1986–91	192	17	25	22	256	164	43	49	72
W. Smith	1991–98	280	33	88	38	379	248	63	68	74
D. Advocaat	1998– date	72	10	6	22	110	77	14	19	76

+   excludes Wilton's period as Match Secretary pre-1899

*   excludes unofficial wartime records

**   includes all major domestic cups, excluding Scottish Cup played in the prevailing period

based on points achieved relative to total available on standard two-point-per-game basis

Honours List

	LEAGUE TITLES	SCOTTISH CUPS	LEAGUE CUPS	EUROPEAN HONS	DOMESTIC 'TREBLES'
W. Wilton+	8	1	n/a	n/a	n/a
W. Struth*	18	10	2	n/a	1
S. Symon	6	5	4	–	1
D. White	–	–	–	–	–
W. Waddell	–	–	1	1 (ECWC)	–
J. Wallace	3	3	4	–	2
J. Greig	–	2	2	–	–
G. Souness	3	–	4	–	–
W. Smith	7	3	3	–	1
D. Advocaat	2	2	1	–	1

+ excludes Wilton's period as Match Secretary pre-1899
* excludes unofficial wartime records
ECWC European Cup-Winners' Cup

52 Mini Moments

Inspirational Mindfulness Techniques To Take You From Stressed To Smiling in Under Sixty Seconds

Clare Josa

Meditation & Mindfulness Teacher | NLP Trainer

Published by Beyond Alchemy Publishing in 2013

www.BeyondAlchemyPublishing.co.uk

ISBN 978-1-908854-44-5

© Clare Josa 2013

A catalogue record for this book is available from the British Library.

The advice in this book is intended for educational purposes only and it is not intended to substitute for professional medical advice. In the event that you use any of this information for yourself, the publisher and author accept no responsibility for your actions. Always consult your medical professional, if you are unsure about whether any of the suggested techniques are suitable for you.

Table Of Contents

Dedication

This book is dedicated to HH Dalai Lama and Thích Nhất Hanh. Thank you for everything you have taught me and for living a life of mindful compassion, inspiring us to see the beauty of who we really are and the interconnectedness of all beings.

Thank Yous

I extend my heart-felt gratitude to some of my greatest teachers, without whom I would never have been able to create this book for you.

To the inspirational Thích Nhất Hanh and HH Dalai Lama – thank you for your life-long dedication to helping people discover how to find the peace they were looking for, deep down inside, no matter what is happening in their lives.

To Chris Barrington and Savitri MacCuish from www.DruWorldwide.com, who have been my meditation mentors: thank you for your decades of abhyasa and your generosity of spirit, sharing so much with us all and helping to inspire me on my journey.

To my children, who have taught me so much about living in the moment, the many ways we curb our true spirit through life, along with how to undo those old choices, and also how to be patient. I wrap you in my deepest love.

To my husband, Peter, and my gorgeous boys, for their flexibility and patience, whenever my need to write and teach is too great to ignore. Thank you for your support – both moral and physical.

To my Dream Team, thank you for believing in the work I share and for being my cheer leaders, when I need you most. Thank you for being there.

To you, my reader, thank you (in advance!) for going and using this stuff. Each time you move yourself back towards feeling at peace, you create a gentle wave that will ultimately change the world. Namaste!

How To Get The Most From This Book

When you're feeling stressed, tired or in need of inspiration, you often don't have time to wade through hundreds of pages in a 'how to' book.

That's why I have written **52 Mindful Moments** for you, to make it easy for you to discover mindfulness techniques (both ancient practices and some modern twists) that can help you to de-stress, unwind, get more clarity, feel calmer and happier, in just a few minutes.

You can either:

- read the book from cover to cover, testing out and learning from your experience of each technique as you go along (perhaps even focussing on one each week?)

- or you can close your eyes, set the intention of finding the technique you need most in this moment, and open the book at random.

My hope is that these 52 ideas will inspire you to have all the stress-busting tools you need, well-practised and ready to use, whenever you need them.

This book doesn't go into the details of 'how to fix stress' or 'how to change your life' – that's not what you have time for, when you're in the middle of 'life' - though these techniques will help you to de-stress and change your life. Whenever you are ready to go deeper, my other books and courses can help.

In the meantime, these mindfulness techniques will be waiting for you, whenever you want to experiment with them, ready to take you back to that place of inner peace and calm, deep inside.

Bonus Resources For Readers

52 Mindful Moments comes with plenty of bonus resources for readers.

By registering as a member of the **Readers' Club** (it's free!), you get:

- **A 15 minute mindfulness meditation MP3**
  It's ideal for those times when you want to take your experience of inner peace even further.

- **Extra MP3s, videos and articles**
  These help you to have an even more powerful experience with the more in-depth techniques.

- **Exclusive private online community**
  Readers' Club members get to join in with a special discussion area for the **52 Mindful Moments** book, in our private online community – Soul-Sized Living. It's a great place to share your experiences, get answers to your questions and connect with others who are enjoying the techniques in this book.

- **Monthly Soul-Sized Living Newsletter**
  Members of the Readers' Club also get my monthly Soul-Sized Living newsletter, packed with the latest inspirational articles, life-changing techniques and members-only goodies.

Register today at:

 www.52MindfulMoments.com/ReadersClub

52 Mindful Moments

Kick-Start Guide

Welcome to 52 Mindful Moments!

To get the most from this book, I strongly suggest you begin by spending a few minutes flicking through this Kick-Start guide, before you dive into the techniques. It doesn't take long and it will lay useful foundations for the rest of this book.

It covers:

- the problem with 'mindlessness'
- what is mindfulness
- how it can help you
- how to avoid the most common life-change excuse
- how to spot the progress you're making

My invitation to you is to enjoy experimenting with these 52 mindfulness techniques. They have been specially designed to be easy to learn, as well as helping you to shift yourself from hectic to calm in under a minute.

Do they with a light heart and a smile on your face. Don't make the mistake of 'trying too hard' or 'forcing' the techniques to work. You'll get the best results by letting the exercises flow and discovering how they work for you. There's no 'right' or 'wrong' with mindfulness.

You don't need to add another 'should' to your daily 'to do' list. **All you need to do is spend a minute, a couple of times a day, playing with the technique.**

Some of the techniques might take more than 60 seconds, the first time you do them. But with practice, they'll be under a minute.

Some of the techniques are drawn from ancient spiritual wisdom traditions. Other are adapted and combined with insider secrets from modern psychology, to make it easy for you to experience mindfulness, every day, no matter how busy your life is.

Just imagine - a couple of minutes a day, each week, for a year and it will transform your experience of life.

Namaste,

Clare. ♡

What's The Problem With 'Mindlessness'?

Being mindful is a state of being – a particular way of choosing to experience life, in the present moment - rather than letting your mind run riot over past mistakes and future worries, whilst sleep-walking through what's actually going on around you.

We're normally too busy doing "mind-full" to be mindful.

Some common symptoms of 'mindlessness' or being 'mind-full'.

- Do you find yourself 'listening' to someone, whilst actually thinking more about your response? Do you realise you didn't really hear what they were

saying?

- Do you find yourself getting to the bottom of a cup of tea or coffee, without remembering drinking it?
- Do you forget where you put things?
- Do you walk into a room, but don't remember why you went there?
- Do you find yourself arriving at a destination, but not remembering the route you took?
- Do you find it hard to remember people's names?
- Do you find yourself getting stressed about not having enough time?

All of these - and plenty more - are symptoms of a mind so full of yesterday, tomorrow and 'what ifs', that it can't enjoy the present moment.

What Is Mindfulness?

I'm going to give you a practical definition of what mindfulness is, rather than a spiritual or religious definition:

Mindfulness is about actually experiencing life, while you're living it.

We tend to spend most of our time running away from our experience of life – hiding from it – perhaps because the stories our Monkey Mind tells us can create pain. Mindfulness is about being present to your experience of life, as it truly is, rather than wanting to change it or believing the drama and the stories.

The 'present moment' - 'here and now' is the only time you have.

10

Yesterday is done and dusted. Tomorrow isn't here yet. If you want to actually live your life, then ***now*** is the only time you can do it. Want to make changes in the future? Then you need to do them ***now***. Want to create a past that you're proud of? Then you need to take action ***now***.

But that's tough, when we don't even notice eating our breakfast or driving to work!

Being mindful means dragging yourself back into the present moment - away from the 'to do' list, the housework, next week's big meeting, last week's presentation and everything else that normally fills your mind to bursting point.

When we are 'mindless', we're living in the past or the future, rather than the 'now'. We are disconnected from the part of us that makes the unconscious choices about how to think, feel and act in every moment. It is hard to see what is 'real' and what is our Monkey Mind's story.

Are you too busy pretending you're a 'human doing'
to be a 'human being'?

We might feel scared that, by being in the present moment: the 'to do' list will get forgotten; the shopping won't get done; the kids won't get fed. (Don't worry - they'll remind you!) But, in fact, *it's the other way round*.

By focussing our experience right here, right now, we can develop a clarity that somehow creates more time in our day, meaning the 'to do' list gets shorter and becomes less of an obsession. It creates more spacing for living and actually experiencing life, as it is happening.

*When you are totally aware of what you are doing –
'doing with awareness' – it's amazing how much
more easily life flows.*

This then gives you the clarity you need to take inspired action, to make the changes that matter the most – more easily and effectively.

As a meditation technique, mindfulness is about using your focus and concentration to be aware of the present moment, rather than being lost in the future or worrying about the past. However **it's not about pretending that there isn't a future or a past**.

*It's about drawing your awareness back into your
physical body and experiencing life through all of
your senses; being truly present – and alive!*

It is the kind of experience you get when you look into somebody's eyes and you really connect. You know that they're there and so are you. Rather than talking to them whilst perhaps thinking about your shopping list and what you have got to cook for dinner, you're really 'present' with them.

Mindfulness is about living life as the sensory experience that it really is, in your physical body, rather than being stuck in your thinking mind.

It's ideal for a multi-tasking mind, because it gives your mind something to do! It gets to help run the process of 'being here'.

12

Just imagine…

- actually tasting your tea, as you drink it
- really feeling that cuddle
- really hearing the birdsong
- really smelling your coffee
- really seeing the beauty of the sun, peeping through the clouds
- really hearing what a loved-one is saying - and seeing the look in their face, when they know they have been heard
- actually feeling the comfort of your clothes on your body
- feeling your feet connect with the earth, with every step

Why settle for half-living?

The back of my business cards has a provocative quote, that sometimes gets me into trouble… It is:

Just because you're breathing, it doesn't mean you're alive.

But it sums up beautifully the difference between a life that is lived from the position of the Monkey Mind and a life that is lived with awareness – mindfully.

Mindfulness can bring your experience of life alive.

It is something you can do at any time, in any place, it feels great - and it's free! One of the great bonuses of mindfulness is that, as you become more familiar with how to practise it, **it doesn't take up any extra time.** You can do it wherever and whenever you want to, no matter how busy you are.

13

How Mindfulness Can Help You

Mindfulness can help you to:
- de-stress
- feel more calm
- feel more relaxed
- reconnect with your sense of inner peace
- think more clearly
- feel more healthy, as your body is no longer flooded with stress hormones and it becomes easier for you to make healthier life choices
- consciously choose how to experience your life
- set yourself free from living on auto-pilot

The power of mindfulness to change the way we think, feel and behave is so strong that even traditional medical doctors are now using mindfulness to help people who are suffering from, for example, clinical depression.

Universities are researching it. Mindfulness is also used in the training for many sports, where athletes really need moment-to-moment concentration and focus.

Imagine living your day actually being 'here' rather than, as I often call it, off on another planet!

Mindfulness is an amazing de-stressing, relaxation technique, which comes with the added bonus that life comes to life.

How Can You Get Back Into The Present Moment?

By getting out of your head and back into your senses.

That's the only way we can experience the present. Anything else – like a thought, feeling, word or action, is a reaction to the physical, sensory experience. And, by virtue of the way our brain chemistry functions, by the time we respond to something, that 'something' is already in the past.

By practising mindfulness, we'll get to a stage where any activity, be it walking, housework, giving a presentation or even picking the kids up from school, can be done with a level of awareness that means we are truly experiencing life and always have a choice.

By allowing the constant drone of "to do" lists and life analysis to fade into the background, it's much easier to feel calmer, less stressed, happier and more in flow with a vibrant experience of being alive.

It's about that split-second choice to come back into the here and now.

Here are some really quick ways you can do this:

- When you talk to someone, make eye contact.
  Actually look them in the eye and allow that connection to take place, just for a moment. It brings you back into the "now" and can transform the outcome of tricky conversations.
- Stop whatever you're doing and take a deep breath in, breathing out with

an "ahh" sound. That's got you back into your body, instantly.

- Stop doing three things at once and choose to just do one – and really focus on it.
- At any moment, ask yourself: "What can I see / hear / smell / taste / feel, right at this moment?"

The **52 Mindful Moments** exercises have been specially designed to help to increase your awareness and become more mindful, in the present moment.

With regular practise, this can easily become your 'normal' way of experiencing life. But it does take practice and an ongoing commitment to choosing to be aware and present.

Dealing with the #1 life-change excuse, once and for all!

But I Don't Have Time!

How do you find time to make changes in your life?

This is one of the most common reasons I hear from people about why they don't make changes... and I have to confess that I have lost count of how often I have used it myself!

When you're stuck in the middle of 'doing' your old habit, it can feel difficult to take the time out to stand back and become aware of what you are doing and which bits you want to change. Yet that time will repay you every single day, for

the rest of your life.

> *Someone I was talking to recently about changing her life was raving about wanting to de-stress. And she was excited about the idea of being able to lay the foundations, day by day, in the comfort of her own home. But when I asked her if she could spare a few minutes a day for it, her answer was, "No! I'm way too busy!"*

> *She was so convinced by her excuse that there was no room left for her to change.*

> *She would rather spend the next fifty years going through the pain of feeling super-stressed – and all the dis-ease that brings with it – than dedicate a few minutes a day to making the shifts she said she wanted.*

Is it really true that our lives are too full to find time to de-stress?

Surely much of our time is used up by the very stress patterns we want to shift?

How To Magically Create More Time

It is true that we often believe that we don't have enough time. But there's a difference between truth and belief.

We believe our stories and excuses, telling them to ourselves so often that they become a pseudo-truth that we no longer question – like 'received wisdom'. We even start to believe in other people's excuses! But is it really true?

It's funny how, for example, if we fall in love, we suddenly find plenty of evenings and weekends to spend with that wonderful new person:

- we watch less TV
- we read fewer magazines
- we spend less time on the internet
- we spend less time on chores
- we use our time more intentionally
- we work more efficiently
- we drop anything that's not essential

Is it really too much for your mind, body and soul to ask for a few minutes of your time each day for something that can dramatically impact your life?

There are many 'important jobs' and distractions during the day that steal our time; things that crop up unexpectedly, where we give them our immediate attention. Everything else falls off the table, including the time we had set aside for working 'on ourselves'. Yet if we were to tell those distractions, "I will come back to you later," it's amazing how they either go away or take up less time.

> *The classic example is a phone call.*
> *You're in the middle of something important, but you answer the phone anyway. The conversation takes ten minutes. Then you go back to what you were doing.*
> *You found ten minutes for the interruption.*
> *So why do we find it so hard to find even a few minutes to change our lives…?*

Little And Often
You will notice a much faster, deeper-acting impact from your mindfulness practices if you do them 'little and often', rather than blitzing them, once in a blue

moon.

I encourage you to remind yourself, each day, to experiment with one (or more!) of these exercises, to allow them to create shifts in your experience of life.

Inspiration can give us the idea. Motivation can get us started. But it's routine and habit that create the change.

Make a commitment to yourself, today, to spend a few minutes learning mindfulness techniques that can shift your experience of life.

It's worth pausing for a moment, just now, to decide **how you are going to remember to do these exercises.**

How To Spot The Progress You're Making

It's easy to miss the changes we make in our lives. We're too busy 'doing the living' to notice them. So make sure you keep a radar on for those shifts.

Some people find it helpful to keep a journal. Others find they like to take time to reflect, every few weeks, to compare how they used to handle life 'in the olden days' with how they're handling it now.

Whatever you choose, it's important to allow yourself to spot those shifts – and to take a few moments to congratulate yourself on those changes. It's the best way to ensure your mind brings you more of them!

Snapshot: Where are you now?

One of the easiest ways to notice the progress you're making is to learn to take a 'snapshot' – to notice 'where you're at' at the moment. If you do this every few weeks, you'll really see the shifts.

Here are some simple questions that can help you to figure that out.

You might find it helps to write the answers down.

1. Which emotions do you feel most often, during a typical day?
2. How would you describe your stress levels?
3. What speed does your mind typically think?
4. How would you describe your energy levels and your physical health?
5. Why are you choosing to learn mindfulness?
6. How often do you actually taste your food, as you eat it?
7. If you could make one change in your life, what would it be?
8. How will you know when you have made that change?
9. If you could give one piece of advice to yourself, right here, right now, what would it be?

Now it's time to dive in and experience the first of these 52 mindfulness techniques.

52 Mindful Moments

The Mindfulness Techniques

The 52 Mindfulness Techniques

1. Three Mindful Breaths

This is such a simple mindfulness technique, yet it has the potential to shift you from feeling stressed to feeling calm in just 3 breaths.

The more often you use it, the more your body and mind will become anchored into its effects and it will begin to work even more quickly for you.

Eventually, you'll find yourself starting to return to equilibrium as soon as you remember to do it – even before you actually do the technique!

- It releases physical tension.
- It releases mental tension.
- It shifts your focus back to 'here and now'.

Not bad for 3 simple mindful breaths?

This '3 Mindful Breaths' technique is a foundation mindfulness technique and it is often used at the beginning of other mindfulness exercises.

It is so core to experiencing mindfulness that perhaps I should have called it technique zero, instead of #1?

It's a great way to bring you 'back down to earth', when you have been stuck in your 'stress-head', getting you ready for the more in-depth techniques. So it's worth practising this one, until it becomes second nature for you – it doesn't take long.

How To Do 3 Mindful Breaths:

1. Stop whatever you are doing and sit or stand with your back fairly straight, rather than slouched.

2. Take a deep breath from your belly area, breathing all the way in through your nose.

3. Breathe out through your mouth, with an 'ahhhh' sound' (it can be silent, if you need it to be!) Really experience the physical sensations in your body as you do this.

4. As you breathe out, imagine you are releasing any stress and tension from your body and your mind.

5. Do this 3 times. Smile. **Notice the difference.**

Once you have practised this a few times, it can help you shift from feeling stressed in just 3 breaths.

The more often you do it during your day, the more you will be anchored into it bringing you back to a mindful state of being and the more effectively it will create that shift for you.

How might you remind yourself to do this?

- Perhaps each time you look at your watch?
- Or each time you hang up the phone?
- Or each time you boil the kettle?

23

2. Have You Forgotten How To Breathe?

Before we start, I invite you to take a moment to notice where in your body you're breathing right now. I know that sounds like a strange question: "Where are you breathing?" But, for most of us, we have no idea where we are breathing and it's often not where it should be.

To test where you're breathing: place your hand over your diaphragm – that is the bit of your belly above your belly button, below your ribcage. Notice whether or not it moves when you're breathing for the next few moments. **Still can't quite tell?** Look in the mirror and see whether your shoulders or upper chest are moving.

Most of us have forgotten how to breathe.

When you watch a baby breathe, it naturally breathes from the tummy area, in a smooth, effortless, gentle rhythm. That's the way our body is designed to breathe: the diaphragm moves down, causing the rib cage to expand, opening up the lungs, filling them with oxygen-rich air. Then as you breathe out the diaphragm moves up compressing everything, naturally expelling the air. It should be a pretty much effortless process.

But when we get stressed or stuck in our thoughts, our breathing tends to move up to the chest area. We end up using the intercostal chest muscles to breathe, instead of the diaphragm. And if we're really stressed our breathing moves up to the shoulders and even the throat. Not only do we end up working too hard to breathe, but we're not getting enough oxygen into the body, which causes physiological stress and starves the brain of oxygen-rich blood, making it harder

to think clearly.

The mind and body are linked, so if the body feels stressed, then the mind starts thinking stressful thoughts, stressful hormones go round, we feel more stressed, we experience stressful emotions and the cycle continues.

You can put a "pause" in this by subtly shifting how you're breathing - mindfully.

As usual do this within your comfortable limits. *If you've got breathing issues or severe asthma you might want to talk to your medical professional first.* **If you can't do this breathing exercise, visualise it, imagine it. It will have a similar effect.**

1. Putting your hands on your abdomen, over your diaphragm, just above the belly button area, with your fingertips lightly touching.

2. Allow your chest to expand as you breathe in. Allow it to gently sink towards your spine as you breathe out. (It's not the time to be thinking about flat tummies, it's ok for your stomach to move!)

3. As you breathe in from just above your belly button, you should notice your fingers slightly moving apart, as your chest expands.

4. As you breathe out they return together, as your abdomen contracts.

5. Feel the cycle – the gentle rhythm – of your breathing. Allow your breathing to continue, at a slightly slower pace than usual, for a minute or two, letting your awareness rest gently on the physical experience of breathing.

Continue until you feel the 'shift' as your body relaxes and you return to the present moment.

3. Turning Your Awareness Inside

We spend most of our time in our heads – or at least not in our bodies. If you were to interrupt someone in the course of their day and ask them how their physical body was feeling, most would be totally unaware.

We take the input from our senses and we analyse it, critique it, compare it, have long discussions with ourselves about it, but we rarely *experience* it.

What's the problem with this?

Your head isn't where your life is.

We are souls, here to have a physical experience of life, not just an intellectual one.

By coming back into your body, you will nearly instantly:

- Cut your stress levels, as you allow your body to stop producing so many stress hormones, rebalancing your sympathetic ('fight or flight') and parasympathetic ('relaxation') nervous systems.
- Get more clarity, as your thoughts slow down.
- Shift your focus from your Monkey Mind's projections and stories to sensory perceptions of "what's real?"
- Feel more centred, grounded and at peace.
- Allow your body to more easily go about its daily tasks, even at a cellular level.

How to turn your awareness inside:

1. Start with 3 Mindful Breaths [from technique #1]

2. Breathe in, with your focus gently resting on the physical experience of breathing. Consciously choose to bring your awareness back into your body.

3. Breathe out and relax into your physical body. Gently close your eyes.

4. As you breathe in and out, gently send your focus around your body, experiencing the physical sensations of being 'in your body' in each area for a few seconds.

5. As you relax into this exercise, you may even become aware of the rhythms of your body, including your breathing, your blinking and your heartbeat.

6. Accept any bits that ache. Perhaps say 'thank you' to each part, as you move around your body with your inner focus.

7. When you feel ready, move your focus to one part of your body, for example, the big toe on your right foot. Allow yourself to become fully absorbed in noticing the physical sensations in that big toe. How does it feel if you wiggle it? How does it feel when you let it rest? Allow all of your focus to rest in that big toe.

8. If your Monkey Mind needs a job, tell it to describe the physical sensations, without judgement.

9. When you feel you are back 'here and now', release this practice.

This is a lovely exercise to be guided through, so there's a bonus MP3 audio of it for you at:

www.52MindfulMoments.com/ReadersClub

4. Is It Time To Be Like A Tree?

Most of us live in our heads, somewhere in the past or the future, rather than in our sensory bodies, in the present moment.

It's a modern epidemic. We're not really 'here'.

There's a side-effect of this. It's as though all of the mental energy we are using stays stuck in your body, like static electricity. Then, just like static, if it connects with something that accidentally earths it, you get a shock.

That shock often comes out as an unexpected emotional outburst or even a physical pain.

So grounding that 'static' is really important.

Here's a mindfulness exercise that works with your breath and with visualisation. Note: if you don't 'think in pictures' and find it hard to visualise, that's fine. You can imagine or get a sense of this technique in any way that works for you.

Time To Be Like A Tree

1.   Stand up and start with 3 mindful breaths [see technique #1]

2.   Imagine there is a cord at the crown of your head, gently pulling upwards, allowing your posture to straighten, slightly tucking under your tailbone, and allowing your spine to lengthen, vertebra by vertebra. When you can sense a tiny space between each vertebra, your spine will still be gently curved, but your posture will feel taller and your centre of balance may have shifted.

3. Tuck your chin under slightly, which releases tension and lengthens the back of your neck.

4. Allow your shoulders to relax and let a gentle smile rest on your face. Your body feels strong, but relaxed and supple.

5. Now send your focus to the soles of your feet. Imagine – visualise / feel / get a sense of that connection - between your feet and the earth beneath you. Feel yourself putting out roots into the earth, growing and anchoring you deeply and firmly. Feel and see those roots getting stronger and deeper, spreading in all directions.

6. When you can sense those roots, imagine you are breathing in from the earth, through those roots, through the soles of your feet. And breathe out through the soles of your feet, back into the earth. Continue for a few breaths.

7. When you feel ready, as you breathe in, draw the anchored and grounded earth energy in through the soles of your feet and up to your chest area.

8. When you breathe out, release 'static' and tension down from your chest area and out into the earth, through the soles of your feet.

9. Continue this cycle for at least 7 breaths.

10. Know that, like a tree, your roots are grounded in the earth and your branches can choose to sway gently in the breeze.

11. When you feel fully grounded, smile and release the exercise.

5. Getting Ready For Your Day

How often do we get up and run our early morning on auto pilot? How often do we taste our tea or coffee? How often do we actually experience getting showered? How often do we remember anything we did, before leaving the house?

Early mornings can be a whirlwind of stress, tension and rush, which sets the tone for the rest of your day. Is that what you really want?

Instead of rushing, fixating on your 'to do' list or worrying and telling yourself stories about things that might never happen, how about using your morning routine as a chance to reconnect with the present moment, cut your stress levels and leave the house with a smile on your face?

Here's a simple mindfulness exercise to get your day off to a great start. And it doesn't take up any extra time.

Brushing Your Teeth – Mindfully

Brushing teeth is something we do (hopefully!) twice a day. Research shows that the average length of time that people brush their teeth for is just 18 seconds – a long way short of the two minutes that dentists recommend.

Yet keeping your teeth and gums healthy is about more than time. If you brush your teeth while you're thinking about your 'to do' list and everything else that is going on in life, the likelihood of you doing a good job is pretty low.

Fortunately brushing your teeth mindfully not only improves your tooth and gum health, but it also helps you to de-stress, relax and smile.

It' really simple:

1. Take 3 mindful breaths, to centre yourself and come back to 'here and now'.

2. Mindfully pick up your toothbrush and put the toothpaste on it.

3. Mindfully brush each tooth, one at a time, brushing the whole tooth and gum area (safely!), before moving on to the next tooth.

4. If your mind wanders, bring it back to brushing your teeth.

5. If your mind needs something to do, how about getting it to say 'thank you' to your teeth and your toothbrush?

6. When you are done, mindfully rinse your mouth out, put your toothbrush away and smile.

Notice how different you feel?

Imagine how you could apply this type of mindfulness to other aspects of your morning routine, all by using mindful awareness?

- Washing your hair
- Having a shower
- Getting dressed
- Having breakfast
- Putting on your coat?

6. How To Make Sure You Never Lose Your Keys Again

I remember, a few years ago, running an NLP seminar for a group of business executives and asking them what the number one thing was that they wanted to learn that day. One of them piped up that he was fed up with losing his keys. He spent ages, each day, hunting for his keys, especially when he was in a hurry. And the rest of the group wanted to fix that one, too.

It wasn't quite what I had expected them to say, but fortunately I was able to share with them a simple mindfulness process that helps you make sure you never lose your keys again, as well as reminding you to come back to the present moment, each time you hold your keys.

It works equally well for anything you handle regularly, which you can't find easily!

The reason we lose our keys is because we are being 'mind-less' or 'mind-full' when we put them down.

We are usually having conversations with ourselves about everything else that needs to be done – or reviewing, analysing and critiquing our day. So it's no wonder that the 'key-thing' is running on auto pilot and we don't consciously remember where we put them.

Here's how to make sure you never lose your keys again:

1. **Before you even start with this one, could you choose a special place to put your keys, whenever you come home?**
   A hook? A shelf? A drawer? Creating a routine around your keys saves

you having to remember where you put them.

2. **When you get your keys to open your front door, allow yourself to take 3 mindful breaths**
[technique #1] (don't worry – you won't need to do this every time – it's just while you're anchoring yourself into this new mindful key behaviour!)

3. **Open your door and then say to yourself: "I mindfully put my keys** _____" – wherever your special place is.

4. **Put your keys there and actually experience it with your senses:** what do you see as you do it? What do you hear? What are the tactile sensations?

5. **When your keys are there, take a moment to see them and know they are there.**
Know that you'll remember it now.

6. **Do this each day for a week** and you'll have created the new habit.

How do you remind yourself to do this in the first place?

You could tie a big and colourful luggage label on your key ring, to tell you to be mindful about them!

You could stick a Post-It by the lock on your front door?

I'm wondering: is there anything else you misplace regularly, where a little bit of mindfulness could help?

33

7. Taste Your Tea

Have you ever drunk a mug of tea or coffee, got to the end of it and realised you have no memory of drinking it?

It's a common symptom of 'mind-fullness', when we go onto auto-pilot, living in your head, not your present moment.

As an antidote, today I am going to invite you to taste your tea. Of course, it's a metaphor for shifting your experience of life.

It's a classic exercise that you can do to practice mindful awareness. And the great thing is that it doesn't take up your time, yet it brings huge benefits - fast.

The next time you make yourself a drink, hot or cold, I invite you to:

1. **Sit down with it.**
    Don't drink it on the run.

2. **Before you pick it up and drink it, actually look at it.**
    Really drag all of your awareness into the process of seeing what you see. Notice the glass, cup or mug it's in. Really see how the light reflects off it. Allow yourself to see the textures. There might be steam or ice-cold bubbles.
    Notice what you notice, in minute detail.

3. **Pick it up and notice the tactile feel of the cup or glass.**
    How does it feel in your hands? Perhaps there is a warmth or a coolness? How heavy is it? Is it smooth? Textured? Really allow your full awareness to

rest in your fingertips for a few moments as you hold the drink.

4. **Before you drink the drink, take a sniff**.
   Spend a moment allowing the smell to fill your awareness, letting your concentration gently rest on your drink.

5. **As you start to drink, sipping gently or gulping, it's up to you, allow yourself to really taste your drink.**
   Taste your tea, taste your water, whatever it is you're drinking. Experience the sensation over your tongue and your taste buds. And, as you swallow, allow yourself to hear the sound.
   Be fully present to the experience of 'tasting your tea'.

Once you are used to playing with this, it takes no time at all. Your cup of tea (or whatever you're drinking) becomes an automatic unconscious anchor to help you remember to be mindful - to come back to the 'now' - to experience life, rather than your mind's story of life.

Even if you are talking to someone or working on your computer, as you drink your tea, each time you pick up your mug for another sip, you can return to that calm place of being mindful, even if just for a few moments.

Normally we would make a cup of tea in a hurry, get to the end of it and wonder where it went. We drink unconsciously, we eat unconsciously, we live unconsciously, as though we are half-asleep.

Practising mindful interaction with every day experiences is the fastest way to learn mindfulness – and shift your experience of life.

8. Raisin Mindfulness (Or Chocolate!)

Surely life is too short to stay stuck in your Monkey Mind's stories and miss out on how fabulous a raisin (or even a piece of chocolate, if that's your thing!) can taste?

Most of us eat raisins by grabbing a handful, throwing them in and giving them a quick chew before swallowing. We rarely even taste them. This next raisin (or piece of chocolate) is going to be a quite different experience!

How To Get A Raisin To Help You With Mindfulness

1. **Grab a raisin – just one.**
   Or a small piece of dried fruit / piece of chocolate, if raisins aren't your thing.

2. **Sit comfortably.**
   It's time to wrap your senses round your raisin.

3. **Look at it. Really see it.**
   What do you notice? Can you see its texture? What about the bumps and lumps? How does the light reflect off it?

4. **Have a sniff. What does it smell like?**
   Let your fingertips really feel the shape and texture. How light or heavy is it? Allow yourself to become fully absorbed in the experience.

5. **It's ok if your mind wanders.**
   If your mind wanders during this experience, just allow it to be gently guide it back to your raisin.

6. **After a few minutes, pop the raisin in your mouth - but it's not time to chew yet!**
   Spend a little while focussing on what it feels like in your mouth, with your tongue and your teeth. Notice what you can taste already.

7. **Then, when you're ready, take a bite, have a good chew.**
   Notice the full experience of the raisin's flavour – how it builds in your mouth. How incredibly sweet it is.

8. **When you have swallowed the raisin, you'll notice you can still taste it for a while.**

How did this experience compare to your usual raisin-munching experience?

- Chances are it was much more vivid?
- Did you notice things you wouldn't normally notice?
- Did you enjoy it more?
- Do you think that you might eat less, if you actually tasted your food?
- What have you learned about how being mindful – aware, in the present moment – can impact your experience of eating a raisin?
- How could you take these learnings and apply them elsewhere in your life?

If you'd like to watch a video to take you through this technique or if you'd like to share your experiences with it via the private online forum, check out the links in the Readers' Club:

www.52MindfulMoments.com/ReadersClub

9. Mindful Eating

How often do you get to the end of a meal without tasting a single mouthful?

Eating is one of the activities that we do most mindlessly. We pile food onto a fork, put it in, chew a couple of times while we're getting the next forkful ready, pop that in (often before we swallow the last one) and load up the next fork.

We all have to eat. It's part of staying alive. So if you think you don't have time to practise mindfulness, how about challenging yourself to take 5 mindful forkfuls, next time you eat?

1. **Start by taking 3 mindful breaths** [see technique #1], to bring your focus back to the present moment

2. **Look at your plate. See your meal.** Notice the colours, the textures, the patterns. Smell your food. Become fully aware of it.

3. **Put some food on your fork, being aware of the physical sensations** as your fingers, hand, wrist, arm and shoulder muscles work together for this.

4. **Put the food in your mouth** and, for a moment, before you chew, allow your focus to rest on the food in your mouth. Put your fork down!

5. **Now chew your food – slowly, mindfully and with full awareness**. Chew for longer than you usually would. Taste it! Be present to the flavours in the different areas of your tongue – and the textures – and even the sounds. *We scarcely chew our food. Yet that's what teeth are for! Chewing your food breaks it down and allows saliva to start the digestion process. If un-chewed*

food enters your stomach, the stomach acids have to do the work of your teeth and mouth, which can lead to digestive problems. It is harder for the body to absorb nutrients from food that hasn't been chewed!

6.   When you are ready, **swallow your food**. **Pause for a moment**, to notice how it feels to eat mindfully. How did your body react to that mouthful?

7.   Now move on to your next mindful forkful.

Deepak Chopra (a Medical Doctor and spiritual teacher) has proved that eating mindfully helps you to be more aware of the body's "I'm full" message. It can help you to manage your appetite and to stabilise at your ideal weight.

Want to take this further?

How about becoming aware of the impact your food has on you? One great way is to spend a few days keeping a 'mood-food diary'.

Draw a line with the hours of the day on it. Write down everything that you eat and drink during the day, against the relevant time. Then, at least once an hour (set yourself an alarm?) write down next to that time how you are feeling – physically, emotionally and mentally.

It doesn't take long for you to be able to spot trends. And, as we've already discussed, awareness is the first step towards change.

There's a bonus article to accompany this technique, called "***Are You Eating Yourself Miserable?***". Check it out via the links in the Readers' Club:

www.52MindfulMoments.com/ReadersClub

10. Coming Back To Your Senses

Just because you're breathing, it doesn't mean you're alive.

I sometimes put this on the back of my business cards. It can get me into trouble, but it does sum up the problem with 'mindlessness'.

When we're in flow, we experience how vibrant life can be. It's as though our senses are on fire.

Henry Miller, who was a prolific and talented writer and artist, summed up how mindfulness can help us enter that state of aliveness:

"The moment one gives close attention to anything, even a blade of grass, it becomes a mysterious, awesome, indescribably magnificent world in itself."

That's exactly what we're experimenting with, when we practise mindfulness.

Giving your full attention - directing all of your awareness - to any one thing creates a miraculous chain reaction:

- It drags you out of your Monkey Mind (the chattering commentary bit!) and back into the present moment.

- It can help you instantly let go of stresses and worries.

- It helps you to reconnect with the Earth beneath your feet, rather than the illusory version of it in your mind.

- It helps you to reconnect with what's 'real', letting go of what is 'story' or drama.

So the effects are so much more than simply being able to see the object.

Coming back to your senses.

1. Choose an object – any object – but if you can choose something made by nature, it seems to work even better.

2. Take 3 mindful breaths [see technique #1], to bring you back to this moment.

3. Now look at this object and set the intention to see it with your heart, rather than your head.

4. Notice what you notice. See every contour, the way it reflects the light, the patterns, the textures, the colours.

5. If you mind wanders, that's ok; bring it back to the object.

6. If it's something you can touch, hold it and feel it under your fingertips or in your palm. Allow yourself to be fully absorbed by observing the object.

Any time you need to de-stress, the easiest and quickest way to do it is to come back to your sensory experience.

It brings you back to the here and now and out of your Monkey Mind, back into your physical body. It helps you let go of the stories and opens you up to creative solutions.

11. Give Your Day An Instant Lift With A Mindful Smile

Sometimes it can be easy to fall into the trap of thinking that we have nothing to smile about, but smiling can be transformational and it can be an amazing way to cut your stress levels and dump life's drama. And smiling mindfully means you'll benefit even more from it.

The sympathetic nervous system is our fight or flight response – the primal part of the brain (the hypothalamus) – which is responsible for short term survival-style decisions, which diverts fuel from non-essential bodily processes and organs, to help give you the energy to escape from imminent danger. It's the bit we drag into action when we're feeling stressed, which floods your system with stress hormones. The parasympathetic nervous system is all about relaxation and allowing your cells to carry on with their vital health-giving moment-to-moment tasks.

When you smile you trigger the endorphins that rebalance those two systems dramatically cutting the stress levels in your body.

> *Smiling, even if you're not in the mood, triggers the release of the body's happy chemicals, which cheer you up.*

Y our body doesn't care whether it's a real smile or a fake one. If we do it for 30-60 seconds, the hormones start flooding round the body and the happier feeling grows, so the smile soon becomes real!

So if you want an instant mood lift, get smiling.

Want to test it out?

- Sit down for a moment and slouch.

  Really get that slopping seating position where your head is verging on doing a nodding dog impression. Yes… that's it.

  Now frown. Look really grumpy. Notice how you're feeling?

Ready for the contrast?

- Sit up as straight as is comfortable for you, lift your chin slightly and scrunch up your eyes tightly for 3 seconds before opening them again – that releases the tension around our eyes, which we need to do before the next bit.

- Now: gently allow the corners of your mouth to turn upwards, ever-so-slightly, then a little bit more.

  You are now smiling! Not a lame little smirk. We're talking full-on smiles – teeth and all, if that's your thing. Smile with your eyes, smile with your mouth. Smile with your heart. Think 'smiley' thoughts. Feel the lift as you do it for a full 60 seconds.

Now let it go and notice what you notice.

Chances are you'll be feeling better. Your face should feel more relaxed, your mood should have lifted and you should be aware that you are generally feeling more positive.

12. Are You Wearing Your Shoulders As Earrings?

One of the most simple things you can do to de-stress is to get more oxygen flowing to your brain. And you can do it mindfully, to help you really notice the difference it makes.

Stress leads to poor posture and stiff shoulders. Anything that we do (or think!) that causes tension in the upper back, the neck or the shoulder area will restrict the oxygen – the blood flow – to your brain, making it harder to concentrate and making you feel tired and even more stressed, as well as potentially leading to long-term health problems.

This mindfulness exercise releases upper back, neck and shoulder tension. It feeds your brain with its life-force: oxygen. It gives you more clarity of thinking and it brings you back to the present moment, by connecting your breathing with the physical movement.

Here's How To Mindfully Stop Wearing Your Shoulders As Earrings

1. **Become aware of your posture** – how are you sitting right now? 'Where' are your shoulders? Are they hanging nice and loosely? Or are they half way up to your ears?

2. **Take three mindful breaths** from technique #1.

3. **Gently (within your own comfort levels) lengthen your spine.**
   Imagine there is a string from the crown of your head gently lifting up, pulling all the way through your spine. It's about subtly lengthening the space between each vertebra until you feel the lift, all the way through the

neck to the crown of the head.

And then tuck your chin under slightly, which lengthens the back of your neck. Can you feel the difference already?

4. **And now, as you breathe in, really lift your shoulders up as close to your ears as you can get them**, both at the same time.

Give them a good squeeze and hold it for a few seconds (keep it safe and comfortable!).

Allow yourself to be fully aware of the physical sensations.

5. **Now give a big sigh as you release your shoulders.**

Just let them drop. Does that feel good?

Do it again! Pull your shoulders up to your ears as you breathe in… and sigh as you let them drop. And one more time, breathe in as you lift your shoulders, scrunching them up to your ears, then sigh as you let them drop.

6. Next, doing this within your safe comfort limits, **roll your shoulders forward, lift them up and roll them behind you in a circle**. Do that two or three times just to release the tension in all of the muscles in that area. And you might find that **you want to reverse directions a few times**.

7. To finish off, give yourself a mindful shoulder and neck rub. And smile.

Can you feel how much clearer your mind feels? Can you feel how much more relaxed you feel? And it was just a few moments of mindfully releasing shoulder and neck tension.

13. Time To Get Hands-On?

Did you know that a decent hand massage activates acupressure points that impact your whole body? Just as with the foot in reflexology, the hand contains tiny pressure points that are connected with the rest of your body. So massaging your hand can help the rest of your body to relax.

And, if you combine the massage with intentional mindfulness, it can cut your stress levels and help you to smile, by relaxing your mind, too.

Mindful Hand Massage

1. **Start with 3 mindful breaths** [see technique #1]

2. **Take a 'snapshot'.**
   Briefly scan your body and mind, noticing how you are feeling and any areas of tension. noticing what kind of thoughts you are thinking and the speed your mind is running at.

3. **Look at the hand you are going to massage.**
   We all know the saying about "knowing something like the back of your hand" – but would you actually recognise the back of your hand – or your palm, if you were shown a picture of it? Most of us wouldn't. So spend a few moments really seeing the palm of your hand – noticing its patterns, its textures, how the light reflects, any old scars.

4. **Now allow your awareness to rest in that hand.**
   Become aware of the physical sensations and any areas of tension, any warmth, any pressure, any tingling or buzzing.

5. **Squeeze that hand into a tight ball.**

   Then release it. Do it again.

   Now stretch your fingers as wide as you can. Release and relax.

   What has shifted? What do you notice?

6. **Begin to use your other hand to massage your hand.**

   Start with the palm and work, mindfully, all over the palm and, one by one, along each finger. Relax and enjoy this massage.

7. **Finish your hand massage.**

   Notice the physical sensations in your hand. How have they shifted?

8. **Take another 'snapshot'.**

   Now repeat that body and mind scan, taking another snapshot. What has shifted? How have the tense areas changed? What has happened to your thoughts?

This is a mindfulness exercise you can do in under a minute, once you have practised it a few times. It can really help to cut your stress levels. Imagine using it next time you're stuck in traffic? The next time you're waiting for the kettle to boil? The next time you're feeling bored and fed up? It might make all the difference.

This can be a potent mindfulness exercise, so if you'd like to share your experiences of it or ask any questions, please check out the link to the Readers' Club forum at:

www.52MindfulMoments.com/ReadersClub

14. Could This Be The Solution To Not Having Enough Time?

How often do we spend our time fretting about not having enough time? It seems to fly by. And the more stressed we are, the faster it goes.

I'd like to share with you a near-magic-wand for creating more time in your day.

No, it's not a time machine. And you don't have to give up sleeping. It's a single gratitude phrase – a mantra - that you can choose to say, with mindfulness. And its effects can feel miraculous.

The way we feel about time is determined by the stories we tell ourselves about it.

When we're hiding away in the realms of the Monkey Mind and its stories of stress, time is a scarce resource over which we have no control. We run the mantra, "I don't have enough time." And we prove ourselves right. In fact:

Whether you think you have enough time or you think you don't, you're right.

Time is largely a matter of perception. When we convince ourselves that we don't have enough time, we trigger the body's sympathetic nervous system's 'fight or flight' stress responses, setting off chemical reactions that pump you full of adrenalin and other stress hormones. These shift your thinking to the primal part of the brain, responsible for life-or-death short-term decision making, meaning it's harder for you to concentrate and you will get less done.

It's as though getting stressed about time steals time form you. Yes,

sometimes we don't have enough time. But mindfulness can help you to make the most of the time you have.

We all have the same number of minutes in a day. And, within reason, we have a huge amount of choice over how we spend them. The whole concept of 'have to' and 'not enough time' is a story concocted by the good old Monkey Mind, based on the diet we have fed it over the decades.

So how can you magically create the feeling of having more time?

By being grateful for the time you have.

Giving gratitude for the time you have lets go of the Monkey Mind's stress-stories and helps time to expand. So if you feel rushed and need more time, here's what you can do:

1. Take three mindful breaths (see technique #1)

2. Allow yourself to settle in your body, rebalancing the body's stress and relaxation systems for a few moments.

3. Now allow yourself to experience the effects of the mantra:
   I am grateful for the time I have.

4. Consciously choose to focus, mindfully, on feeling grateful for the time you have. Notice the shift – you'll feel it in your body and mind.

After all, this moment is all the time we're ever going to get, so why on earth waste even a moment of it by feeling grumpy about it?

15. One Mindful Minute

This mindfulness technique is lovely because it not only helps you to return to the present moment, coming back 'here and now', it also helps you to practise acceptance.

Acceptance is crucial for cutting your stress levels and feeling happier.

Most of the time, feeling bad about things is a result of the stories we have been used to telling ourselves. We want things to be different, we want people to behave in other ways, but we're too busy telling those stories to be able to actually change things – or we want to change things that are beyond our control.

Acceptance is about acknowledging – in this moment – how things are and pressing pause on the stories. Then you can choose whether or not to take inspired action.

Then you can choose whether to stick with that sense of "It's ok" or to use mindfulness techniques to get clarity over which actions you *could* take.

There's a difference between 'acceptance' and 'acceptable'. If something is genuinely unacceptable (rather than what I call 'stroppily unacceptable'!), then it's important to take action and to make changes.

You can accept that something is currently unacceptable, without condoning it or pretending that it is ok. (Brain in a spin yet?!) But if you haven't accepted how

things currently are, how can you make changes?

It's like refusing to accept what your SatNav tells you is your current location, but expecting to plan a successful route.

Here's an exercise to help you practise mindful acceptance.

1. Take 3 mindful breaths [see technique #1]

2. Whatever you are doing, pause and simply be still for a minute.

3. Allow yourself to be 'in your body' and to experience what is happening, in this moment. Slow down.

4. See what you see. Hear what you hear. Feel the sensations. Smell what you smell. Taste what you taste. If your mind wanders, gently but firmly bring it back to this mindful moment.

5. Allow a wave of acceptance – of 'ok-ness' - to wash through this experience, in this moment. It is how it is and – in this moment – it's ok.

6. Allow your breathing to relax and your mind to slow down, as that wave of acceptance of this moment helps you to let go – in this moment - of any need to control or to change your experience. Feel the relief as you let go and relax into this moment.

7. Notice what has shifted, as you release this exercise.

51

16. Breath Awareness

Full breath awareness, often called 'mindful breathing', is one of the foundation techniques for learning mindfulness meditation.

It is something you can do wherever you are, whatever is going on around you, and no one will notice.

It also has the potential to transform your experience of life. And it's free.

Not bad for such a simple idea?

Mindful breathing helps you to gently move out of your 'Monkey Mind', with its stories, dramas and stresses, back into the present moment, experiencing life 'here and now'.

By becoming aware of your breathing, you are helping yourself to:

- Learn how to concentrate – it's amazing how your mind can wander, even with such a supposedly simple task. It's great brain training.
- Calm and slow your mind, as it switches from multi-tasking to a few moments of just concentrating on one thing.
- Rebalance your body's stress hormones - as your focus on your breathing, and only your breathing, gives your body the signal to stop flooding your system with adrenalin and other stress hormones, allowing your body's relaxation response to come back into play.

This technique is a wonderful de-stressing tool, as well as being useful mindfulness practice. The benefits are huge. Want to give it a go?

1. Stop whatever you are doing and take a deep breath in to your belly, just above your belly button. Breathe out with an 'ahhhh' sound, as you relax your body and mind (you can make this silent!). Do this 3 times.

2. Now allow your breathing to settle into a natural, comfortable rhythm.

3. Bring all of your focus to your breathing. Allow your mind to rest, watching, listening to and feeling the physical sensations of your breath.

4. If your Monkey Mind needs a job, as you breathe in, you might like to mentally say, "I breathe in."

5. As you breathe out, you might like to mentally say, "I breathe out."

6. If you are feeling particularly stressed, you might choose phrases such as "I breathe in relaxation; I breathe out stress and worry."

7. If your mind wanders, that's ok. Gently bring it back to following your breath.

8. Repeat this for at least a minute. Do it in a relaxed way, with a gentle smile on your face.

You might find it easier to concentrate if you close your eyes.

Even if you're not feeling stressed, you can still benefit hugely from regular practise of mindful breathing throughout your day. It can help you move into the present moment much more easily. And the more you practise it, the easier it gets. It has a subtle, profound impact on all aspects of your experience of life.

17. Ten Mindful Steps

Practising mindfulness while you walk is amazingly powerful, as a way of training your mind to come back into the present moment, but without taking up loads of your time.

You may have 'done' mindful walking before, or it may be new to you. Either way, I invite you to let go of any preconceptions and release anything you have previously tried, coming to this 'ten mindful steps' process with fresh eyes (or feet!).

Walking, mindfully, is a potent and incredibly useful, for 3 main reasons:

- Walking is something we all do, every day, so there's no excuse not to practise! Even if you can't walk, you can visualise walking, and achieve the same benefits.

- Many people find 'silent sitting' meditations difficult, because their Monkey Mind chatters. Combining mindful meditation with movement quietens your mind more easily – and gives it something to do.

- Walking is a very physical process, which most of us do on auto-pilot, so it's perfect for training ourselves to come back into the present moment and to increase your awareness of physical sensations – the sensory experience of life.

And, rather than aiming for 10 minutes of mindful walking, how about going easy on yourself and doing just ten mindful steps? It's simple to follow. Don't 'try' too hard. Just flow with it and let it be enjoyable.

START: This walking can be done anywhere - outside in nature or even walking up the stairs or around your kitchen. Choose somewhere that you can be on your own, for the first few times. **Take a 'snapshot' of how you are feeling ~** physically, emotionally, mind-wise. We'll come back to this at the end.

1. **Take 3 Mindful Breaths** – to centre yourself and come back to the 'here and now'.

2. **Start walking.** Slow your speed down by at least 50%.

3. **Focus all of your awareness on your feet.** Become fully aware of the physical sensations of your feet on the floor, as they connect with the Earth. [Doing this barefoot on grass or sand is a special treat - though not essential!]

4. **Take ten slow and mindful steps.**

5. **It's ok if your mind wanders.** If your attention wanders, **gently guide it back to feeling the physical,** tactile connection of your feet with the earth.

END: when you feel ready, release your practice and take that snapshot again. How are you feeling - physically, emotionally, mind-wise? Compare that to the snapshot from the beginning. With practise, you'll notice that the mindful steps make a tangible difference.

At first, just do this for ten truly conscious, 'present' steps. As you get used to it, aim to build up to a full minute. Walking up and down stairs, for example, is an ideal way to experience this technique.

18. Mindful Walking

Building on the ten mindful steps [technique #17], full-blown mindful walking has many variations. In this one, I want to share with you a way you can turn any walk, whether in a beautiful forest or the car park at work, into a sixty second mindful de-stressing meditation.

START:
Take a 'snapshot' of how you are feeling ~ physically, emotionally, mind-wise. We'll come back to this at the end.

1. **Slow down.**
   As you walk, at a slightly slower pace than usual, allow your awareness to rest in the soles of your feet. If your mind wanders, that's ok, bring your focus back to your feet contacting with the earth beneath you.

2. **Feel the physical sensations.**
   When you're in the rhythm of walking, become aware of the physical sensations in your body.

3. **Notice your balance.**
   Feel those amazing muscles, tendons, ligaments, bones, joints and nerves doing such an incredible job of keeping you safe and upright.

4. **Notice your arms moving.**
   You don't have to change anything; just become fully aware of the physical movement.

5. **Notice your posture.**
   Feel the physical sensations, if you tweak the way you are holding your body.

6. **Really feel the soles of your feet with each step.**
   Feel it, as they take your weight as you walk.

7. **Connect with the Earth.**
   Then, when you're ready, return to simply being aware of each step, connecting with the Earth.

8. **Say 'thank you'.**
   Once you are comfortable with this process, you might like to add in a silent 'thank you', perhaps to the Earth, for supporting each step, without agenda or judgement.

END:

Take that snapshot again. How are you feeling - physically, emotionally, mind-wise? Compare that to the snapshot from the beginning. With practice, you'll notice that the mindful walking makes a tangible difference.

There are so many different ways to approach mindful walking that you could spend years studying it.

If you'd like to learn more, Thích Nhất Hanh has written a beautiful book on it. You can find out more via the Readers' Club area on this book's website.

www.52MindfulMoments.com/ReadersClub

19. Emotional First Aid – Time To Come Back Down To Earth?

Here's a mindfulness quick fix for whenever you're feeling stressed or worried. You can do it any time, any place – even when you're surrounded by people.

And once you know how to do it, it will become second nature, helping you to gently let go of whatever is bothering you, in a matter of seconds.

I call it a 'grounding breath' because it is as though you are physically grounding – or earthing (like an electrical cable) – the emotions that have been stuck whizzing around.

✓ By consciously connecting with the emotions and choosing to release them, you help to quieten your mind and your thoughts.

✓ This then impacts the chemical reactions in your body that had been fed by your Monkey Mind's stories.

✓ Your body can then return to its equilibrium state of relaxed alertness, rather than being stuck in its 'fight or flight' mode.

Grounding Breath

If you are feeling tense, stressed, worried or annoyed, this mindfulness exercise takes less than 60 seconds to release those feelings.

*If the emotion you want to let go of is particularly strong, imagine you are looking at another 'you' on the other side of a glass screen, and imagine watching **them** going through this process, until the feeling diminishes. The first few times you practise this, I suggest you pick emotions no stronger than a 5 out of 10 on your emotional scale.*

1. Sit or stand still and close your eyes.

2. Focus on your feet contacting with the floor and imagine yourself growing strong roots, deep into the earth, like a tree. You might imagine seeing or feeling these roots growing, anchoring and grounding you.

3. Focus for a moment on the feeling. Ask yourself, "Where in my body do I feel this?"

4. Repeat again: "Where in my body am I feeling this?"

5. Breathe in to that area, with the breath absorbing all of that emotion. Breathe out, down through your feet into the earth, letting that emotion go.

6. If the location of the emotion moves that's fine.

7. Breathe into that area of the body: breathing in, the breath absorbs the emotion; breathing out through the legs and the feet into the earth, feeling the sense of relief flooding through you as you let go of that emotion.

8. And when you're ready, take a deep breath in, breathe out with a sigh (it can be a silent sigh, if you are in a meeting or with other people!) and smile a gentle smile, as you release this exercise, coming back to the here and now.

9. Now, is there any inspired action you need to take, as a result of this?

Much easier than spending the day wallowing in that old emotion? Want to share how you got on? Check out the forum link in the Readers' Club:

www.52MindfulMoments.com/ReadersClub

20. The Magic Of The Mundane

I had a friend who was a Buddhist monk. He told me a story about when he was in his earliest days of training. The newest students had to do all of the ironing for the rest of the monastery. With the flowing robes of the monks, that meant an awful lot of ironing. And this young monk didn't enjoy it.

He went to his master and complained. Why should he do the ironing for the other monks? Why couldn't they do their own? It wasn't fair! He was feeling bored and fed up.

It's amazing how often we begrudge day-to-day tasks.

How often do we do things with a heavy heart? With a sense of resentment? And how does it feel when we do it that way? Do we enjoy it? Does it feel good? Or does the burden become heavy beyond the weight we would expect for such a task?

The simple act of choosing, instead of feeling obligated, sets you free to experience that everyday task in a revolutionary way. And if you do it with mindfulness, it can help you to de-stress and feel happier, too! Instead of being a burden, it becomes a path to freedom.

And the student monk? One day he had done enough ironing that he realised that the ironing was teaching him to experience the 'here and now', to let go of the stories his Monkey Mind was telling him and to feel truly grateful for life, with each breath. And, funnily enough, as soon as he 'got' the lesson, he was taken off the ironing rota.

The Magic Of The Mundane

I invite you to pick an everyday task that perhaps bugs you a bit. That way you'll experience the shift this exercise creates even more clearly. Whether it's taking out the rubbish, clearing up after the kids, doing the washing up or cleaning the toilet, it doesn't matter.

1. Start by remembering some of the recent times that you have done this task. Remember how it feels. Remember the kinds of thoughts you think while you are doing it. Remember how your body feels, physically, while you're doing it. Where are you holding tension?

2. Now, do that task, but instead of feeling obligated, start by saying to yourself:

    I choose to do this.

3. As you carry out the task, wear a gentle smile on your lips, soften your jaw and eyes / eyebrows and each time an irritated or grumpy thought comes up, say a silent mantra: "It's ok. I choose to do this."

4. You might find it helps to use this mantra slowly, throughout the task.

5. Allow yourself to be fully present and aware, experiencing the task with all of your senses (yup! Even the toilet cleaning. Ok, definitely not your sense of taste!)

6. When you have finished, pause and say a heart-felt "thank you" to yourself, for having completed the task. How different did that feel?

21. What Are You Thinking?

Despite the fact that your Monkey Mind is racing at the speed of thought, we are very rarely aware of what it is actually thinking.

Yet those thoughts have a direct link to the body's hormones and chemical reactions. Think a sad thought and your body fires off its 'sad stuff' auto-pilot responses, filling your system with all the bits that are needed to create 'sad', physically and emotionally. Think a happy thought and your body triggers endorphins, so you end up feeling good.

There's more… Your Monkey Mind filters your experience of life: it chooses how to interpret what is happening, based on its own set of assumptions and beliefs.

We usually don't spot the story until the body has already done its bit. And we have spent a lifetime learning to ignore its behaviour and pretend it isn't there. But do you really want all of that running on auto-pilot?

When you consciously observe your thoughts, without judgement, it becomes easier to choose which to feed and which to let go.

Although you might not be aware of where the thoughts come from, you can do something about them. You can gently, but firmly, train your Monkey Mind to choose thoughts that bring relief and happiness, rather than stress and gloom.

Becoming aware of your thoughts is the first step to reclaiming your power to choose.

Sometimes your Monkey Mind is trying to get a message through to you. It might be worried that you're going to forget to do something; sometimes it's telling you about things we are afraid of; sometimes it's just used to filling in the chatter, to avoid us feeling lonely; sometimes it has just got into the habit of running an unconscious commentary about everything we are seeing and doing. Often, if you listen without judgement or interaction, the Monkey Mind can have its say and then relax.

If we fight our thoughts, or try to ignore them, chances are your Monkey Mind will shout louder. So here's a mindfulness exercise to help you take the first steps towards becoming the conscious observer of your thoughts – and eventually choosing which ones to feed.

1. Take 3 mindful breaths, to centre yourself and return to the present moment [see technique #1]

2. Sitting or standing quietly, take an imaginary step back from your mind and allow yourself to observe the thoughts that are running through your head. Don't interact with them. Don't try to change them. Simply observe them and accept them, without judgement or commentary.

3. If a thought that makes you feel good comes up, enjoy it. If a thought that makes you feel bad comes up, let it go.

4. Any thought, left to its own devices, will drift on through in a matter of seconds.

22. How To Tame A Multi-Tasking Mind

When did multi-tasking become such a prized skill? Most of us are addicted to it. We have trained our minds to need to think of many things at once. It's a real skill. Unfortunately, it can make you feel tense and stressed and it can make it harder to get things done well.

But thinking itself isn't the problem. **Thinking isn't bad.**

An out-of-control mind produces thinking that is 'unconscious' and 'unaware'. This feeds our love of drama, creating painful emotional states and keeping us stuck worrying about the past or stressing about the future.

So it is 'untamed' thinking that is the issue, not the presence of the thoughts. And it is our attachment to the thoughts that causes the pain, not the fact that they exist.

It's believing what you're thinking that's the problem.

Want to find out how to press pause for a multi-tasking Monkey Mind? It is based on an interesting question (that sends your mind into a spin!)

1. Take 3 Mindful Breaths [see technique #1].

2. Rest for a moment and observe your mind. Notice how it is thinking, without commenting on or engaging with any of your thoughts.

3. Ask yourself the question:

What won't happen if I don't think of three things at once?

What won't happen if your mind doesn't chatter three conversations at once? Just let an answer bubble up for you, without analysing or judging it. This can help you to unlock the key of why you have been telling your Monkey Mind that it needs to run at full-speed. And notice where you feel it in your body. Chances are there will be an area that tenses up, in response to this question.

Are you scared of silence? Are you scared things won't get done? Are you trying to avoid thinking about something else?

Usually the answer to that question contains hints on how to set yourself free from that old grasshopper mind habit. If the answer feels uncomfortable, don't dive into the drama.

4.   When you know what has been keeping you stuck, multi-tasking with your thinking, then you can start to take action about it.

5.   Be gentle, but firm, with your Monkey Mind.

It's ok to think of just one thing at a time. The world won't come to an end.

6.   Remember that with every breath we can choose to make a fresh start. Anything the Monkey Mind is telling us about our past belongs just there.

Having chosen to go on a mindfulness journey, you're already taking positive steps towards creating a new future.

All you need to do now is to remember to practise!

23. Do You Really Want To Feed That Thought?

It is a fact of life that we tend to get the things that we give our attention to.

I remember when I was learning to drive that I would unconsciously steer towards whatever I was looking at - in the direction of my focus. If I looked over at my driving instructor, he knew that he was going to have to grab the steering wheel – fast.

Life is just the same. We tend to move towards that which has our focus and attention. But most of the time we're running on auto-pilot, so we don't even notice where that focus and attention is. We are at risk of thinking our way into a future we don't really want, without even noticing!

You can choose which thoughts to feed.

You don't have to be at the mercy of thoughts you're not enjoying. Whilst it can be really difficult to totally empty your mind of thoughts or to control which thoughts pop up, you can gently, but firmly, train yourself to choose which thoughts to feed. Without being fed, a thought – left to its own devices – will disappear.

For most of us, our Monkey Mind is like a tantruming child – constantly doing whatever it takes to grab our attention. If that means it needs to shout and crank up the drama, it will. If that means it needs to focus on quiet worrying, to create anxiety, it will.

It doesn't mean that our Monkey Mind is 'cruel' or 'unkind' or wants to hurt us in any way. It's simply that we have spent decades teaching it to tell us the stories that we, at some deeply unconscious level, want to hear; need to hear. While we

let our mind run riot like an undisciplined child on a sugar-rush, we will experience the effects of its chaotic stories.

How do you return to choice with your mind's thoughts?

The first step is to become consciously aware of them. And that's where this mindfulness technique comes in.

The first step to choice – and change – is awareness.

1. Start with 3 Mindful Breaths [see technique #1]
2. For the next few moments, sit quietly, having done your 3 mindful breaths.
3. Let your body settle and allow yourself to become aware of your thoughts.
4. There's no need to engage with them or to hold a conversation. This exercise is simply about observing them.
5. Accept each thought as it arises and be a compassionate observer of it, without judging or trying to change anything.
6. Then, when you are used to observing your thoughts, you are ready to ask yourself, do I want to feed this one? Do I want to let it create my reality? If not, let it go and wait for the next thought.
7. Notice that there is a gap between your thoughts.

The second step?

Choose to believe that you can influence the thoughts you feed.

It's a choice. That's it. And mindfulness makes it easier.

24. Floating Through The Sky Of Your Mind

I have lost count of how many times students have complained to me that they can't "shut up" their Monkey Mind. And I remind them that very few people can.

In our modern society, where we bombard ourselves with stimuli from every direction, all day long. It's no wonder our minds are chattering. Then you need to add in the decades of training we have given our Monkey Minds, to critique, to analyse, to judge, to re-tell stories and to keep a running commentary of our day. It's no wonder we can feel like our mind is teeming with thoughts.

The great news is that you don't have to make your mind go completely silent, to be able to de-stress and feel happier.

All you need to do is to accept your thoughts and perhaps allow them to slow down.

You might be surprised at the sense of relief that brings.

Is it time to remind your mind who's boss and calm it a little? You are the boss of your Monkey Mind, whether it accepts it or not!

Here is a mindfulness exercise that can help.

1. Come back to the present moment by taking 3 mindful breaths [see technique #1]

2. Imagine that your thoughts aren't fixed, but are floating through your mind – like clouds in the sky or like boxes on a conveyor belt.
    If you choose to be still and just observe them, without interacting with

them, they will simply float on by.

3. **If your thoughts are mainly words:**
How about telling your thoughts to slow down?
Cutting the speed at which your mind is speaking can help cut your stress levels.
And when you have played with that, how about changing the volume, making it quieter?
You could experiment with changing the tone of the conversation that you are hearing in your head and making it sound kinder and softer.

4. **If your thoughts are mainly pictures:**
How about slowing down any movement in the pictures? This can really help you to relax.
If the pictures are bright and colourful, you could tone them down a little.
If they are big, you can make them smaller.

5. **Got stories running wild in your Monkey Mind?**
How about telling yourself one of my favourite quotes from HH Dalai Lama:

"This too will pass."

Nothing lasts forever – life changes. If we keep telling ourselves yesterday's stories, chances are that our experience of tomorrow will stay the same, even if life changes. So reminding yourself that current stresses are transient, not permanent, can help you feel more at peace with the situation – and more empowered to do something about it.

25. Are You Running From A Mountain-Sized Molehill?

Sometimes in life we face problems that are genuinely big. But usually we don't.

The size of the problem is dictated by the stories we tell ourselves about it.

And the bigger the problem feels, the more likely we are to run from it – to try to avoid it.

"What you resist persists." ~ Carl Jung

It's all about the situations, the conflicts and even the thoughts that we would do anything to avoid, which cause us massive amounts of stress – and we all have them… What they all have in common is the effort that's required to keep resisting them and the low level, or sometimes even the high level, stress that this can cause.

If you run from something that makes you feel uncomfortable, it will still catch up with you, even if just in your mind. You are giving it power over how you feel. When we think about that problem – when we imagine it – we trigger those same physiological reactions as if it were actually happening. Your body fires off the same stress responses as though the event were real, here and now.

Things are rarely as bad as the stories your Monkey Mind tells you.

It seems crazy to tell ourselves these stories; to run away from these molehills and to build them into mountains, making us feel stressed and miserable. But it's

a habit that most of us have

If you take a deep breath and mindfully turn to face that mountain-sized molehill, you'll find it's much smaller than you thought it was – you can begin to live the life that is real, that's nowhere near as stressful as the one in the stories.

Not only do your Monkey Mind's stories instantly lose their power, but our inner drama disappears and our responses to the situation change.

> *When we run from the molehill, it becomes the size of a mountain. When we turn to face it, we regain perspective, cutting it back down to size.*

1. Take 3 Mindful Breaths [see technique #1].

2. Is there a situation for you at the moment where you might be running away from a molehill sized mountain?

3. Instead of running, turn to face it. [Note, if it's a 'biggie', do technique #19 first!]

4. Imagine setting yourself free from that old stress and fear, by taking a deep breath and deciding, just for a moment, that you are going to stop running and deal with it? Or at least look at it and see what's true.

5. What inspired action could you take? Even a baby step? Today?

It's an amazing way to cut your stress levels – simply by shifting the stories that your Monkey Mind is telling you.

26. It's Ok To Let Your Thoughts Slow Down

When your mind is racing, it prompts your body to chuck out adrenalin, cortisol and other stress responses, getting your primal 'fight or flight' system running at full pace.

There's a difference between low-stress 'quick thinking' and 'mind racing'.

When you're 'quick thinking', it feels as though you have the clarity of a mountain stream as the snow melts in spring – and you can easily leap from one stepping stone to the other, making fast progress.

When you're 'mind racing', you are in that 'fight or flight' near-panic space.

You can't keep up with the thoughts as they arise, your breathing shifts to your upper chest, so your brain gets less oxygen (its 'thinking food') and your hypothalamus takes over (the primal bit of your brain), which specialises in short-term survival-type decision making, rather than clear strategic thinking.

One of the simplest ways to move from 'mind racing' to 'quick thinking' is to use mindful breathing and to allow your thoughts to slow.

Here's how.

1. Take a moment to do a 'snapshot' – to notice how your are feeling, in your body, emotionally and in your mind.

2. Start with 3 mindful breaths [see technique #1]. Allow your breathing to settle and slow down a little.

3. As you rest in the 'here and now', allow yourself to become aware of your thoughts and the speed at which they are running.

4. As you breathe in, say to yourself:

"I notice what I am thinking."

5. As you breathe out, say to yourself:

"I accept what I am thinking."

6. Continue this for a few breaths.

7. Now that you have linked your breathing with your thinking, slow your breathing rate down a little (keep it comfortable!). Keep saying to yourself the phrases as you breathe in and out, slowing your speed down a fraction.

8. Now pause and observe your thoughts for a few moments.

9. Take a moment to do another 'snapshot'.

What has shifted? How has the speed of your thoughts changed? What impact has that had on your body? And your emotions?

27. Relax Your Face!

When I'm running a meditation class, one of the really important things we do before we meditate is a deep relaxation. In fact, I sometimes wonder if it's the main reason that most people come to the class! If you're tense, you can't concentrate, so it's hard to meditate.

One of the favourite guided relaxations we do involves tensing each area of the body in turn, with full awareness, and then relaxing it, to release tension.

We start with the feet and move up through to the crown of the head. But where is the area that produces the biggest sighs of relief and the most smiles as people let the tension go? The face.

When you are feeling tense and stressed, it's likely you'll be holding tension in your jaw, you might be clenching you teeth, you'll probably be holding tension around your eyes and your eyebrows, you'll most likely hold tension between your eyebrows and you can even hold tension around your ears and in your scalp.

So if you'd like to combine deep relaxation with mindfulness, to help you de-stress, here's a sixty second technique that can help you to feel better, fast.

1.   Take a snapshot of how you're feeling, right now. If you were to concentrate on your head, where are the areas of tension?

2.   Move your focus to your neck and throat and when you next breathe out, imagine releasing the tension from your throat. Become fully aware of the physical sensations in your neck.

3. Then move to your jaw and give it a wiggle – slowly – side to side, up and down, round in a circle. Let your focus mindfully rest on releasing tension from your jaw.

4. Stick your tongue out and trace the letters of your first name with it (sorry if it's a long one for you!). This releases tension from the tongue, mouth, jaw and even the bottom of the ears.

5. Move up to your eyes and scrunch them closed, then release them. The open them wide and release. Raise your eyebrows as high as you can. Then release. If your mind wanders, bring it back to the physical sensations in your face.

6. Scrunch your whole face up really tight – and release. Then open / stretch everything really wide – and release.

7. Finally give yourself a face and scalp massage with your fingertips (visualise it or get a sense of it, if you're somewhere that this wouldn't be safe!). Finish with a gentle smile on your face.

8. Take a snapshot. How do you feel? What has shifted? How have your tension levels changed? How are your thoughts now?

There's an MP3 audio in the Readers' Club, if you'd like to be guided through this exercise:

www.52MindfulMoments.com/ReadersClub

28. Are You Still Telling Yesterday's Story?

When we get stressed, we tell ourselves stories about it. Those stories go round and round in your head.

And, just as in a game of Chinese whispers, the way those stories started out isn't necessarily how they'll finish up. Your good old Monkey Mind tends to embellish those stories. They get little nuances added. We add in some 'what ifs' which, over the space of a day ,are no longer 'what ifs'; they feel quite real.

The more we tell the story, the more real it feels. Researchers have proven that we believe the stories we tell ourselves – and we would even pass a lie detector test for them, we are so convinced by them.

The problem with the story is that it triggers exactly the same chemical reactions in the body as if the event were actually happening. So we might have had a stressful event first thing in the morning, but if we tell ourselves that story all day, we keep that physiological and emotional stress alive, well beyond the point when it might have been useful.

While you keep on telling yesterday's story, how will you create a different tomorrow?

How Can You Stop The Story Cycle? Err… Mindfulness…

Becoming aware of what's 'story' and what's 'Truth' is key to pressing pause.

And luckily there's a simple question you can ask yourself, to take you back to the Truth of things, fast – as long as that's where you're prepared to go. (Many of us

are addicted to our stories, so letting them go can be a challenge).

1. Take 3 mindful breaths (from technique #1)

2. Think of a story you've been telling yourself. [Note: if it's a big emotional drama, you might want to use technique #19 first].

3. Consciously set the intention to press pause on the story cycle.

4. Now ask yourself a question and be very honest about the answer:

    What specifically is the problem?
    When we tell the story, we're generalising. And we use things like 'always' and 'never', which might not be the case at all:
    "He always does that!" or "She never gets it right!"
    That just keeps the drama going.
    The word 'specifically' helps to break through these generalisations, helping you to get to the root of what's 'real'.

    What, specifically, is True, right here, right now?

5. If you find your mind diving back into the drama, with stories and blame and 'not fair' and 'but', then ask yourself the question, again.

When you know what the issue is, it helps you to get out of the drama and to be clear about the issue. When you are clear and mindful about the Truth of the issue, rather than re-telling the old story, you will find it easier to have clarity in your thinking and to spot inspired solutions.

29. Getting Into The Gap Between Your Thoughts

Your mind is doing its best. And it doesn't realise the hassle it's causing. In fact, it's doing exactly what we have trained it to do – over the decades.

It tells us stories. It passes comment. It evaluates. It tells us what to do and how to feel. But it can only speak from the perspective of the filters, experiences, beliefs, habits, hopes and fears it has picked up over the years. So its view is biased.

If it tells us we can't do something, we believe it. If it tells us that our dreams are unrealistic, we believe it. If it tells us that things will go wrong, we believe it. If it tells us that something is stressful or that we should feel stressed, we believe it.

Just because your mind tells you something is so, it doesn't mean it is.

Don't believe everything your Monkey Mind tells you.

It's ok to question what our mind tells us. It is full of opinion, prejudice, assumptions and leaped-to conclusions, based on a lifetime of practice.

When it sees a stress trigger, it automatically dives into telling us stories about previous stresses. It triggers the unconscious mind's auto-pilot programmes for reacting to those stress triggers. It effectively removes our choice.

And if we're in the habit of feeding that adrenalin with more stories, then we're likely to indulge in telling ourselves (and others) stories about that stress trigger that keep the hormones running high and the adrenalin pumping. We all love a good drama; and the more emotionally charged, the better! In fact, many of us are so attached to our stories that it becomes an addiction.

But there's some good news: All you need to do to reclaim your choice over how to respond is to spot that you are telling yourself a story – then you can choose whether or not to feed it.

How do you get things back under control?

Look for the gaps between your thoughts.

When you get into the gap, you reclaim your power of choice over which thoughts to feed.

How to get into the gap between your thoughts

1. Start with 3 Mindful Breaths [see technique #1]

2. Sitting quietly, allow yourself to become the conscious observer of your thoughts. Don't interact with them. Don't critique or analyse or engage with the thoughts. Simply let them pass through.

3. Watch a thought arise, grow, begin to fade and then pass through.

4. When you have done this for a while, you'll notice that there can be gaps – pauses - between your thoughts.

5. When you spot a gap, don't try to cling to it – it will disappear. Simply acknowledge it and enjoy it, while it lasts. It might be a split-second gap or one that lasts quite a while.

6. And when the next thought pops up, repeat #3.

7. Over time, you'll easily be able to relax into that gap and to feel the peace and stillness, whenever you need it.

79

30. A Secret Truth Your Unconscious Mind Needs You To Know

There's a truth about your unconscious mind, which could be keeping you stuck where you don't want to be, if you don't know it yet.

And most people don't. It's a trap that most of us fall into.

It keeps you thinking about what you don't want; it keeps you looking for signs and experiencing life through the filters of what you don't want; it stops you from moving forwards and can keep you feeling miserable.

Your unconscious mind doesn't understand 'not'.

What do I mean by this?

Whatever you do, right now, don't think about a pink donkey climbing up a prickly purple tree with a yellow dog barking at the bottom.

What happened…? Point made?

To be able to do a 'not' or a 'don't', your mind first has to imagine the 'thing' or 'scenario' and then adds in the 'not'. It is how it is wired.

"Don't run!" is processed as "Run!" and then "Don't!"

"Don't mess up the presentation!" is translated as the instruction to "Mess up the presentation!", triggering all of your auto-pilot scripts for imagining (and creating) messing up the presentation. The 'not' gets lost in the footnotes.

All those times when we're talking about what we don't want, guess what we have to imagine first? And that imagining triggers off the same emotions and

physical hormone and chemical reactions in your body as if it were actually happening.

We get what we focus on. If we keep thinking and talking about what we don't want and what we don't like, that's what we'll see more of in our lives.

What has this got to do with mindfulness? Well, spotting the thoughts that cause us to fall into the 'negative' trap is the essential first step to breaking free from this habit. Awareness is the first key to change.

By practising mindful awareness of your thoughts, you get a chance to press pause and to ask yourself the magic question that can help to turn this around:

What do I want instead?

Then use your answer as a spring-board for taking inspired action.

1. If you catch yourself thinking or talking about what you don't want, press pause.

2. Take 3 Mindful Breaths [see technique #1] to help you get out of the story and drama and back into what's 'real', here and now.

3. Ask yourself: **"What do I want instead?"**

4. If more 'not' phrases come up, or if more drama resurfaces, go back to #2.

5. Once you are clear about what you want instead, decide on one action – even if just a baby step, which could take right now to move towards it.

31. Is Your Monkey Mind Telling You The Truth About Stress?

Have you noticed how your Monkey Mind likes to tell stories about stress? Even when you're not feeling particularly stressed, if it spots a stress trigger, it uses it as an excuse to start up the story machine again.

And it likes labels. It likes to put things in boxes: "That's a stressful thing. That's a difficult thing. That's a happy thing." When the stuff is in boxes, it makes life easier for your Monkey Mind, because then it knows which auto-pilot scripts and old habitual behaviours to run.

Is this really stressful? Or am I just telling myself it is?

Life is an objective, sensory experience, until you label it and attach the event to a story. As soon as we use a label or put an experience into a particular box, we lose our flexibility and choice over how to respond.

The experience is automatically connected to your body's chemistry set, triggering the hormones and chemical reactions that impact your physiology and emotions. The label – the story – impacts every cell in your body, without you consciously doing a single thing about it. But it's all a fib, because:

'Life' isn't stressful. The stories we tell ourselves about life create
the stress. It is believing your thoughts that causes the pain.

The phenomenon of 'stress' comes from believing the stories your mind is telling you about it. Yes, some events have the power to trigger more stress than others, but ultimately it's up to us to choose how to experience life.

You are the author of your own story. So you can choose which story to write.

How to get your Monkey Mind to tell the truth – and reclaim your choice.

1. Start with 3 Mindful Breaths [see technique #1]. This brings you back into the present moment and into your body.

2. Say to yourself: "I choose to press 'pause' on the story." And mean it. Wait for the gap to arrive.

3. Ask yourself: "What is *real* in this situation?"

4. Be firm with yourself. If stories and drama surface, press pause on them and ask yourself again what's real.

5. If you get stuck, go back to describing the physical sensory experience, e.g. *"When my boss said I have to do a presentation next week, I noticed the pit of my stomach tensing up and I clenched my jaw."*

6. Sensory descriptions bring you back to what's real and helps you to drop the label-addiction.

7. When you distil the situation back to the essence of the sensory experience, and let go of the labels and the stories, it always feels better.

8. If you want to try out solutions to the problem, imagine them and ask yourself how they *feel*. Your body will tell you whether the solution creates physical sensations that feel worse or whether it brings genuine relief. It's easier to make decisions, when you work with your body's internal barometer.

32. Are You Suffering From 'Should-Itis'?

When you go to do things, are you usually thinking about how happy you feel about doing them? Or are you thinking about how fed up you feel about them?

Are you telling yourself stories about everything you 'have to' do? Are words like 'should' and 'must' your best friends?

Then you're probably suffering from 'should-itis'. It's a modern epidemic.

With a mild case of should-itus, there's just a general feeling of dis-ease. You're feeling ok and happy, but you feel like you don't get to be in control of how you spend your time, very often.

As should-itus progresses, the symptoms get stronger. We feel more and more out of control, as though life is 'happening *to* us', and we feel that we have no choice or freedom. Simple tasks become a burden that we resent. And we tell ourselves stories about it, to justify how we're feeling.

Sounds familiar?

Fortunately there's a mindfulness-based solution to all this.

How are you feeling about your choices? Our choices in life (whether it's the laundry or your career) are usually made from a place that is far from freedom. You can spot it in the language we use:

I have to… ~ I must… ~ I ought to… ~ I should…

But these are just phrases we use to ourselves. They're not 'real'.

Freedom is a matter of mindset.

Why do we set our minds to feel trapped and not free? Habit. And because we believe the stories we tell ourselves about it.

Could it be as simple as flicking a switch, to make that shift? Yes!

I have lost count of the number of times I have used this technique with myself and with clients - and it works every time – if you choose it to!

"Any choice made from freedom creates more
freedom." ~ James Twyman

Note: *Some of us are quite attached to feeling trapped. If that's you, please go and get some professional help to let go of that old habit.*

Here's the not-so-secret antidote to should-itis:

1. When you spot yourself thinking "I have to…" or one of its friends, press pause and take 3 Mindful Breaths [see technique #1] to help you come back to what's 'real', here and now.

2. Swap your 'should', 'have to', 'must' and 'ought' for 'I choose to…'
    Try it out now – even with something mundane!
    Do you prefer: "*I **have to** do the laundry.*" or "*I **choose** to do the laundry.*"
    Which one feels better?

3. Put a smile on your face and mindfully make that choice. If it helps, you could practise technique #20, while you're at it!

33. How Does This Choice 'Feel'?

If you're feeling stuck about which decision to make, there's a mindfulness exercise you can do to get an insight into the answer.

It's about handing the decision over to your body.

We normally think that we have to make decisions with our heads, but your body is much better at telling you which answers resonate for you than your Monkey Mind will ever be.

And mindfulness is, as you have probably experienced by this stage of this book, a great way to reconnect with your body, in this moment.

Your body never lies to you. If you come back to the 'here and now' and allow yourself to become aware of the physical sensations you are experiencing, you'll quickly learn how to tune in to your body's barometer.

How to make more mindful choices.

Your body can help you not just with the big decisions in life, but with moment-to-moment responses to what's happening, here and now.

A scary amount of our behaviour is running on auto-pilot – quick-fire responses and behaviours triggered by the re-running of old memories. Some, like taking action to avoid an accident, are useful. Others, like responding emotionally to someone's behaviour, can be destructive.

They are based on 'old programming' from past experiences and can get out of date.

It keeps us stuck in old behaviours and habits, long after they have finished serving any useful purpose.

Taking a deep breath and relaxing can give you a moment to consider how you really want to respond this time, giving you back your choice.

And if you're not sure about which choice to make, here's a mindfulness exercise that can help you tap into your body's inner wisdom, letting you know – loud and clear – which option to choose.

1. Ask your body to give you a sign, whenever an old habit that you're ready to release comes back to play.

2. When you feel – sense – that sign, pause and take 3 Mindful Breaths [see technique #1]

3. Ask yourself:

   Do I really want to respond that way this time? Or would I like to choose another path?

4. Your body will tell you the answer. Pay attention to feelings of tension and feelings of relief.

5. If a choice is in alignment with where you're at or ready to 'be', then your body will feel good. If it's not – and if it's going to create inner conflict for you – then your body will give you a clear signal to warn you!

Your body holds the answers, if you learn to mindfully tune in to it.

34. Be Careful Who You're Letting Rent Space In Your Head

When you spend your time and energy telling yourself stories about someone else's behaviour, you're giving them power over how you feel. If you're feeling irritated and stressed, whenever you think about the situation, then your Monkey Mind's story machine is in overdrive.

If you're spending time talking to others about it, then you're reinforcing the thought patterns that are making you feel bad. That person has moved in, set up their furniture and hung their pictures on the walls.

You're letting that other person – who is bugging you! – live in your head, rent-free, and you're letting their issues impact your thoughts, emotions and actions.

Watch out who you're letting rent the space in your head. It's ok to evict any tenant who's dragging you down.

It's a surprisingly common problem. It can lead to stress and worry, with a massive dollop of negative thinking and generally feeling bad.

What can you do, when someone else is camping out in your head?

Let go of the story!

It's not about rejecting the other person. It's not about saying that the other person's behaviour was ok. It is about setting clear boundaries (with yourself!) and accepting responsibility for the fact that who and what you let hang around in your head will impact your experience of life – and we always have choice.

Here's a quick – but highly effective - mindfulness exercise to help you.

1. **Start by taking your 3 mindful breaths.**
   Allow your body and mind to settle for a few moments.

2. **Ask yourself (very honestly!): what's true in this – and what's drama?**
   Let go of everything that's drama, not matter how 'right' or 'vindicated' or 'good' the drama has been making you feel.

   It will feel better – instantly – especially if you do this from a place of compassion, rather than anger. [Remember: all criticism is borne of someone else's pain – see technique #39.] This isn't about pretending the other person's behaviour is ok. It's about you taking charge of whether or not you want to live in the drama.

   Ask yourself: do I need to take any specific action to improve this situation? If yes, do it. If no, let go and move on.

3. **Each time that person pops back into your head space, lovingly remind yourself that you have chosen not to play that game any more.**
   Choose to think of something else. If you find that hard, you can always experiment with the 'waterfall meditation' exercise [see technique #35].

If this exercise is challenging for you, it's time to look at 'secondary gain' – what are you getting from letting the other person hang around in your head? How is it supporting your position, perhaps as being 'right' or being a 'victim'? The answer might surprise you.

Mindfulness can help you gain insight into the deeper patterns you're running, giving you back your choice, so you can take action to set yourself free.

35. Magic Mindful Scissors For Moving On

Sometimes, even if we want to let something go and move on, it can still hang around. It goes round in your head. You tell yourself stories about it. You keep it running on repeat. The harder you try to get rid of it, the more firmly it stays.

Fortunately there's a really simple technique you can use, to send it on its way. Interested?

When it's time to let go of an old habit, belief or thought pattern – or a memory from the past – all you need to do is grab your imaginary scissors….

The past – be it habits, beliefs or memories – can feel like it is tied to us with invisible bits of string. No matter how often we tell it we are done with it, it can pop back and keep us stuck.

Earlier in this book I mentioned that mindful awareness is the first step towards making changes. Well, here's a great next step: **my favourite 60 second process for finally letting go** (though it might take you more than 60s the first time!).

1. **Take 3 Mindful Breaths**, to bring you out of the story and drama and into the present moment, [see technique #1]

2. **Notice and acknowledge that old pattern, habit, belief or memory.** Notice where in your body it is hanging out. Let your focus rest in that area, becoming aware of the physical sensations.

3. **Then, rather than rejecting it, it's important to accept it – not to resist.** If you're pushing it away, then you are still giving it your power.

90

4. **Does it have a message for you?** Be mindfully aware; open to hearing it.

5. **It really helps to be able to say thank you to it.** It doesn't mean you have to feel happy about it or pretend that that old experience was ok, but everything we experience can be used for our growth and learning, at some level. You might choose to imagine you can talk to this old thought, belief, habit or memory and perhaps say something like:

   "Even though I might not fully understand why you were part of my life, I thank you for however it was you were trying to help me. Now I choose to let go and move on. Our work together is done."

6. **Then imagine you can see the invisible cord of energy, connecting you to that old belief / memory.** Take your big imaginary scissors and cut that cord – all the way through. Fill both ends with love, as they melt away. Then allow that old habit / belief to drift away, gone and finished.

   Reclaim your power. Feel the power you gave to that old thought, belief, habit or memory returning to you, as you finish cutting those old ties.

When you cut the ties, you are making a choice to let go and release. You can use this process with 'stuck emotions', too. it's exactly the same and it can instantly improve your mood. When you experiment with this, you'll notice you end up with a wonderful sense of relief, when the job is done.

If you're still holding on to the old issue, you can always run the "Eightieth Birthday Test" – it normally sorts things out! You'll find the link at:

www.52MindfulMoments.com/Readersclub

91

36. Mind How You're Standing (Or Sitting!)

When you're feeling unhappy or stressed, it's not just in your head. Chances are you'll be slouching over, with your back curved and your head down. Our movements tend to be tired and sluggish. Yet the mind and the body are linked.

So getting mindful about how you're using your body can help you to shift the thoughts that you're not enjoying in your mind. And getting mindful about your thoughts can impact how your body performs.

Want to prove it?
1. Sitting in a chair, keep repeating the following phrase in your head:
   Tired and weak… Tired and weak…
   Do it about 10 times. Really *feel and experience* 'tired and weak'.
   Now try to stand up.
   Kind of difficult?

Now for the contrast – give yourself a shake to let go of the last part.
2. Sitting down again, repeat this phrase 10 times in your head:
   Powerful and strong… Powerful and strong…
   Do it about 10 times. Really *feel and experience* 'powerful and strong'.
   Stand up.
   Did you almost fly across the room?

Did you notice the difference? **As I said: mind and body are linked!**

One of the easiest ways to feel happier and less stressed, right now, is to become mindfully aware of your posture – and to make changes that impact your mood.

There's a video to take you through this exercise in the Readers' Club:
www.52MindfulMoments.com/ReadersClub

START: Take a snapshot of how you're feeling – your thoughts, your emotions and the physical sensations.

1. If you're reading this somewhere where you can stand up, then stand up and give yourself a shake. Have a stretch and a yawn. Do this with mindful awareness for maximum benefit!

2. Now move your body:
    *   start with flicking your fingertips, then wiggling your wrists, wobbling your elbows, shaking your arms and shrugging your shoulders.
    *   then move to your feet (one at a time!) and wiggle your toes, shake out your ankles, kick your legs and wobble all the way up to your hips.
    *   Gently free up your torso with some jiggles and some mindful spinal twists.
    *   Gently tilt your head from side to side, to release tension in your neck.
    *   Then give yourself a big stretch and a yawn. This wakes you up.

3. Either standing or sitting, imagine a cord from the crown of your head gently pulling your spine and creating a tiny space between each vertebra. Lift your head up and tuck your chin in slightly (to lengthen your neck) and wear a gentle smile on your face (*all within your own comfortable range, of course*).

END: Take that snapshot again. How have things shifted?

37. Is It Time To Dump Your Spinning Plates?

Do you ever get to the stage of feeling overwhelmed? As though you're one of those circus acts who has all those plates spinning on sticks, running to and fro to keep all of the plates spinning, because if one of them drops, it'll smash on the floor?

When my 'to do' list gets that way, I call it 'spinning plate syndrome' – where everything we know we *ought* to be doing [see technique #32!], becomes a low-level energy drain.

When we put something off – when we avoid thinking about it or doing it – we might believe that we are free from it, but **the reality is that we have handed our power over to that 'something else'.**

It is probably waking us up at 3am and we're probably feeling guilty about avoiding it – or stressed. We have given 'it' the power to change our emotions – to knock us off our equilibrium.

To justify this, we might tell ourselves stories about how difficult a task it really is, about how unpleasant it will be, about how much we are dreading it, about how unnecessary it really is. So although we're not actually doing the thing, we're still giving it plenty of attention. [See technique #25 – Are you turning things into a mountain-sized molehill?].

The secret to stopping the plate from spinning is to stop telling yourself stories about it and take action.

That action might be as simple as changing a thought, or as tangible as actually

doing the thing we had been putting off.

Here's a mindful awareness strategy to set yourself free from spinning plates:

1. **Take 3 Mindful Breaths.** See technique #1 – this brings you out of your 'story head' and back into the present moment.

2. **Is it really your plate?** Before you go any further, be really honest with yourself: if it really your plate to spin? Or are you doing it for someone else? Could you give it back to them?

3. **Answer – honestly – "What is it about this task that I am *really* avoiding?"** This might surprise you. Be honest. You're not looking for 'why' or justifications. You're looking to identify what your block is.

4. **Answer – again, honestly – "No matter what I have been avoiding, will I feel relief when the task is done?"** Almost always it's a yes.

5. **Then choose whether or not to do the task.**
   If you choose to do it, take the first baby step now, so that the actions are in motion, breaking the thinking / feeling stress cycle.
   If you choose not to do it, assuming that is an option for you, it's important to cut the energetic ties you had to the task. Imagine a cord, connecting you and the task. Gently, but firmly, cut it. Allow the two ends of the cord to be filled with light, to dissolve any fear. Then allow the task to disappear away from you [see technique #35]. Feel the relief!

Is it time for you to get back in the driving seat on this one and get 'active', instead of 'stressing'?

38. Do You Need To Press 'PAUSE'?

If you're feeling stressed or there's a powerful emotion running for you, you can use this mindfulness exercise as a kind of 'First Aid', to help you get back to a sense of equilibrium – then it's much easier to see solutions. It is one of my favourite 60 second mindfulness de-stressing techniques.

It's all about pressing 'PAUSE':

P Press the 'Pause' button & breathe. Visualise pressing 'pause'. Then take 3 deep mindful breaths, breathing in from your belly to your chest, then breathing out with a releasing 'ahhh' sound.

A Accept - accept where you're at. Become aware of what's 'real' – rather than the story your mind was telling you. What's physically 'here' for you, in this moment? What is happening in your body? With your emotions? With your thoughts? Accept it - there's no need to change it. Let go and relax into accepting.

U Understand – a kind of deep knowing – that this too will pass. Nothing lasts forever. Whatever is 'real' for you right now will pass, in time. You may need to take inspired action, but it will pass.

The pain is amplified by the stories we tell ourselves about the situation. The stories aren't real. They're just stories (even if they're good'uns!).

Let go of the story and allow your deep understanding – your inner wisdom – to

wash through the situation.

Smile – even if just a gentle half-smile.
Smiling, even if you're not feeling like it, releases endorphins (or little dolphins, as my friend's son used to say!) into your bloodstream, giving you a very natural high.

After just a few seconds of smiling, those hormones start to trigger chemical reactions that produce happier emotions, also reducing your stress levels. It doesn't matter if you're faking it, smiling shifts your emotions, mind and body to a better space.

Need encouragement? There's an article in the online Readers' Club with a little experiment you can use to prove to yourself why it's so important to choose to smile, when things get tough.

www.52MindfulMoments.com/ReadersClub

Enjoy! Whatever is going on in your life, allow yourself to enjoy this moment.
Right here, right now, allow yourself even just a few seconds to enjoy this moment. Let go and relax into it, knowing that this space is waiting here for you, 24/7, whenever you need it.

I know this technique can take longer than sixty seconds, the first few times you do it. But the more often you practise, the quicker it will become, until all you need is a mindful moment.

97

39. Why Are They Being So Mean?

Sometimes people do stuff that's really unacceptable. Yes, there's a sliding scale to 'unacceptable', but it's still not ok.

It's our tendency to want to retaliate in some way – perhaps by behaving unkindly or even doing something nasty to them. It's easy to hold resentments and grudges and to allow those to taint our experience of relating with that person. We tell ourselves (or anyone else who will listen) stories about their behaviour, to try to make ourselves feel better. We can direct all sorts of painful emotions towards them give them the power over how we feel. But…

There's a difference between the person and their
actions – a person is not their behaviour.

The behaviour – the actions – are the outward appearance of the person. What is deep down inside, the essence of that person, is different from their actions. At some level, they are running the same kinds of auto-pilot responses that we do. At some level, they just want to be happy, just like us.

Everyone has been through tough experiences. Everyone has experienced pain. Everyone has experienced loss and sadness. And these experiences colour the way we think and the way we behave.

Deep down, most people (no matter how bad their behaviour) are just muddling their way through life, without much of an instruction manual. Their choices might be bad, but that doesn't make them a bad person – any more than it would make you a bad person, when you make choices you later regret.

There is a difference between the actor and the actions.

Like actors in a play, what we show the outside world isn't necessarily the truth of who we really are, but is a script – a series of behaviours – that can change.

When we remember that, we can set ourselves free from much of the pain. We create a space between their action and our response, which can allow us to choose a response for the long-term higher good, rather than short-term retaliation.

All criticism is borne of someone else's pain. ~ Native American saying

A happy person doesn't do unkind things. So if someone does something unkind to you, it's likely to be because they're feeling pretty bad, deep down inside. Lashing out and projecting that pain onto someone else may seem easier for them than facing and dealing with that pain.

So the next time you feel tempted to lash out and do or say something unkind to someone who has done or said something unkind to you, how about allowing yourself a moment to choose whether that's what you really want?

1. Take 3 Mindful Breaths, to help you to reconnect with your inner wisdom.

2. Pause your Monkey Mind's stories for a moment and ask yourself: "If I choose this thought / action, will it bring me peace or pain?"

3. Let your body (not your very clever and crafty mind!) give you the answer.

4. It's It gives you back your personal power and helps you to be less impacted by others' actions. And it's the key to cultivating compassion.

99

40. What's Going On Around You?

When we're busy and overwhelmed, the last thing we want to do is to open our awareness up to more 'inputs' from the outside world.

Our tendency, instead, is to 'shut down' and disappear back into our heads –the realm of the Monkey Mind.

But what if opening up to what is going on around you could cut your stress levels, help you think more clearly and even relax your body?

Those are some of the benefits of the mindfulness exercises that allow us to practise accepting our environment, rather than rejecting it.

In just sixty seconds you can relax into the present moment, letting the noises, smells, sights, sounds and other distractions bring you back to a place of stillness, rather than stressing you out.

As I have already said in this book:

"What you resist persists." ~ Carl Jung

and

"Acceptance is the first step towards change."

So letting go of fighting or resisting what is going on around us and accepting how it is, in this moment, just in this moment, is a powerful strategy for making the shifts you are looking for.

The key is to turn down the volume on your Monkey Mind's story for a few moments, so you can experience the calming Truth of what's 'here'.

Accepting what's going on around you

1. Take 3 mindful breaths [see technique #1] to help you come back to the present moment. Gently close your eyes.

2. Allow your breathing to settle into a slightly slower speed than it usually would be, to allow your parasympathetic nervous system (the 'relaxation' part) to balance out the stress of the 'fight or flight' sympathetic nervous system.

3. Allow yourself to experience, for a few moments, the physical sensations in your body, bringing your awareness fully into your physical form, tuning in to its rhythms.

4. Now gently open up your senses to become aware of the world around you. You might initially want to focus on what you can hear, or perhaps the vibrations in your chair as the lorry drives past, or the smell from the coffee machine – whatever it is that is in your environment right now. It's often easier to do this with your eyes closed.

5. Allow a wave of acceptance – of 'ok-ness' to wash through this awareness. It is how it is, and that's ok.

6. When you feel that acceptance is complete, move on to noticing another element of your environment and accepting that, too.

When we let go of the need to control things that are beyond our influence, it's amazing how much easier life becomes.

41. My All-Time Favourite Mindfulness Mantra

You will already have experienced the impact of mantra in some of the earlier mindfulness exercises. A mantra is a phrase (often a sacred phrase, but sometimes an affirmation) that we can use to keep the Monkey Mind focussed on what we are doing. It helps us to concentrate and it also sets our intention for our practice. It has the potential to change your life.

We have already used phrases like "I breathe all the way in" as mantras and you will have felt how they can shift your experience.

In this mindfulness exercise, I'd like to share with you my all-time favourite mindfulness mantra. It's one that anyone can use, whatever their beliefs or cultural background, and it can work like a magic wand, to bring you back to a sense of peace in the present moment. And it's much more simple than you might be expecting:

"It's ok."

This two-word mantra came to me at a time when I needed it most – and it produced the most incredible shifts in a very difficult experience. The wave of 'ok-ness' it helped me to create was the first step that I needed, to return towards peace and happiness.

The more often you practice a mindful mantra when things are going well, the more effectively it will work for you, should life present you with challenges.

Of course, you can pick any mantra of your own to work with whilst meditating. However, I strongly suggest that you work with an experienced meditation

teacher or mentor, before choosing a mantra of your own. It's easy to accidentally pick one that makes things more difficult.

A few years ago, I started working with the mantra "Make me a channel of your peace," from the prayer of St. Francis of Assisi. Within days, my inner peace turned into outer chaos, as life seemed to fall apart and everyone wanted to rage war with me. It wasn't until later, when I worked with my meditation mentor, that I realised I had been putting out a prayer to attract situations where peace was needed – in other words I was asking to have to be a channel of peace!

Practising mindful mantra is simple, yet it can feel profound.

1. Take 3 mindful breaths [see technique #1]

2. Allow yourself to be really present, in your physical body.

3. Starting in your heart area, as you breathe in a natural rhythm, gently repeat to yourself: "It's ok." Use a soothing tone of voice. Say it slowly. You can say it out loud or silently in your head.

4. As you feel you can connect with this sense of 'ok-ness', allow it to naturally grow. Sense it expanding beyond your heart space, gradually filling the rest of your body with a wave of peaceful ok-ness.

5. When you feel ready, still saying "It's ok", you might like to allow this wave of peace to expand beyond your body, effortlessly filling the space you are in and connecting with all the other ok-ness and peace in the world.

6. Enjoy it for as long as you want to!

42. Connecting With Your Heart

Contrary to what you might think, your inner wisdom doesn't 'live' in your head. That's the domain of the Monkey Mind. And the Monkey Mind's job is usually to tell us all the reasons why we can't achieve our aim - reminding us of all those limiting beliefs and fears, whilst critiquing and passing judgement on our experience of life.

Your inner wisdom comes from your heart. Your head can come up with the most amazing ideas, but if they don't feel 'right' to your heart, they won't work.

How can you connect with your heart's wisdom?

Quieten the Monkey Mind for a few moments, before asking a question about which actions to choose or which decisions to make. Then, of course, you have to do the one thing that most of us forget to do...

...Listen for the answer.

Most of us spend our time asking, asking, asking. Our chatter feeds the drama of the Monkey Mind and drowns out our inner wisdom, which speaks the language of whispered intuition, rather than brash shouting.

Here's a quick and simple mindfulness technique you can use to calm your Monkey Mind and to help yourself get into a heart-space, to connect with your inner wisdom:

1. **Take 3 Mindful Breaths** [see Technique #1] to bring you back to the 'here and now'.

2. **Allow your awareness to come back to your physical body**, resting gently in the area of your heart. Perhaps imagine that you are **breathing in and out of your heart.** Allow yourself to feel calm and relaxed.

3. **Ask your question** - talking directly to your deepest wisdom, like a trusted friend.

4. **Stop asking**! It's time to listen.

5. **Let go and trust**. You might get an answer immediately, or it might take a few days (or longer!). But it will come.

Your answer might not arrive in the form that you are expecting. Yes, it might be a thought, but it also might be a feeling or something that someone else says, or the words of a song. Be open to receiving your answer, however it arrives.

How do you know the answer is from your deeper wisdom and not your Monkey Mind? **I can always tell a 'wisdom answer' from an 'ego answer' because:**

The wisdom answer always seems so simple, so obvious and yet so profoundly right.

If the answer is complicated and difficult, or causes someone else to lose out, then it comes from the thinking mind. Make friends with your inner wisdom. It is there to help you in every way in life.

Being able to take inspired action, from the viewpoint of your inner wisdom, helps you break through limiting beliefs and get past old fears. It truly is your secret helper.

105

43. Are You Really Who You Say You Are?

By this stage, I'm guessing you're getting pretty good at being mindfully aware of your Monkey Mind's chatter – including how you talk to yourself.

We run a habit in our self-talk, though, that can keep us stuck where we least want to be.

When we're beating ourselves up about life, there are two little words we use that keep our problems running. Think about typical self-talk phrases for a moment:

"I am rubbish at that."

"I'm not clever enough."

"I am so tired!"

When your mind hears "I am..." it takes it as an instruction.

"I am …" is your mind's unconscious instruction to run its pre-programmed auto-pilot scripts, to match whatever comes after the 'am'. It's like placing an order in a restaurant. You get (usually!) what you ask for.

For your unconscious mind, whether the next word is lazy, happy, angry, rubbish, stupid, bad, tired or inspired, your mind dives into its old, well-rehearsed thoughts, feelings and actions, to match the instruction you gave.

It's an essential process, helping us to take short-cuts on life's learning curve – just imagine having to relearn how to walk, each time you stood up! But the whole "I am…" thing is even more important. You are making a statement about

106

who you are – about your identity – and it colours your entire experience of life.

"Ok, so that's the role we're playing today! Cool! I can handle that for you." says your unconscious mind. Imagine being on a diet while telling yourself, "I am fat," or studying for an exam while complaining, "I am stupid"?

The auto-pilot scripts mean we don't have to make conscious choices, which helps us to get through the day in one piece (how to cross the road safely is another one of these auto-pilot scripts). But if you don't really want to keep what is after the 'am', then it steals your freedom.

The label keeps you stuck.

A mindful solution – when you fall into the "I am..." trap:

1. Start with 3 Mindful Breaths [see technique #1] to come back to the present moment.

2. When you catch yourself saying "I am...", pause for a moment. Ask yourself, **"Am I? Really?"** and notice what bubbles up.

3. It can help to rephrase your commentary, getting specific about the behaviours and emotions, rather than making generalised judgements about your deepest identity. Talk about "I do... " rather than "I am..."

4. Then ask yourself, playfully, "Is that really who I want to be? No? Who am I? Who do I want to be?" and then choose thoughts, feelings and actions which align with that choice.

44. Are You Listening To Hear? Or Listening To Reply?

Are you really listening? Or are you just pretending? When you have a conversation with someone, is your inner dialogue talking to you about what the other person is saying? Or is it telling you what to say back?

It's amazing how easy it is to fall into the habit of 'listening to reply'.

And yet, not feeling heard is a painful experience in any relationship. Not feeling heard can push our buttons and provoke all kinds of behaviour that we'd rather avoid – from yelling and sulking to lashing out or shutting down.

Not feeling heard can undermine trust, prevent real communication and damage relationships.

Fortunately, there's a simple technique you can use to become someone who listens to hear: **Mindful listening, with compassion.**

Listening mindfully, with compassion, requires us to:

- Suspend our Monkey Mind's running commentary – few of us can listen to two conversations at once – and concentrate on understanding them.
- Resist judging the other person – you can't listen with compassion if you're criticising the other person in your head.
- Accept 'where' they are – and that what they are saying is valid for them, based on their map of life.
- Let go of the need to prove our point – most of the conversations we have in our heads, whilst listening to others, are about what we will say next to

prove we are right. We need to let go of our attachment and be present to what is 'here' and 'real'.

Bringing your awareness back to the present moment, focussing on the other person by making eye contact, makes mindful listening easier. If your mind needs to chatter, how about telling it to repeat the intention, "I hear you."?

*"We must learn to listen to one another with understanding and compassion, to hear what is being **felt**." ~ Thích Nhất Hanh*

Want to practise mindful listening?

You don't need to wait until you're talking to someone. In fact, it's easier to develop this skill when you don't need to reply – such as listening to the radio.

1. Start with 3 Mindful, to bring you back to the 'here and now'.

2. Gently close your eyes and bring your awareness to the sounds you hear.

3. Spend a few moments noticing the sounds, becoming totally focussed on them, without judgement or commentary. Accept the sounds you hear. Really tune in to them.

4. If you are practising this exercise whilst listening to a person, let your attention rest on the sound of their voice – become fully absorbed by what they are saying, without the need to analyse or form an opinion.

5. Notice how, despite the fact you haven't been multi-tracking in your head, what the other person said is clearer and replying is easier than if you had been 'listening to reply'.

45. How Are You Talking To Yourself?

We've all got one – that critic on your shoulder who makes sure you know exactly how rubbish you are in life, just when you most need to find your cheerleader-in-a-closet. And we do everything we can to eliminate that inner loudspeaker of negative self talk. But what if there were a way to sort your inner critic, once and for all? What if there were a way to turn that inner critic from something that feels lousy to something that feels great? And what if you could get started – and make a noticeable difference – in the next minute?

That inner critic works 24 hours a day. Most of us run self talk patterns that can leave us feeling yucky. And there seems to be nowhere to hide. We all know the kind of thing:

I'm rubbish at that… I'm never invited… I'll look terrible in those jeans… I don't have enough willpower… I'm stupid… It never goes right for me…

Self talk that makes us feel bad limits our ability to live as the amazing Being we really are. It stops us from taking action. It creates and feeds our excuses. It nourishes our fears. It sabotages our success. Yet most of us aren't even consciously aware of what our self talk tone is – or that we can change it.

How can you deal with that inner critic and change negative self talk?

Your inner critic is simply a commentary, based on what you have trained your Monkey Mind to think, over the years. That's it.

It's not a 'nasty person' or 'bad'. It's simply the way you have previously chosen to talk to yourself – and that can shift – in any moment.

You are the boss and the inner critic is not. Over time, it's even possible to shift your inner dialogue from critic to cheer leader. All it takes is mindful choices about which thoughts to feed– little and often.

A mindfulness technique for calming your inner critic.

1. Take 3 Mindful Breaths [see technique #1].

2. Tune in to your inner critic; that voice in your mind. Let it slow down the speed at which it is talking. It doesn't have to rush. It can let go and relax.

3. Gently shift the tone of voice it is using or the images it is showing you, to one that feels more gentle and compassionate – or even comical – whatever works for you. Play with this one.

4. Turn down the volume a little. Adjust the brightness of the images. Keep going until it feels more comfortable.

5. If your inner critic is saying something unkind, let that thought drift on through, without rejecting it or feeding it, just like any other thought [see technique #24].

6. Make friends with it and ask it to find things to say that help you to feel good about yourself.

By accepting your inner critic as being part of you – and worthy of love and compassion – you might be amazed at the miracles that start to happen.

There's a special discussion thread in the Readers' Club for this topic:
www.52MindfulMoments.com/ReadersClub

46. Seeing Who They Really Are

When we're feeling angry with somebody, it's easy to get stuck in the drama of the story. We see them as an actor in a play, giving an Oscar-winning performance in annoying us.

But seeing them that way has a nasty side-effect – it gives them power over our emotions – over how we're feeling. And it doesn't do the relationship any good.

There are many, many mindfulness practices that focus on cultivating compassion for others, especially when they have wronged us, and most of these are beyond the scope of 52 Mindful Moments. But I do want to share with you a mindfulness technique that can help you to let go of the drama and pain, as well as potentially improving that relationship (if that's what you want) or at least setting you free from the stress of it.

In technique #39 we talked about how a person is not their behaviour – how the person deep down inside is not the same as the outer actions.

You are not your behaviour. Your personality is just a
set of clothes you wear when you're awake.

When you see who someone really is, deep down inside, rather the seeing them through the 'armour' of the personality you both 'wear', you connect with them at a much deeper level. You can see past the ego, past the old pains and hurts, past the fears and worries, to who they really are. And that can be transformational.

It's something you can do, with mindfulness, at any time, even if the person isn't there with you.

1. Take 3 mindful breaths [see technique #1] and set your intention to 'see' the other person, for who they really are, underneath the behaviour.

2. Allow yourself to feel calm and choose to wear a gentle smile.

3. Choose to let your assumptions drop.
    > Be in this moment
    > The past doesn't count, right here, right now
    > The future isn't here yet

4. Let your armour drop. You are safe, in this moment.

5. Imagine connecting, heart to heart, with the other person. Realise that they are just like you – full of old hurts, pain, confusion, trying their best.

6. They are not their behaviour. Who they are, deep inside, is just like you.

7. Know that, in this moment, you can calm the emotions you have been feeling towards them. Connecting heart to heart you can feel compassion and understanding, even if their behaviour has been unacceptable.

8. Imagine looking into their eyes. See the humanity.

9. Release the practice, but perhaps choose to take this compassion with you, throughout your day.

There's a special discussion thread for this topic in the Readers' Club:
> www.52MindfulMoments.com/ReadersClub

47. Setting Your Intentions

If you don't set your intention, you are leaving your happiness to chance.

Yet we are rarely mindfully aware of the intentions we set.

Setting an intention is like telling your unconscious mind which mental radio station to tune in to. If we set the intention to have a positive week, we will spot the things that go well and even challenging situations will feel more easily handled.

Imagine stubbing your toe as you get up in the morning: with no intention set, it's possible that this could set the tone for your day, with you continuing to notice everything that's going wrong – the classic 'woe is me' experience. But with a clear intention set that 'life is ok' or 'I choose to experience this moment', the stubbed toe remains a stubbed toe and doesn't ruin your day.

Without setting our intention, our experience of life is at the whim of our mind's mood.

Setting an intention for how you want to experience the day is a powerful way to create the life you are looking for.

And when you set an intention, and commit to it, the Universe can send miracles your way.

> *Until one is committed, there is hesitancy, the chance to draw back, always ineffectiveness. There is one elementary truth, the ignorance of which kills countless ideas and splendid plans: that the moment one definitely*

commits oneself, then Providence moves too.

All sorts of things occur to help one that would otherwise not have occurred. A whole stream of events issue from the decision, raising in one's favour all manner of unforeseen incidents and meetings and material assistance, of which no man could have dreamed would have come his way. Whatever you can do or dream you can, begin it. Boldness has genius, power and magic in it.
Goethe

How do you set a mindful intention?

1. Take 3 Mindful Breaths, to bring you back to the present moment [see technique #1]

2. Ask yourself: "What is my intention in this?"

   Pause and rest, observing your thoughts, allowing the answer to surface.

   Or

   When your mind and body feel calm, tell yourself what your intention is.

3. Experience that intention flowing through your body, through your mind, washing through your emotions and tuning in to every cell. Get a sense of it flowing in front of you, throughout your day.

Not sure what kind of intention to set? How about something like: "For the next few moments, I choose to experience life from the viewpoint of love"?

48. Is It Time To Say 'Thank You'?

There's something about feeling grumpy about everything that's going wrong that drags your mood down instantly – and not just for a few minutes.

Turning your perspective around – and consciously choosing to think of things you feel happy about or grateful for – is one of the most effective ways to re-programme your thought habits. So how do you do it?

It's about mindfully focussing on what you have,
instead of what might be missing.

1. **Take a 'snapshot' of how you're feeling, right now.**
   Just a quick 'tour' of your body, your thoughts and your emotions.

2. **Grab a piece of paper and a pen.**
   This works better if you write it, rather than type it, because it gets your creative brain running.

3. **Make a list of 10 things you feel grateful for, right now.**
   This might feel tough, if you're feeling down. But there will be ten things. No matter how bad things might seem, you're still breathing…
   Getting beyond 7 things is important – it helps you to go more deeply into your unconscious mind, making this technique even more powerful.

4. **One at a time, go through the items on your list and focus on them.**
   Be really mindful and 'present' as you let your awareness rest on each item. Give it your full attention, mindfully experiencing - the emotion and the physical sensations of gratitude, as you work through the list.

5. **Now let go of the practice and notice what you notice.**
Repeat that 'snapshot'. What has shifted? How much better are you feeling now? Are more things to feel grateful about suddenly coming to mind?

Are you ready to kick the habit of feeling grumpy about what's missing – choosing, instead, to feel grateful about what's already here?

How To Easily Create This New Habit

Do one of these lists each day. It works really well, first thing in the morning, before you get out of bed. Many people find it helps to have a special journal, to write these lists in.

You could even get into the habit of sharing some of the items on your Facebook status – we use the hashtag #miracleofgratitude for ours. It's a great way to connect with others who are also choosing to feel gratitude, mindfully.

Some days it feels easy, other days it's more of a challenge. But either way, it sets the tone for your day and gives a clear instruction to your unconscious mind that its job is to find more things to feel good about.

Just imagine the difference that will make.

You could even find your favourite things to feel good about and write them on small pieces of paper, sticking them in a jar, so you can pull one out at random, whenever you need a mood lift, and focus on it for a mindful minute.

117

49. Allowing Peace To Grow

Whatever is going on around us in life, there is always the option to return to experiencing it from a place of peace.

The key is to practise resting in that peace, regularly, so that it becomes easy for you.

If you dive straight from drama and expect to find nirvana in the midst of raging adrenalin and other stress hormones, you're unlikely to be rewarded with sustainable inner peace. It's a big shift. As you will have experienced by this stage of this book, little and often brings big rewards when it comes to mindfulness.

For this mindfulness exercise, I'm going to assume that you're used to experiencing mindful breathing and body awareness. If you're new to those, it's worth going back to the earlier techniques to practise those first, though this one will still bring you results, even if you're a newbie.

It's about resting in your heart.

Your heart doesn't chatter, unlike your Monkey Mind. And you'll always find a sanctuary and stillpoint there, waiting for you, when you need to return to it.

"You can always rest in your heart." ~ Chris Barrington

By connecting with your chest area and letting your awareness settle there, you can reconnect with the peace in your heart.

Then, if you want to, you can do some pranayama breathing – where you consciously change the way you are breathing - to bring stillness and

compassion throughout your body and your day's experience. See the online Readers' Club for more on this: www.52MindfulMoments.com/ReadersClub

Resting in your heart

1. Begin by taking 3 mindful breaths [see technique #1].

2. Allow your awareness to come back into your physical body. For the next few moments, notice the physical sensations as you rest and just breathe.

3. When you feel that now-familiar shift (the release or relief of coming back 'here) allow your focus to rest on your chest area; around your heart.

4. Without doing anything or changing anything, let your awareness rest in your heart, knowing that this is your sanctuary space.

5. After a little while, you might get a sense of connecting with a peaceful energy within you. It doesn't matter whether that peaceful feeling is huge or tiny, it's there, waiting for you. Breathe in and out at your heart.

6. Once you have a sense of this peace, allow your focus to rest in that peace, as you let it be there for you, as you breathe in and out at your heart.

7. You might want to slow down your breathing and say to yourself, "I breathe in peace," as you inhale and, "I breathe out peace," as you exhale.

8. Notice how, as you breathe in and out peace, this feeling gently grows.

9. Allow yourself to settle into a rhythm of breathing in peace and breathing out peace into the world around you.

50. The Mindfulness Mysteries Hidden In A Candle Flame

Do you need more light?

One of the body's ways of regulating our sleeping patterns and our activity levels is through the hormone melatonin, via the pineal gland. The pineal gland is in the centre of the brain and it is light-sensitive. This means that lower light levels, for example in winter or if you're stuck in an office all day, impact the production of melatonin, which makes us want to be less active and to sleep more – and it also impacts your energy levels, which makes it harder to handle stress.

The great news is that you can bring light to the pineal gland in many ways. You can go for walks outside – even on a dull day. You can buy Seasonal Affective Disorder lights, which many claim have helped. Or you can buy a candle – somewhat cheaper!

The simple act of gazing at a candle can impact the pineal gland, reducing the production of melatonin slightly, helping us to feel lighter, more awake, more energised and even happier – as yogis have known for millennia. It's often called "Tratak".

Here's a simple Tratak mindfulness exercise:

1. Find yourself somewhere still to sit, where you won't be disturbed for a few minutes.

2. Light a candle (safely!) about an arm's length from your head, at about eye level, if possible. Dim the lights, to make it easier to focus on the candle.

3. Sit upright, comfortably but with a straight spine. Gently close your eyes and take 3 mindful breaths [see technique #1].

4. When you are ready, open your eyes and gently let your gaze rest on the candle flame – it's about relaxed focus, rather than staring.

5. Try to blink less often than usual – allowing your eyes to stay open for as long as possible, without straining. It's easiest if you relax your eyes, rather than forcing them to stay open.

6. Every time your mind wanders, gently guide it back to mindfully concentrating on the light of the candle flame.

7. Allow your breathing to remain relaxed, as you continue to rest your awareness on the light of the flame for as long as it feels comfortable.

It's a great way of relaxing, clearing your mind and improving your concentration levels. Plus the light of the candle acts on the pineal gland in your brain, helping to balance the hormones and even help you feel happier!

And there's an added benefit: while you're gazing at the candle, focussing your whole concentration on it, you are 'in the present moment'. So any time you're near a candle, you can practise mindfulness.

When you experience this technique, you'll notice how resting all of your awareness on the candle causes any stresses or worries to melt away. And it's up to us whether we choose to pick them back up again, afterwards.

51. Remembering The Sunshine

Earlier in **52 Mindful Moments**, we talked about how the unconscious mind can't tell the difference between something that is actually happening and something that you're imagining, for example, a stressful situation.

Whether real or fictional, it fires off the same chemical reactions in your body, producing the expected physiological and emotional responses.

Your unconscious mind can't tell the difference
between what's 'real' and what's 'story'.

You can use this to your advantage by replaying a happy memory.

When you need to add a bit of sunshine back into a cloudy day, you can consciously choose to remember something that makes you feel happy.

When you do this with mindful concentration, it will cause your body to produce endorphins (its 'happy chemicals'), to rebalance your nervous systems and to let go of stress, calming your mind. And, with mindfulness, you can then anchor those feelings here in the present moment.

1. **Take 3 Mindful Breaths [see technique #1].**

2. **Close your eyes.**
   It makes it easier to engage the creative part of your brain.

3. **Go back to a memory of a really happy, sunny time…**
   … just let yourself relax and flick through your mind's photo album until one appeals to you.

4. **Really see that memory clearly in your mind…**

   … stepping into the event, feeling the warmth of the sun, hearing the sounds that were around you, getting back into the feelings you had in that sunny memory. Allow yourself to sink into those happy feelings until you feel your mood lift. Re-experience the physical sensations. And stay with it for a few moments.

5. **Visualise those sensory experiences and emotions washing through you…**

   … lifting up every cell in your body - enjoy resting in this state for a few moments.

6. **See and feel those experiences and emotions washing into your future…**

   … filling your path with sunshine.

7. **And, when you're ready, come back to the here and now…**

   … bringing those happier feelings back with you.

Any time you need to get back to that happy memory, you can return there in an instant, by closing your eyes.

Or perhaps, if you have a photo or memento from that time, you could keep it on your desk at work or windowsill at home, so it reminds you to feel happier, whenever you see it?

52. The Power Of A Sixty Second Gratitude Spiral

Sometimes in life, especially when we're stressed, it can be difficult to fall asleep. It's as though the worries of daily life just keep going round and round in your head.

Rather than fighting your thoughts, which just feeds them and keeps them at the centre of your attention, here is a simple technique that costs nothing, but can make a huge difference.

Bedtime Gratitude Spiral

The last thing we're thinking about at bedtime – and the last emotion we're feeling – can have a major impact on the quality of our sleep and even our dreams. It's as though those final pre-sleep thoughts give our mind the unconscious message about what we want to focus on for the next few hours. It then tends to send us dreams that match the emotions we were feeling as we fell asleep – and we're also likely to wake up with those feelings, too.

So it makes sense that mindfully creating a happy mood as we fall asleep can make a big difference. And it's easier than you might think.

One of the simplest ways to achieve that is to think about things you're grateful for. It's amazing how quickly a couple of things you feel thankful for can grow – triggering other things you feel grateful for and creating an ever-growing spiral.

Note: It's not about pretending that everything is ok, when life is feeling tough. It's not about "rejecting" any worries or negative thoughts you're having. It is about mindfully allowing happier thoughts to creep in and have centre stage for a while.

1. As you relax in bed, think about something that you feel grateful for. This might be people, experiences, opportunities, weather – it's up to you!

2. Once you have identified something specific, allow yourself to gently rest in the feeling – the emotion – of feeling grateful.

3. Really dive back into the experience that you're remembering – seeing what you would see, hearing what you would hear, feeling the physical sensations you would feel.

4. Allow the intensity of your gratitude to ramp up, perhaps imagining you are turning a dial to increase it.

5. Then think of something else you feel grateful for and repeat the process. You'll notice that the more things you think of, the more things you can think of to think of!

6. Keep finding more and more things you feel grateful for until you feel the shift in your mood or – most likely – fall asleep. zzzzzzzz…..

Once you're used to doing this, to help cement the new habit, reminding yourself to do it each night, pick something you do shortly before going to sleep to act as a trigger. For example, if you read a book before falling asleep, you might like to choose the act of closing the book and putting it down, to remind you, or maybe it's turning off your bedroom light, or putting your head on the pillow.

If you enjoyed this technique, you might like to find out more about **The Miracle Of Gratitude** – via the Readers' Club:

www.52MindfulMoments.com/ReadersClub

What's Next?

There is so much more I want to share with you!

The hardest thing about writing **52 Mindful Moments** was deciding what to cut out. Each time I created another mindfulness technique for you, there was so much more I wanted to say, to give you. But my focus here has been very clear – to offer you techniques that work fast, without you having to trawl through hundreds of pages of a 'how to' guide.

I hope that these mindfulness exercises have inspired you and perhaps you might be interested in taking things to the next level?

This book is just the beginning. I encourage you to dive in and discover how ten minutes a day (instead of one minute!) of mindfulness and meditation could change your life. You might be interested in **How To Meditate – Made Easy**.

It's an online course (and a paperback /Kindle book) that guides you through, step by step, how to easily create a daily meditation habit, over the course of 28 days.

It brings you all you need to know about how to meditate, but it also uses an inspired blend of ancient wisdom and modern psychology, to help you get past the blocks that would normally cause students to give up.

To find out whether your heart is calling you to take things to the next level, go to:

www.HowToMeditateMadeEasy.com

More Resources

I hope you have found the techniques in **52 Mindful Moments** helpful.

Please make sure you have grabbed all the goodies that are waiting for you in the online Readers' Club. To register (it's free!) go to:

www.52MindfulMoments.com/ReadersClub

If you'd like to take your journey further, here are some ideas.

1. **Want to take things to the next level?**
   How about joining in with our '**Soul-Sized Living**' community? As a member, you will receive:

   - exclusive access to all the goodies and conversations in our invitation-only private online community
   - all the extra articles, members-only MP3s, worksheets and other life-changing treats via ClareJosa.com
   - discounts & priority booking on courses (online and workshops)
   - my monthly Soul-Sized Living newsletter (it's the *only* way to get this!)
   - moral support on your life-changing journey from other members of the community
   - the chance to get answers to your questions – and a place to share your insights and to celebrate your successes
   - there's even a **52 Mindful Moments** readers' club
   - and much, much more…

You can join today – it's free – as my gift to you: www.SoulSizedLiving.com

2. Let's connect on Facebook & Twitter

Join me at our Soul-Sized Living page and connect with others who have enjoyed this book.

www.Facebook.com/SoulSizedLiving

www.Twitter.com/clare_josa

3. Find a local class

If you live anywhere near Forest Row in East Sussex, UK, you could join in with one of my regular face-to-face meditation & mindfulness classes. There are also weekend seminars and workshops, if you live further away.

You can find details at:

www.ClareJosa.com/workshops

If you're not local to Forest Row, but want to find a good meditation and mindfulness teacher, I have written an article that will help you:

"Looking For A Meditation Class? 10 Must-Ask Questions For Newbie Meditators": www.52MindfulMoments.com/ReadersClub

And, to give you an idea of the kinds of answers you should be looking for, I've written a second article with the answers I would give. This is at the same link. I hope these help!

4. Want to do an online course?

I have created a range of online courses that you might enjoy – from a 10 week mindfulness course (*How To De-Stress With Mindfulness*), through to *6 Weeks To Spring Clean Your Life* and even Mastermind Groups, where you can

work with me on live calls and Skype workshops. You can find details of all of these here: www.ClareJosa.com/online-courses

5. **Check out some of my other books?**
    I have written a number of other books that might be of interest to you, if you enjoyed this course. I have also created a range of meditation, mindfulness and deep relaxation CDs. You can find an up-to-date list here: www.ClareJosa.com/Clare-Josa-Books-CDs

Before I sign off, I'd like to say a huge thank you to you for sharing your journey with me.

No matter how often you have practised these techniques, you will have taken you a step closer towards the life you want. None of it is wasted. It all makes a difference.

Wishing you inner peace and happiness on your journey.

With love, Namaste,

Clare. ♡

www.ClareJosa.com

About Clare Josa

Clare Josa is a certified NLP Trainer, a Meditation & Mindfulness Teacher, a Seminar Leader and a Breakthrough Mentor, who feels passionately about helping people to fall in love with who they really are.

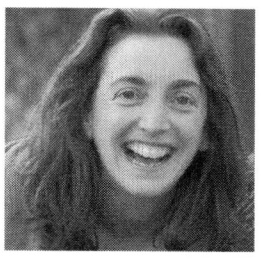

She is the author of numerous books and the creator of a wide range of online courses, as well as face-to-face workshops. They help you to dump your old excuses, let go of limiting beliefs that have been keeping you stuck and give you the kick you needed, to take inspired, practical action towards living the life of your dreams.

Her career began with a Master's Degree in Mechanical Engineering and German, spending a decade in diesel engine manufacturing. She enjoyed discovering how things worked and figuring out how to fix broken processes, but she realised that what she loved most was making people smile. So she combined her problem-solving skills with her passion for psychology and 'how people tick' to move into helping people remember how to feel happier and how to be who they really are.

She studied Neurolinguistic Programming (the 'user manual for your brain' / 'Practical Psychology' - NLP), qualifying as an NLP Trainer (training students up to Master Practitioner level) in 2003. She built on her 20-year enthusiasm for meditation by training to become a Meditation Teacher in 2008, as well as continuing her life-long passion for writing and teaching.

Her engineering background means that the inspirational work she shares is always grounded in practical common sense – to which she adds an intuitive and light-hearted approach.

Clare lives in Sussex, UK, with her husband, three young sons, six very mindful chickens and a bouncy Jack Russell.

Today's choices create your tomorrows.

With each and every thought, you can choose again.

With each and every breath, you can choose thoughts that inspire you and make your heart sing.

Wishing you love and laughter.

Namaste.

Clare, ♡

Index Of Mindfulness Techniques

Made in the USA
Charleston, SC
12 August 2013